The
Lake Erie Quadrangle
WATERS OF REPOSE

Dave Stone and David Frew

Erie County Historical Society
Erie, Pennsylvania 1993

The "Ghost Ships of Long Point" and "Ghost Fleet of the
Quadrangle's South Shore" Charts shown on the endleaves of this
book are available in a poster 22 inches x 38 inches from:

Dave Stone
Long Point, Ontario, Canada
            or
Erie County Historical Society
417 State Street
Erie, Pennsylvania 16501

Erie County Historical Society
417 State Street
Erie, Pennsylvania 16501

THE LAKE ERIE QUADRANGLE

The dangers and mysteries of the Bermuda Triangle pale by comparison with those of the Lake Erie Quadrangle! The Bermuda Triangle is a 14,000 square mile area off Florida which has been the sight of some 112 disasters. The Lake Erie Quadrangle is much smaller, only 2,500 square miles, but has had 429 maritime disasters. By statistical comparison this makes the Quadrangle 21 times more dangerous than the Bermuda Triangle!

Located within Lake Erie's central basin, the Quadrangle extends from Conneaut to Barcelona on the U.S. shore, and from Port Burwell to Nanticoke on the Canadian side. This work catalogues and dates the disasters, and details the adventures. It explains the mysteries and reveals the reasons for the world's most dangerous waters. "Waters of Repose" is about the regional maritime history of central Lake Erie. It is an organized collection of oral history from the Erie and Long Point regions. The tales of schooners, steamers, boat building, rum running, commercial fishing and lifesaving are set in the historical context of two developing nations through the 19th and 20th centuries.

ACKNOWLEDGEMENTS

We complete this work with a new found appreciation for the work of professional historians. Neither of us has had enough formal academic training in history or in methods of historical research. We do, however, have a great respect for the often unsung work of these heroes of our culture. Without them we would, as it has been said, be doomed to continue repeating our errors. So with apologies for our amateur attempts at the chronicling of oral history, we offer the following "story" of Lake Erie's central basin and its important maritime history.

We must also offer thanks to the following people whose time and wisdom have made our efforts come to life. They shared their time and their knowledge with us helping to create the volume which follows. Dr. Robert Allshouse (Gannon University History Department), Rich Aranos (Erie County Sheriff's Diving Team), The Backus Conservation Area of Port Rowan, George Backus (who piloted the airplane for the aerial photography), Harry Barrett (Port Dover's resident historian and author), Bill Beckman (Deceased), Elizabeth Beckman (Erie County Historical Society), Bowling Green University's Great Lakes Institute, David Bierig, Donald Buscombe, The Canadian Wild Life Service, Scott Cook (Olmstead Foods), James Crow (Canadian Consulate), Christine Detzel, Mary Dibble (Westfield Library), Dan Dundon, Bob Ellis

(STELCO Steel), Mrs. Harvey Ferris, Mike Fletcher (commercial diver and Canadian discoverer of the *Atlantic)*, Cheryl Frew, David A. Frew, Kristin Frew (our editor), Mary Ann Frew (who helped with most of the writing), The Great Lakes Historical Museum of Vermillion, OH, Bill Greulich, Barry Hazlett, Mary Howard, Tim Hughes, Detective Sergeant Carl Kalinowski, (Erie Police Dept. Retired), Craig Latimer, Roger Kenyon (Biologist for the PA Fish Commission), Dr. Carl Lechner (Gannon History Dept.), Thomas Leonardi, Harry Leslie (Presque Isle State Park Superintendent), Rev. Robert Levis, Dr. Betty Jo Licata, The Long Point Company, Dr. Gary Mahan, The Mariner's Museum of Newport News, VA, Chuck McCain, Ron McConnell, Judy Mickol, John and Nadine Mitchell (Port Dover Yacht Club), Don Muller (Erie County Historical Society), Don Murray (Port Dover Fish Co.), Bob North, The Ontario Ministry of Natural Resources, Bob Osborn (Ontario Hydro), Dr. Tom Ostopowski, Sgt. Al Pede (Erie Police Dept. Retired), The Pennsylvania Department of Environmental Resources, The Port Dover Harbor Museum, The Port Rowan *Good News*, Seaweed, Pat Shoup, Bruce and Tony Schnider (The Erie Beach Hotel), Sidney and Sandy Smith (Erie Sand Steamship), Jean Stone, Julie Stone, Gerry Urbaniak, John Veber, Dr. Robert Wall (Canadian historian and author), Ash Winter (Barrister and Solicitor from Port Dover), Dr. Bob Wallace, Terry Walsh, Dr. Charles Watkins, Stan Zagorski (Gannon University Limnologist), Harland Zeller, and all those whose names we have forgotten.

A Word About The Book

*B*efore you begin reading we feel that it is important to bring two unique aspects of this book to your attention. First we have been told by many of our proofreaders and technical advisors that they were a bit confused by our sense of history. They had expected a typical book about regional history. But they were surprised, if not perplexed, by our inclusion of relatively recent events. We do not find these comments in the least disturbing. In fact, we are delighted by them since that particular reaction highlights our sense of what history is all about. Perhaps this is a comment on our status as "amateur" rather than academic historians.

Neither of us feels that history is something which exists in a vacuum disconnected from the present. To us, events of yesterday are as important to history as those of a decade or a century ago. What makes history come alive is its connection with present day experience. Perhaps Isaac Asimoff, the science fiction writer, said it best when he constantly alluded to historians as the heroes of culture for their proclivity to integrate the events of the past with the issues and technology of today.

In each of the primary chapters we have made a concerted effort to organize chronologically, and then to move topically from past to present. Sometimes it was impossible to stay on chronological track, but there is always a general path leading from yesterday to today.

The second and perhaps more unique feature of the book is its design as a participation manual. We believe in experiential learning. Therefore, in each chapter we have included activities intended to bring the contents to life. Each of us has spent countless hours and days traveling the lake shore on both coasts. Our experience tells us that some of the very best possible vacation and getaway trips are hiding right here under our collective noses. Many of our activity suggestions involve travel. If you listen to our advice you will ultimately be driving all the way around the lake, getting out of your car in places where tourists rarely go and experiencing Lake Erie as few visitors ever do.

Hopefully, our American readers will venture across the lake and experience the uniqueness and beauty of the Long Point area. Likewise we hope to encourage our Canadian friends to visit the U.S. shore. There are parks, nature preserves, islands, museums, harbors and shipyards to be seen along both coasts. In individual chapters we will be making recommendations which are appropriate to the topics. When you do finally set off (book in hand) on an automotive circumnavigation, we urge you to go slowly. Find the secondary roads which follow the lake shore (this may require careful study of road maps and some questioning en route) then stop at each possible point of interest. Our recommendation regarding the rounding of the west end of the lake is to skip the traffic and hassle of Toledo, Detroit and Windsor and take the automobile ferry between Leamington, Ontario and Sandusky, Ohio. This will add some maritime spice to your trip and give you a first hand look at the island area of the lake.

Lots of our adventures involve short field trips to lookouts, museums or harbors. Some of these can be planned as day trips. We also hope that this book will inspire you to keep reading. In most of the topical areas herein, we have only scratched the surface. A visit to bookstores, museums and libraries en route will quickly provide you with more book lists and references. It is not critically important to proceed through the adventures in order. Just make a list of the things that you wish to do and get started. And while you are out there seeing things, don't be surprised if you run into one or both of us on our 50th time through!

TABLE OF CONTENTS

THE WATERS OF REPOSE

To the waters of repose
he leads me,
there he revives my soul...
Psalm 23

*W*e must appear to be the oddest of
friends. I am a generation younger than Dave Stone. I am an American and Dave
Stone is a Canadian; I am a College Professor, and Dave is an agricultural products manufacturer and salesman; I am a sailor and Dave is a diver; Dave Stone
spent four years on the North Atlantic during WWII before I was born. There are
clearly more differences between Dave and myself than similarities. Yet, the first
time we met we bonded. And the glue that brings us together is the fabric of this
book. We share a love for Lake Erie and of the Long Point to Erie area in particular. Our shared obsession is more than a feeling for the geology, nature or history
of the area. It is, in fact, a spiritual love, which makes our affection difficult to
articulate. We both have had a lifetime of experiences drawing us to the shores of
the body of water that the Iroquois called "the great water spirit." And each of us,
in individual ways, has resonated with the spirits which have both taken life from
these waters and given their lives to them.

Beginning with the Native North Americans, who inhabited Lake Erie,
there has been a continuous flow of people to the edge of the shore and over her

David Frew.

waves. The stories of these souls are, in a very real way, the history of North America. But these stories make up much more than just a disconnected history. For in their evolving, they are also our stories—the stories of people who live and work along the shores today, their children, and their children's children.

The waters near Long Point and Erie, Pa. gave life and sustenance to the Indians, the voyagers, the fur traders and the pioneers. They held warships and collected artifacts of 19th century naval battles. They became waters of commerce dictating the lives of schooner captains and crews, followed by steamboaters and commercial fishermen. They have seen the French, the English, and then the birth and evolution of two great countries, the United States and Canada. And as the 19th century progressed with its steamship commerce, Lake Erie became the center of transportation for two growing nations.

Most notably, the Long Point/Erie area became one of the most fearsome and difficult navigational passages in all of the world's waters. During a time when transport by commercial sail or steamboat was the primary mode of conveyance, the area speedily developed a reputation for shipwrecks and adventure. Sailors the world over spoke of the difficulty of making way up Lake Erie in a November blow.

This book honors the spirits of all those who have lived on or about the lake. We dedicate our efforts to the sailors and fishermen who have given up their lives making a living on the Great Lakes.

AUGUST 1992

It was August 18th, 1992. The two of us were returning to Dave Stone's cottage on Long Point after a day-long search of the beaches along the south shore. For several days the wind had been blowing at 25 knots from the east and we were anxious to look for shipwreck debris on the beaches. Aside from spotting hundreds of balloon ribbons and a few fish net floats, our trip across the south shore beaches had proven uneventful. This entire area is closed to the general public and currently under the management of the Canadian Wildlife Service (it was donated to them by the Long Point Company). Dave has had an archeological permit for a number of years and shares his findings with them. But Dave was not at all discouraged. As he has said, whenever anyone would listen, it takes thousands of hours of beachcombing to uncover a single shipwreck lead. Discovering a wreck is like getting a hole in one!

We returned Dave's boat, *Beachcomber*, to its boathouse along Long Point's Hastings Cut and detoured away from his cottage toward Port Rowan. As we entered Dave's favorite restaurant, The Coop, the proprietor greeted Dave with his standard request, "When are you going to write another book Dave?" The Coop is one of several retail outlets for Dave Stone's first book, *Long Point Last Port of Call*. After we finished our meals, the owner pointed to his rack of books and said, "Dave, just about everyone who reads this book comes back and asks if you have another one out yet!"

Dave Stone, if truth be known, is just too busy living the life of the Long Point Beachcomber to write books. His wife Jean says that she had to put him in irons to finish his last two page newspaper piece. He has too much fun walking the beaches, giving slide presentations, and cruising the shores in his dive boat to want to sit down and write.

Dave and I had talked about a collaboration for years. I assured him that he could do most of the talking and that I would do the bulk of the writing. But he has only recently recovered from the job of writing his last book some 4 or 5 years ago.

As we drove back down the causeway past his boathouse to Long Point and his cottage, I broached the subject another time. "What do you think?", I asked. "With the resources of Gannon's history department, editing people and a University Press, we could do this easily." Unable to focus on administrative details, Dave muttered something about pencil-necked academics and pulled up to the rural mailbox in front of his cottage.

Schooner Ribs on the beach.

The top item was a package from the Great Lakes Historical Society in Vermillion, Ohio. "Wow," he said with the enthusiasm of a 5 year old at Christmas, "its finally here!" He ripped open the package to reveal a new book, a catalogue of shipwrecks on the Great Lakes with listings in alphabetical order. The front cover featured a list of the special sections within the book and our attention was immediately drawn to one heading, "The Most Dangerous Place on the Great Lakes."

We opened the volume to that page and were shocked to see that the author had concluded that, it was the "thumb of Lake Michigan." "Just doesn't seem right," muttered Dave. "What about Long Point and Erie's Presque Isle" he asked? There were far more wrecks between those two areas over the years." "There is not enough published material about Long Point or central Lake Erie," I responded. "Someone better write some more books." So, grudgingly, kicking and screaming about how busy he was going to be—he would be chasing wreck leads over the next few months and could be called on as an expert witness in the controversy surrounding the wreck of the *Atlantic* and its salvage—Dave finally conceded. The fruit of this collaboration was shaped into the book which you are about to read.

As we planned the book, we began to envision a rectangular shaped area in Lake Erie. The area is bounded by a line extending from Conneaut, Ohio north to Port Burwell, Ontario, then east through Port Rowan, Port Dover, and Nanticoke, and south again to Barcelona, NY. The southern boundary passes back through Erie, Pa. and completes the loop at Conneaut. Our collective experience suggested that this area contains some of the most exciting lake lore available, and our research was not to disappoint us. Adventure, pirates, war, shipwrecks, heroism, fishing stories and more have all occurred within this region.

We decided to call our area the "Lake Erie Quadrangle," in the tradition of the Bermuda Triangle and to construct a book describing the region and its maritime history. The history and stories from the Quadrangle are rich with the economic and cultural development of both shores. It is from this oral history that all of us who currently inhabit the shores of Lake Erie can come to understand our place in the events of history. As we continued the project, we were reminded repeatedly of the rich and adventurous history which has taken place right here, on our own shores. We hope that as you read this book you come to share in our amazement and discovery.

David Frew

Dave Stone and Dave Frew in the **Beachcomber**.
Photo by NADINE MITCHELL

Dave Stone.

For me, the romance began more than 60 years ago in 1933 when I was introduced to the Long Point area. My family had a cottage at Turkey Point, and it was here that I first laid eyes on the mysterious sickle shaped sand spit stretching half way across Lake Erie. I was enchanted by the stories of shipwrecks, lost treasure, murders and adventure on this forbidden land.

World War II separated me physically from Long Point, but my time in the Royal Canadian Navy chasing submarines in the North Atlantic stirred my love for the water. I returned to the area, completed my university education and built a cottage at Long Point.

Walking the beach one day I spotted the remains of a shipwreck. Looking at the buried ribs raised many questions in my mind. What ship was this, What happened to it, etc? I was hooked! From that day on I was obsessed with maritime history. I began to involve myself in underwater archeology, diving, photography, ship construction and history. There was not much published information about Long Point in those days and I had to do quite a lot of digging to get little bits and pieces

When I met Dave Frew several years ago I knew that I had found a kindred spirit. He clearly shares my love of the Lake and of Long Point. And when he invited me to Gannon to talk about my work, I was more than impressed with the warmth and hospitality of the Erie community. Since that time we have spent many hours walking the beaches of Long Point and talking about maritime history.

When Dave asked me to share my life's experiences with him in the form of a book there was no hesitation. Until recently my focus has only been on the Canadian shore, but the opportunity to include both shores in one volume convinced me that a collaboration was a great idea. This venture is hopefully, not only a rich and unique documentation of the maritime history of our area but the outcome of a very special and lasting friendship with my co-author.

Dave Stone

THE SETTING OF NORTH AMERICA:
WATERWAYS AS HIGHWAYS

*I*t is important to build a foundation for our stories about the Lake Erie Quadrangle. To accomplish this, we hope to put the area in perspective by helping the reader to visualize the state of the world in the "old days." We recognize that most people have little theoretical interest in History, but even a regionally focused work such as this is incomplete without a historical context. To understand central Lake Erie and its many nautical adventures, it is important to see its place in history.

In geological time, the Great Lakes were formed by the retreat of the Wisconsin Glacier. This ice sheet began to recede in about 13,000 BC, leaving a series of escarpments and lakes, including a ridge line from today's Lake St. Clair to Erie, Pa., as well as an escarpment line from central Lake Huron to the southern end of the Niagara River. By 10,000 BC, the ice sheet had further withdrawn to form a line from the northern tip of Lake Huron to Montreal. By this time, the waters of Lake Erie were flowing over Niagara Falls.

THE EARLIEST SETTLERS

Archeological evidence indicates that the current shape of Lake Erie was formed by the year 2000 BC. We can also deduce, from anthropologic findings, that Native American people had begun to inhabit both sides of Lake Erie almost as soon as the Wisconsin Ice Sheet withdrew. Prior to the influx of the Europeans, there is clear evidence that the Iroquoians (although not yet fully organized as a nation) inhabited both the north and south lake shores. The early Iroquoian peoples (all of whom spoke a common language) were located in four general areas. These included (1) the Hurons north of Lake Ontario, (2) the Iroquois who lived south of Lake Ontario (in today's upstate New York) and the tribes which settled both the (3) south and the (4) north banks of Lake Erie. The Lake Erie tribes included:

1. The Erie Indians … along the south shore from Erie, Pa. to Buffalo
2. The Wittlesey Indians … along the south shore from Toledo to the Pa. line
3. The Parker Indians … along the north shore from Detroit to Nanticoke Ontario
4. The Tobacco (Petrun) Indians … who lived north of the Parkers and shared access peacefully to the lake

During the early years of the arrival of the Europeans, there was conflict among these tribes. Eventually the Iroquois tribe from New York absorbed the four tribes from the Lake Erie area. While it is unclear how violent this Iroquois action was, there is evidence that members of the four Lake Erie tribes were somehow absorbed by the Iroquois groups.

By the time that Verrazzano (1524) sailed from Europe to verify the "theory" that the land which Columbus "discovered" was in fact a continent, Native North Americans living in the region of Lake Erie and Lake Ontario had formed the Iroquoian Confederation, the forerunner of the Iroquois Five Nations.

As a group the Iroquois peoples (13 tribes as of the early 1600s) represented an advanced culture which was at least as large as the combined European nations. They had a highly evolved agricultural system including crop rotation, and a vast variety of cultivated plants, fruits and vegetables. They had perfected the use of fertilizer. In addition, they were skilled boat builders who used their craft for fishing, trade, transportation and communication with other tribes. In the winter, they used boat building technology to build efficient toboggans.

They also developed a system of trails for traveling to fishing sites and other tribal locations. They dried fish and fruit, then stored it for winter usage. They had a sophisticated system of government. They did not, however, read, write or have gunpowder.

Most modern North Americans do not know that the Iroquois were evolved as a nation prior to European settlement. They also generally see themselves as either Americans or Canadians, thus misunderstanding two important Iroquoian perspectives. For Native North Americans, (1) the U.S./Canadian border is a meaningless line drawn through water by late-comer Europeans and (2) the conflicts between the various Iroquoian tribes were as meaningful as the earlier European wars.

THE ARRIVAL OF THE EUROPEANS

As the French, Dutch, and English arrived by the boat load to settle the new continent, they gravitated to the North East. They arrived by boat and faced the problem of settling or exploring a wild new land. From their vantage point on the Atlantic coast, they could not relate to the scope of North America and its native people. The imminent reality for them was survival in a new land. For the settlers, this meant survival without the infrastructure of European culture. For the explorers (voyageurs), the issues were different. Their mission was to claim new lands for the European nations, which sent them on various quests to the new world, as they searched for passages to the Pacific and the Gulf of Mexico.

To understand the problems of the settlers and explorers, it is useful to ponder our immediate experience of the 20th century world. Invariably we think about day to day activities such as going to work, driving to the store, or visiting friends. The thing that almost all of us take for granted as we do these things, however, is the system of roads and highways which allows such easy access. Especially for those who were born after the development of the modern North American thruway system, it seems that the existing set of roads and highways has always been in place. For modern folks, it is almost impossible to imagine a world without roadways.

For the Europeans, the highways to exploration and new settlements were the waterways. Chief among these in the early years were the Hudson and the St. Lawrence rivers. The explorers made their way up stream through both of these waterways and sent back word about the wonderful western lands. There were resources beyond the wildest imaginings and opportunities for land owner-ship and development. As the east coast settlements began to bustle with settlers, more and more were motivated to "go west." But, in those days, the "west" was not Colorado, or California. It was the area of North America which could be reached by following either the Hudson or St. Lawrence rivers away from the east coast. To put this notion into perspective, it was estimated by military strategists during the War of Independence (1776), that 75% of North American colonists lived east of the Hudson river.

Figure 1-1 is a representation of the major waterways at the time of European colonization. Both the Hudson and the St. Lawrence, which were at least somewhat navigable for the largest ships, were connected by established Indian portage systems to the Great Lakes. The Great Lakes were, in turn, connected (sometimes by portage) to all of the continent's major eastern and midwest-ern river systems. This ultimately allowed explorers and settlers access to the Allegheny/Ohio river systems as well as the Mississippi/Missouri. In addition to the major river systems, there were countless smaller waterways, which made the potential for settlement of an apparently infinite area seem quite attractive.

As the Europeans settled into North America, there were two cultural epicenters in the north. The first was the French settlement of Quebec which became the central focus of exploration for the voyageurs and their missionary companions. The voyageurs traveled the St. Lawrence, quickly reaching Lake Ontario and finding the barrier of Niagara Falls. While they did some exploration of Lake Erie, they were quick to recognize that a land trail across today's Ontario would most expeditiously get them to Lake Huron. Essentially, the voyageurs were most interested in exploring and claiming new lands to the south and the west, as they searched for passages to the Gulf of Mexico and the Pacific Ocean.

The Iroquois were in possession of charts and maps which gave rough estimates of the locations and the relative sizes of the Great Lakes and showed portage access to the river systems. The voyageurs utilized this information to launch their explorations and claims of the new continent. En route, the French moved into the Ohio and Mississippi river systems; and in a very short time, they had claimed lands as far south as the Gulf of Mexico.

The English were much slower to move west. They seemed preoccupied with the formation of permanent settlements. From their vantage point in New England, they used the Hudson river system and its tributaries to push to the west. They also ultimately arrived at Lake Ontario, but with visions of the creation of permanent canal navigation systems for moving goods and people to the west. At first, these missions put them in conflict with the native people, but a strong English/Iroquoian alliance was eventually developed.

The English notion included navigable canals in conjunction with the existing river systems, which would ultimately join Lake Erie with the Atlantic

Figure 1-1
Great Lakes/St. Lawrence/
Hudson/Allegheny –
Waterway System

colonies. They immediately understood the importance of reaching Lake Erie rather than Lake Ontario in order to avoid the impediment of Niagara Falls.

Both the French and the English understood the strategic influence of Presque Isle. The Indians had established a portage system leading south to (today's) French Creek, approximately 12 miles south of Erie. This provided access to the Allegheny and then the Ohio/Mississippi river systems. The area along the south shore of Lake Erie, from today's Erie, Pa. to Buffalo, NY, was of vital importance to the English settlers since it was clear that a system of canals and rivers could ultimately connect the Atlantic coast to Buffalo, and then the Presque Isle area to the Gulf of Mexico. This would make trade with the Spanish possible, as well.

NATIVE AMERICANS MEET THE EUROPEANS

As the inevitable migration to the west began, the explorers and settlers increasingly came into contact first with the Hurons and then with the Iroquois peoples. As the Europeans traded with the Hurons, to the East, the Iroquois began to realize the usefulness of European goods. The competition for trade with the Europeans soon escalated old hostilities between the two tribes and propelled the Iroquois and Hurons into war. Eventually the Hurons were driven North and west and the Iroquois became the primary point of contact between the Native North Americans and the Europeans. Unlike earlier contacts with the Hurons, the Iroquois welcomed the Europeans. They were, as a people, relatively willing to share their knowledge about North America and about how to survive in the new frontier. The Iroquois had developed an elaborate transportation system that utilized the canoes which they had been building for generations. They taught the Europeans how to build their own canoes using bark stretched onto cedar frames. They also helped to guide the Europeans through the established systems of lakes, rivers and portages, teaching them both to survive in the new world and to explore its western boundaries.

For some reason, the Iroquois seemed to have an affinity for the French voyageurs during the earliest days of exploration. The two cultures seemed, at first, to establish a mutual respect. The French, with their Jesuit sponsorship, shared stories of the great "chiefs of Europe," while the Indians helped them to become established in the wilderness. They also assisted the voyageurs in the acquisition of furs for trading. Unlike the English settlers who originally seemed to threaten the Native Americans, the French voyageurs traded with the Indians and hired them to work as guides.

The Iroquois had knowledge of the Great Lakes waterway systems, including the western and northern lakes such as Superior. Beyond this frontier, however, the Iroquois seemed to have little or no information. The French, who were obsessed with reaching the Pacific as a part of their quest, developed a vague notion that the western-most boundary of Superior might lie just a short distance from the west coast. Many historians now feel that one reason that the Iroquois were so friendly toward the French was that they were made to believe that once they had guided the French to the frontier and the great ocean beyond, that the europeans would, in effect, go away, leaving the Iroquois with only the direct benefits of their brief encounters with the Europeans.

Historical accounts of the settling of North America from the early 1800s are incredibly telling and biased documents. The extent to which recorded history ignored the importance of the Iroquois to the commerce and the explorations of the day is unbelievable and appalling. Many recorded accounts painted a picture of the Indians as savages with little or no intelligence who were barely able to survive due to the lack of European refinement. Much of this distortion is due to the subsequent competition between France and England, and to the role of Native Americans in the French and Indian wars. Since the English won, eventually they recorded the history of the settling of North America.

From the perspective of the French voyageurs, however, it was the use of the huge birch bark canoe, clearly an Indian invention, which allowed the early explorers to move en masse up the lakes and waterways. They returned with cargoes of furs for trading in Europe to fund the explorations. The large version of the Iroquoian canoe could carry more than three tons of cargo and still cope with conditions on Lake Erie.

Within a relatively short time, however, the French managed to alienate the Iroquois. The Indians realized that the French were taking advantage of them. Once the voyagers had moved on, it was the English who developed more lasting trade relationships with the Indian peoples of Lake Erie. This commercial bond was soon to form the basis of a long term relationship which helped, first, to enlist the Iroquois's support of the English (the winning faction) during the French and Indian wars. The Iroquois were loyal to their allegiance to the English during the war of American independence, although the English lost.

After the American War of Independence (1776), the boundary area between the United States and Canada became a "real" international line. Essentially this line, which had been laid out after the French and Indian war to designate the territory of Upper Canada, bisected the Great Lakes (except for Michigan). The only important Native American presence on Lake Erie created by these historical events was the creation of what was to become today's Brantford, Ontario. This land was granted by England to Chief Joseph Brant, a fierce and loyal supporter during the war. At the time, Brant's Ford (Brantford) became the chief portage on the Grand River which flowed from the north into Lake Erie at Port Maitland some 30 miles east of Long Point. This portage was an important economic link on the trail system from Quebec to Toronto to Detroit and the west. Joseph Brant, who was educated at Dartmouth and visited Europe, took his Iroquoian followers and escaped the probable wrath of the Americans, who he had fought against on behalf of the English by moving to Brantford. The Iroquois nation that was established there remains today, and is or was the home of Native North American actors Jay Silverheels (Tonto in the Lone Ranger series) and Graham Green (Dances With Wolves).

THE FINAL STEPS IN THE WATERWAY

Although it took many more decades, the early visions of both the French and English were finally achieved. The first and major step was the completion of the Erie Canal in 1825. This waterway allowed settlers bound for the American or Canadian mid-sections to move from New York to Buffalo. Here they were loaded onto a rapidly growing fleet of Lake Erie passenger ships (both schooners and steamships) for the trip west. Thousands of immigrants who settled Michigan, Wisconsin, Ohio, Illinois, and central Canada made their way from Europe via this route.

By the year 1844, the Erie Extension Canal opened, linking Erie with Pittsburgh. This important linkage provided access from Lake Erie through Pittsburgh, to the Gulf of Mexico. In the years of the Extension Canal, it was possible to reach Pittsburgh by Packet Boat in 36 hours. Unfortunately for the economy of the canal, by the time the waterway was completed, it was no longer commercially viable. The Extension Canal declared bankruptcy in 1870 and ceased operations in 1871 when an aqueduct (overhead) section of the canal broke and funds to repair it could not be raised.

There were three more important problems in the creation of the Great Lakes waterway system, (1) a waterway to connect Lake Ontario with Erie, (2) access to the Atlantic through the St. Lawrence River, and (3) a means for navigating Lake Superior.

The original version of the Welland Canal opened in 1829, allowing much needed commercial access between the ports of Lake Ontario and the other Great Lakes through Lake Erie. By today's standards, the first Welland was quite small and inefficient. It was expanded slightly in 1887 and enlarged significantly in 1932 and again in 1959. The final increases allowed vessels of 730 foot length and 75 foot beam to pass around Niagara Falls.

In 1855, the St. Mary's Locks opened allowing navigational access to Lake Superior. This addition created a major upsurge in freight interests on the Lakes,

Ziemia Zamojska, a salty,
locks through the Welland Canal.
Photo by TOM LEONARDI

since large vessels could be used to move the vast quantities of natural resources which were available in the northern states. The locks were expanded significantly in 1970 (with the addition of the new Poe Locks) allowing vessels up to 1100 feet long with beams of 105 feet to move from Lake Erie to the west. Since vessel size on the Great Lakes has been governed by the dimensions of the locks, the new possibilities at Sault Ste. Marie motivated a trend in shipbuilding during the 1970s and early 1980s. A series of super lakers such as the *Stewart J. Cort* (built in Erie, Pa.) emerged, to take full advantage of the increased lock size. A number of existing ships were "jumboized" during this same period.

The last piece in the waterway puzzle was completed in 1959 with the official opening of the St. Lawrence Seaway system. This connected the Atlantic Ocean, via the St. Lawrence and a system of locks which bypassed the river rapids, to Lake Ontario. Ocean going ships (saltys) could use the Seaway in conjunction with the Welland Canal to get to Lake Erie and the rest of the Great Lakes system, including Superior. In addition, the coal fields of Newfoundland were connected to the Great Lakes. While a number of smaller locking systems had been developed around the rapids in the St. Lawrence, the final opening of the seaway system did not officially take place until 1959. The Seaway created a waterway well beyond the wildest visions of the early Europeans. Together, the Locks at Lake Superior, the Great Lakes and the St. Lawrence, now represent a major seaway which is, in fact, almost as large in linear miles as the trip from England to the Atlantic coast.

Lake Erie Adventures

1. Rent the recent video "Black Robe" and watch it. This is an exceptional Canadian film which depicts the era of French exploration and the new world as it presented itself to the Voyageurs and the Jesuits.

2. Drive to the Canadian side of the Niagara Falls area and visit the locks on the Welland Canal. The best lock to observe is #3 at St. Catherines. There is a museum there with an explanation and history of the canal system. On the American side of the Peace Bridge you will be able to see the Black Rock Canal which is the entrance to the Erie Canal and points east such as New York City

3. In the city of Erie, Pa. you will still be able to find vestiges of the Erie Extension Canal. There is a placard at 26th and Zuck Avenue depicting that end of the waterway. From there, it ran diagonally to the canal basin just west of the Public Dock at the foot of State Street. The canal way passed approximately 50 feet to the west of the existing Gannon University Recreational Center at Fourth and Peach, and ran diagonally through the block which now contains the Gannon Football field, crossing Sixth Street between Sassafras and Myrtle.

4. Drive south on Parade Street (Route 97) to Waterford and Lake LeBoeuf (immediately south and west of the town). This was the Indian portage to French Creek. You can follow LeBoeuf Creek out of the south end of the lake and under Route 19 as it meanders toward Cambridge Springs to the South. Use a road map to help you, and you will be able to follow French Creek to the Allegheny and see how you could get to Pittsburgh, then to the Ohio River and finally to the Mississippi like the Voyageurs. Before you go stop at the Erie History Center and pick up the *"Driving Tour of the French Trail and French Creek."*

LAKE ERIE AND
HER TWO GREAT SAND SPITS

*L*ake Erie is 254 miles long, approximately 50 miles wide, and 210 feet deep (at its deepest point south of Long Point). Although it is the second smallest and the shallowest of the Great Lakes, it is a major body of water. The voyageurs and settlers wrote that it had the appearance of a sea, rather than a lake since it was a large enough body of water to have substantial waves during storms and a water horizon (its width prohibits seeing the other shore under most conditions). Lake Erie is also deep enough to permit navigation by large ships. The Europeans and Native North Americans regarded the lake as a seaway and utilized its waters for both transportation and commerce.

Lake Erie was one of the last Great Lakes to be discovered and developed. Because of its southernmost location, however, and its connections to both the Hudson and St. Lawrence Rivers, it soon became the most important Great Lake in the development of North America. It bounds both Canada and the U.S., and it provided access between the established cities of the east and the developing west.

As a body of water, the lake behaves both like a river and a sea. Since its axis runs from southwest to northeast (in the direction of the prevailing winds) its most unique characteristic is that it is a sea with currents like those of a river. Its

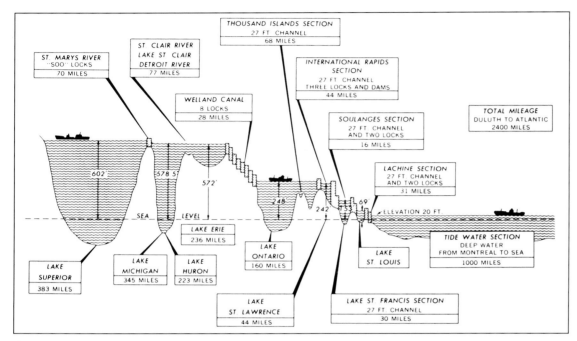

Figure 2-1
A profile view of the St. Lawrence
Seaway System water levels.

relentless flow is driven both by the prevailing southwesterly winds and the gravity-fed waters running from the higher lakes (to the north and west) toward the Atlantic Ocean. Waters from Lake Huron, for example, which are 579 feet above sea level, eventually pass from west to east through Lake Erie (570 feet above sea level), go over Niagara Falls and into Lake Ontario (245 feet above sea level). There they join the Atlantic at sea level. (See Figure 2-1)

The continuous current from southwest to northeast is responsible for the geology of the lake. It is also the culprit in much of the navigational difficulty which plagued Lake Erie's sailors over the years. Since the prevailing south-westerly winds have historically averaged approximately 11 knots, and current is related to wind velocity, the lake acts like a variable speed conveyor carrying everything in it, from southwest to northeast. During violent storms, when winds have been recorded at up to 90 knots, the conveyor belt velocity increases significantly. Even in a fresh sailing breeze of 15 to 20 knots, the effect of the current is substantial.

The two most important things that have been carried along the lake's axis (for the sake of this book) are sand and sailors. The relentless motion of the sands, which are in solution in the water, is responsible for the formation of the two great central basin sand spits, Presque Isle and Long Point. In addition, current and wave action (especially during storms) have been responsible for the navigational difficulty, shipwrecks and mayhem which have occurred in the Lake Erie Quadrangle.

SAND SPIT GEOLOGY

Navigators think of Lake Erie in terms of three different sections, the eastern, central and western basins (Figure 2-2). The Long Point/Presque Isle corridor is, essentially, the dividing line between the eastern and the central basins. Interestingly, it is this region which has historically represented a major trouble spot for sailors. Often, the navigational difficulties were caused by the presence of either Long Point or Presque Isle.

The two sand spits are unique within the lake. There are a few significantly smaller spits (Pelee and Rondeau) on the north shore, but nothing to rival the size or potential for navigational hazard of the two central basin peninsulas. Essentially the two peninsulas are mirror images of each other with Long Point being about three times larger. Geologically, this means that structures on Long Point, such as dune ridges are identical to those on Presque Isle but three times bigger, longer, and higher. Long Point also juts into the lake at more of an angle than Presque Isle, probably due to the shape of the lake's shoreline to its west. This creates more of a navigational hazard on the north shore, because this angle of exposure, coupled with Long Point's size, results in a distance of roughly 20 statute miles between the tip of the point and the shoreline immediately to its north. On summer days, when visibility is a bit hazy, it is impossible to see the north shore from the tip of Long Point. The southern tip of Presque Isle, on the other hand, is only 3 miles from the south shore.

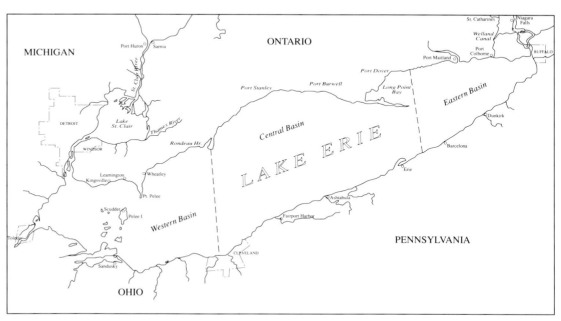

Figure 2-2
Overall view of Lake Erie and its Three Basins.

Pond structure on Presque Isle.

Both Presque Isle and Long Point were created approximately 1000 years ago by the action of sand moving from west to east along the lake's axis. Geologists suspect that the sand stopped and built up in these two specific places because of shallow (30 to 40 feet below the surface) semicircular rock ledges left over from the glacier. The rocky reefs are located just to the west of the two sand spits and apparently influenced migrating sand along the shorelines to slow down and congregate at these two spots.

Geologists believe that the spits have slowly changed shape over the years, systematically wandering to the east with the westerly current. The natural rate of movement at Presque Isle has been estimated to be approximately 50 feet per year. It is also theorized that, if for whatever reason, all of the sand and structure from either of the two sand spits were to be eroded and pass into the deeper eastern basin, it would simply disappear. The shoreline would then eventually look just like the shoreline along most of the rest of Lake Erie with little or no deposited sand or beach structure.

Since Presque Isle is one third the size of Long Point, it is much more vulnerable to the possibility of ultimate erosion and disappearance. Over the past 100 years, there have been many instances of water breaking through the western arm of the sand spit and creating an island out of the Peninsula. In some cases, the rupture was significant enough to threaten the ongoing use of Presque Isle as a break wall for Erie's harbor. For this reason, there has been a continuing effort by the Army Corps of Engineers to stabilize the Peninsula and in particular, to protect its narrow arm. In the 1920s, the Army Corps built a massive seawall along the arm of Presque Isle which finally seemed to halt migration to the east. Since that time, they have added sand to the beaches on a yearly basis. In 1992, the Army

Corps completed a controversial program in which they placed a series of rock-rubble barriers parallel to the shoreline and approximately 300 yards off shore. The people of Erie seem determined to keep Presque Isle where it is!

Although there have also been occasions over the past years when waves created a channel through the arm of Long Point and into its Inner Bay, the larger size of the land mass along its thicker western arm has precluded concern that it could wash away entirely. Also, since Long Point is not a public park with a road system leading to recreational areas, there have been no frantic engineering efforts to stabilize it (as on the south shore at Presque Isle). Fortunately, Long Point (probably because of its size), has survived the winds and waves of time.

To understand the two great peninsulas it is important to recognize that the geological and biological processes which created them continues to resculpt their contours. During prevailing southwesterly winds, sand is carried northeast by waves down the lake's axis. The bulk of the sand is carried along the shores in the shallows. As the lake's waves travel from west to east they bend toward the two shorelines. To observers standing on either shore during prevailing southwesterly winds, it appears that the waves curve toward shore. Waves which are well offshore travel straight down the lake, while those which are closer to shore seem to angle almost onshore. The closer the wave is to the beach the more it appears to be traveling almost at right angles to land rather than down the lake's axis.

In hydrodynamic terms the bottom of the wave structure, which is as high as the top of the wave, is tripping on the shallow lake bottom close to shore. The effect is to slow the inshore end of the wave and to aim it, with its contents, toward the beach. Waves carry the sand, which is suspended in the water, up onto the beach and deposit it. This process is called "nourishment." Sand piles up on top of itself and forms a mini-sandbar at the edge of the beach. Inevitably, natural materials such as sticks, debris from the water, and dead fish deposit themselves on the newly formed mini-sandbar.

The eastern tip of Long Point.

Mature inland ridge line on Presque Isle.

Two other phenomena are required to develop a mature sand spit. First an occasional reversed wind of relatively high velocity is needed. For either Long Point or Presque Isle this means a nor'easter (a storm with winds from the northeast). These occasional reversed winds of high velocity sculpt the new little sandbars with their accumulated debris from the long calm summers, into ridge lines with trapped shallow water pools behind them. In the spring of the following year, a second phenomena takes place, the annual pollination of cottonwood trees. Fluffy seed pods from the cottonwoods, which are characteristic of both peninsulas, blow into the water and become trapped in the sculpted ridge lines formed by deposited sand after the fall northeasterlies. Cottonwood seeds can only pollinate in moist shore line sandbar ridges. When they do, the small seedlings which emerge anchor the sand ridges upon which they are growing, making them relatively impervious to wave damage.

Therefore, the cottonwood trees, which are the quintessential species of both Presque Isle and Long Point, grow in orderly arch (wave) shaped rows, looking almost as though someone planted them that way. Once the trees begin to mature, their bases and root systems trap biological materials, including their own leaves, and then attract insects and animals. Sooner or later, a mature ridge line is formed with soil on both sides, a variety of plant and animal species and then a combination of trapped water, and wetlands between it and the next ridge to the west. An aerial view of either Long Point or Presque Isle reveals several sequences of ridge lines with cottonwood trees growing on their tops. The height of a ridge and the size of the trees growing on it is an indicator of its age.

Both sand spits are of great interest to biologists because the secession from beach to sandbar to dune ridge to mature forest can be seen between successive ridges to the west. The dynamics of the growth of both Long Point and Presque Isle are characterized by the carrying of sand from the western-most portions of the sand spits (erosion) along the beaches, where it is slowly deposited (nourishment), and finally to the eastern tip of the point, where it is sculpted into cottonwood ridge lines as the spit grows in an eastward direction.

LAKE LEVELS

Another important dynamic at work on the lake and its sand spits is the fluctuation of water levels. On the gradually sloping beaches of either Long Point or Presque Isle, small fluctuations in lake level can either expose or bury tremendous volumes of sandy beach. An increase of one foot, for example, may result in a loss of 100 yards of beach. There are three sources of water level fluctuations in Lake Erie. First, is the predictable annual shift of water levels, resulting from seasonal variations in rainfall and the resulting shifts in the water table. Typically, water levels are at their maximum in spring and fall, then recede over the summer and winter months. The highest water level is in June and the lowest is in February. These seasonal differences have historically averaged almost two feet. This fluctuation is critical to the pollination of cottonwood seeds and the formation of the ridge lines at the shore which hold the young trees.

The second source of fluctuation which can create substantial short term problems for the stability of the sand spits, is called a "seiche" or bathtub effect. This commonly occurs during the fall when storms with reversed (northeasterly)

Low water levels expose a beach at Presque Isle.

High water damage in 1975 to the cottages of Long Point.

wind patterns push surface water from one end of the lake's surface to the other. The seiche effect has been described as a phenomena similar to holding a pan of water in the air and then shifting it from one direction to the other. The resultant stacking of extra water on top of the surface of the lake can (during high winds and storms) create sudden increases in water levels of five or more feet. This seiche effect, in combination with high winds and waves, can instantaneously tear away sand dunes, ridge lines, and vegetation which have taken decades to develop. The final and least predictable source of water level fluctuation is the year to year variation which seems to occur in cyclical patterns. There are many theories about how and why these shifts take place, but few definitive answers to the ultimate problems of erosion which they create. In the mid–1980s, for example, water levels were so high that large portions of Long Point seemed to be doomed. Buildings were lost, and even the lighthouse on the tip was at risk. By the early 1990s, however, water levels had fallen by almost 4 feet throughout the lake. Sailboaters from Port Rowan's Inner Bay, who had gradually grown accustomed to average depths of 10 feet, were suddenly faced with an average seasonal depth of only 5 to 6 feet of water. Many had to remove their deep draft boats prior to the fall low water cycle. Currently, most large boat sailors have abandoned their docks in the Inner Bay. The water is simply not deep enough to make sailboating with more than a 4 foot draft practical.

NAVIGATIONAL PROBLEMS

For old time sailors the currents also created some difficult navigational problems. As we will see later, most of the shipwrecks and problems in Lake Erie have occurred near the Erie-Long Point Corridor. One of the primary reasons for this problem (which will be elaborated later), is Long Point, itself. The point is a navigational hazard because of its position as gateway to either the eastern or the central basins (depending upon the ship's direction).

But, before we get to the adventures and shipwrecks, a word about the navigational dilemma of travel by sailing vessel, or for that matter, by the early (and relatively slow) steamships. Most ships were traveling the length (rather than the width) of the lake, heading from east to west or visa versa. Great Lakes sailors call the westward trip "upbound" and the eastward voyage "downbound." And for good reason! Given the relentless effect of the current toward the east, and the fact that storms would often increase the current velocity precipitously, it should come as no surprise that many of the early vessels which plied Lake Erie, had quite a difficult time going west.

It is important to note (for those who are not familiar with sailing) that sailboats cannot go directly upwind. To get upwind, a sailboat must tack back and forth at the closest possible angle at which it can "point" to windward. Modern America's Cup type sailboats can sail within 40 degrees of the wind. For them, a trip up the lake would be fairly easy. Given the prevailing south westerly breeze they would make a series of tacks at 40 degrees to the actual wind direction. Since modern racers can make speeds of 15 to 20 knots, Dennis Conner and his crew could leave Buffalo and be at the western end of Lake Erie (after several tacks) in about 20 hours (assuming an 11 knot breeze).

Lake Erie's first schooners were neither as fast as this nor as efficient, with respect to pointing (sailing close to the wind). Most were barely able to sail upwind at angles of 60 or 70 degrees to the wind. As a result they would sail a much longer up wind distance than modern sailboats. To make matters worse, top speeds for the schooners were usually in the neighborhood of 5 to 7 knots. Given that their speed over the bottom was much slower than that of modern sailing yachts, the old time schooners could find themselves laboring to make upwind and up-current progress. Revisiting the Dennis Conner example, a typical 19th century schooner might have taken 90 hours under ideal conditions.

In stormy weather, as the velocity of the wind rose to 30, 40, or even 50 knots, the old time sailing boats would find it increasingly hard to make headway. Boat speed could be only slightly more than the effect of the current or in extreme conditions less than zero. Many a captain went afoul off Long Point or Presque Isle as he drove his boat toward the shelter of the sand spit, or tried to round it, only to find that he was trapped by wind and current and driven onto it.

The plight of the early steamers was not much better. While they did not have to tack up wind, the steamships of the 1800s were also limited by speed. Most of them labored to reach velocities of 10 knots through the water. This meant that during storms, speed made good across the bottom could be reduced to 4 or 5 knots, giving plenty of opportunity for navigational difficulty. For the schooners and steamers alike, a trip up-current could be an arduous task. A down-wind, down-current trip, on the other hand, was an exciting ride. In addition to grains of sand, the two sandy peninsulas collected a large number of ships, sailors, and cargo over the years.

Lake Erie Adventures

1. Locate a nautical chart of Lake Erie and study it. Note the distances and depths as portrayed on the chart and try to imagine the problems of the early navigators.

2. Visit Presque Isle. Drive around the Peninsula slowly looking for sand ridges and dune lines. There is a good example of a mature sand ridge on the left side of the road, immediately after the intersection where the main road loops around toward the bay side of the Peninsula, just after the marina road intersection. This ridge line is on the path which begins just before the bridge which crosses the marina outlet to the lagoons.

3. Try to find and attend a lecture on succession forest on the Peninsula. The state park has a regular lecture series. Call and ask for a schedule.

4. Wait for a stormy day and take a field trip to a place where there is a panorama of the lake. Sit for a moment and imagine the difficulties of the early sailors. Can you tell the wind direction (the two most important things for sailors are wind direction and velocity)? Try to observe the phenomena of waves twisting toward shore.

5. Even though it is generally impossible to see across the lake, there are exceptions. On cool clear days in the fall, Americans can see the Canadian shore from elevations just south of Erie. The best place is at the junction of Routes 89 and 90. Go south of Route 90 on Route 89 about 600 yards to the first right turn. Follow this road to the top of the first hill and you will have an excellent panorama of the lake. On clear days from this vantage point, you should be able to spot the Long Point Lighthouse almost directly across from you, the 680 foot stacks at Nanticoke's Generating Plant, and the coal delivery conveyor at Stelco Steel. It is also possible to see these landmarks from other high spots in and around Erie, Pa. (West and East Grandview for example). Remember as you gaze, that Long Point is about 15 degrees to the east from Erie as you look across the lake. Take binoculars!

6. On the Canadian side it is even easier to see the U.S. on clear days. This is because of the glacial escarpment south of Erie which creates the appearance that there are mountains behind the city. On clear fall days, an observer from the Port Dover or Port Rowan areas can see a blue-grey ridge line above the water horizon. This ridge line starts west of Erie and reaches a maximum height near the New York state line. Two excellent observation posts on the Canadian side are: (1) the clubhouse at the Turkey Point Golf Course, and (2) east of Port Dover on the Old Lake Road.

7. Visit the Long Point area and walk the beaches at the Provincial Park.

8. On Kelly's Island in western Lake Erie you can see the marks made by the glacier as it withdrew from the area.

THE LAKE, HER PORTS AND THE QUADRANGLE

The purpose of this chapter is twofold. First we hope to build an overall perspective of the lake and her ports, and then we will present a detailed description of the Quadrangle. In the first two chapters, some general history and geology were presented. To fully appreciate the lake, however, it is important to clearly visualize its overall shape and size.

Figure 3-1 is a representation of the entire lake and its primary ports (current and historic). In addition, major commercial routes have been designated using dotted lines. Most commercial traffic proceeds either along the lake's axis or on straightline routes between major ports. This is why it is essential to understand both past and present port locations.

While most traffic patterns remain the same, there are a few notable exceptions. The first is the shift, on the eastern end, from Buffalo to Port Colbourne as the primary port of entry. This occurred as a result of the gradual transition from the use of the Erie Barge Canal (connecting Buffalo with New York City) to the Welland Canal, which exits the lake at Port Colbourne. Most of the traffic which used to depart and return to Buffalo now uses the Welland. So, it proceeds up and down the lake at slightly different angles with respect to the eastern basin.

A second fundamental change is caused by the disappearance of commercial sailing vessels. Sailboats loaded with cargo no longer tack up the lake. Because of the evolution to engine driven shipping, it is possible for trade routes to be clearly designated on nautical charts. This helps to minimize the likelihood of collisions at sea (previously a significant danger). Nautical charts now clearly designate boundaries for both upbound and downbound traffic. These designated zones insure that most of the commercial traffic, which still moves west or east along the lake's axis, is arranged like highway traffic. Upbound vessels, for example, all move along the same corridor, so that they are unlikely to encounter each other.

These days, the only traffic crossing patterns are the few predictable routes where shipping moves across the lake in a north-south direction. Interestingly, there has been a significant increase in this cross traffic within the Quadrangle during the past 20 years. This has been created by the Stelco Steel and Nanticoke Power Plant industrial development, approximately 10 miles east of Port Dover. Both operations burn coal as a primary power source. The volume of coal burned is substantial. To support the continuous requirement for coal, special unloading docks were constructed at the Stelco plant and Ontario Hydro's Nanticoke Works near the town of Nanticoke in the early 1970s. Approximately two lakers per day tie up at these piers to offload coal and iron ore.

Since most of the coal that is delivered to the Nanticoke piers comes from Sandusky, Conneaut, and Ashtabula, there are currently three significant traffic crossing patterns in the area of the lake just north of Erie. Not only must the ships within this North/South corridor cross the established upbound and downbound traffic routes, but they must successfully negotiate a rounding of the shoal waters off Long Point to make port at Nanticoke. To complicate matters, they must also drive through the north shore's largest commercial fishing fleet, as well as a busy recreational route in the process.

PORT DEVELOPMENT

Settlers to the lake area were drawn to the water's edge, and collected at places where river or creek outlets met the shoreline. Almost every major city which was to become a port along Lake Erie developed near a creek outlet. Commercial sailing began on an ad hoc basis. It was obvious to the early settlers that water travel held the potential for transport between neighboring cities. It could also connect them to both the eastern (old) and the western (new) worlds.

At the beginning of the 1800s, there were no ports, as we know them, on the lake. There were a few "natural harbors," such as the bay in Erie, which provided shelter for the outlet creeks and enabled maritime commerce to develop. The Cuyahoga River basin in Cleveland, the bay area in Sandusky, and Toledo were the only other natural harbors on the U.S. side. Of these, Erie was by far the best natural harbor. Erie seemed destined to become the most prosperous city on the Great Lakes. On the north shore, the Grand River area at Port Maitland, the Inner Bay behind Long Point, and Rondeau/Erieau were the only natural harbor areas. But even these few places were riddled with shallows, sand bars and other navigational hazards.

There were schooners doing trade before the development of harbors along the lake, but they worked their way in and out of natural harbors or took their chances by anchoring near the outlets of creeks along the open lake. On trade runs, they had to anchor in the open waters of the lake in front of a destination city and unload by row boat or by wading ashore. Often, the early commercial schooners were built by entrepreneurs right in local outlet creeks. The captains would make a number of runs during the summer months, and then pull their schooners back up the creeks to winter, sheltered from the fury of fall and winter storms.

The lack of regular harbor facilities significantly limited the growth and development of commerce along the lake shore. At the end of the War of 1812, when attention was called to the potential for shipping on the lakes, pressures were

Nanticoke.

brought to bear on both the U.S. and British governments to appropriate monies for harbor development.

Perhaps the single most important catalyst for this action was the launching and subsequent success of the first steamship, the *Walk In The Water*, at Black Rock in 1818. The four year tenure of that pioneering venture was greeted along Lake Erie's south shore by a tremendous interest in shipping and commerce. Unlike schooners, the steamboat made regular scheduled runs and traveled directly up and down the coast. Townspeople could go to the lake shore and count on seeing her steaming by.

City officials recognized the merits of steam travel. They quickly understood that the cities which built commercial ports would attract steamers, and that the existing schooners would also do business in these cities. By the mid–1820s, the U.S. Government had begun the systematic appropriation of funds for harbor development. Such funding grew through the century. By the 1900s, there were several established ports, such as Buffalo, in places where there had originally been almost no access. Canadian ports development lagged behind by almost a decade because of the extra layer of bureaucracy involved in securing permissions from Britain.

Port development proceeded in three stages over a 50 year period. First, there was dredging to establish a navigable channel. Often, this was followed by the construction of protective piers which extended into the lake. The final stage in many of the major port areas, such as Cleveland, Ashtabula, and Buffalo was the construction of a series of sea walls.

In the following sections, the developing ports are listed. The lists which follow proceed from east to west, and include both historic ports (which may no longer exist) and present day ports, which (in some cases) are not mentioned in the early history of the lake. Some minor ports and most small landing sights, which are often frequented by fishermen during the summer months, are excluded. The following legend is provided to assist in classification:

H – A former port of historic significance
L – A large port capable of berthing commercial freighters
M – A medium sized port able to berth some commercial vessels
S – A small port available for smaller non-commercial vessels

NORTH SHORE PORTS

Moving from east to west, the following represent the ports along the Canadian north shore:

N01. Point Abino [S]
N02. Crystal Beach [S]
N03. Port Colborne [L]
N04. Port Maitland [M]
N05. Ontario Hydro Docks [L]
N06. Nanticoke [S]
N07. Stelco's Pier [L]
N08. Port Dover [M]
N09. Port Ryerse [S]
N10. Normandale [S]
N11. Turkey Point [S]
N12. St. Williams [S]
N13. Port Rowan [S]
N14. Port Royal [H]
N15. Port Burwell [S]
N16. Port Bruce [H]
N17. Port Stanley [M]
N18. Erieau/Rondeau [M]
N19. Port Crow [H]
N20. Wheatley [S]
N21. Leamington [S]
N22. Kingsville [S]
N23. Colchester [S]

Normandale.

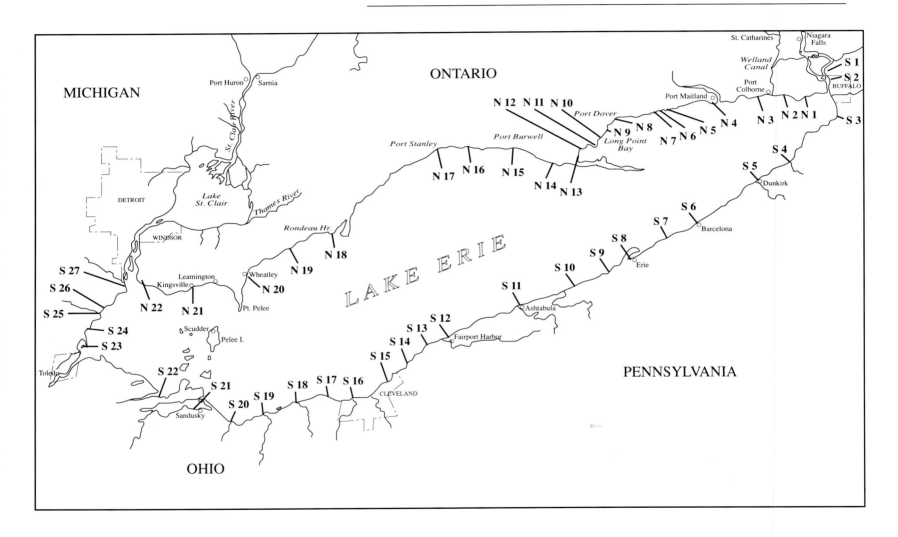

SOUTH SHORE PORTS

Moving again from east to west, the primary ports along the United States coastline include:

S01. Tonowanda [S]

S02. Black Rock [H]

S03. Buffalo [L]

S04. Cattaraugus Creek [S]

S05. Dunkirk [M]

S06. Barcelona [S]

S07. Safe Harbor Marina [S]

S08. Erie [L]

S09. Walnut Creek [S]

S10. Conneaut [L]

S11. Ashtabula [L]

S12. Fairport [S]

S13. Mentor [S]

S14. Chagrin River [S]

S15. Cleveland [L]

S16. Rocky River [S]

S17. Lorain [M]

S18. Beaver River [S]

S19. Vermilion [M]

S20. Huron [L]

S21. Sandusky [L]

S22. Port Clinton [M]

S23. Toledo [L]

S24. Otter Creek [S]

S25. Bolles Harbor [S]

S26. Monroe [S]

S27. Swan Creek [S]

The Ontario Hydro Plant's 680 foot stacks near Nanticoke.

THE THREE BASINS

Navigators think of Lake Erie in terms of three distinct sections: the eastern, central and western basins. The eastern basin is the portion of the lake ranging from the Niagara River near Buffalo to a line drawn between Long Point and Erie. This portion of the lake generally consists of deep water off shore. But, there are a few rocky reefs on the northern coast, namely the Tecumseh reef near Port Maitland, and a series of rocky reefs near Nanticoke. For deep draft vessels traveling the shipping lanes, there are no obstructions along the center line except for the tip of the point itself. A vessel that remains a mile or two to the south of the lighthouse would be in 150 to 200 feet of water.

Port Ryerse.

Conneaut Harbor.

Barcelona Harbor.

The central lake basin is generally regarded as the area between Long Point and a north/south line drawn between Cleveland and Rondeau/Erieau. This basin, while not as deep as the eastern basin, is generally sandy bottomed with few navigational difficulties. The shipping lanes continue down the center of the lake (as in the eastern basin), but in this area there is a navigational hazard created by cross traffic. The continuous flow of coal carriers from Ashtabula, Conneaut, and Sandusky to the Stelco and Ontario Hydro piers near Nanticoke creates crossing patterns within the central basin. These converge just east of Long Point in the center of the Quadrangle, where vessels are slowing to turn around the point while crossing both upbound and downbound traffic.

The western end (Cleveland to the Detroit River) is quite unique relative to the central and eastern basins. First and foremost in its differences is a string of islands ranging from Sandusky and Cedar Point (on the south shore), across the lake in a northerly direction to Point Pelee. In addition to the quaintness of these islands, each of which has its own distinct personality, the existence of the land masses present a navigational challenge for large ships.

The western end of the lake is also characterized by its relatively shallow depths. In the western end, there are large expanses of offshore water with depths of only 10 to 15 feet. This makes many of the between-island and slightly off-shore shallows a navigational hazard to large boats. The shallow waters also create a zone in which storms can quickly whip up a major chop, causing discomfort and danger to pleasure boaters and commercial shipping alike.

The Pelee Passage is an ongoing problem for commercial shipping. Steamers must "thread the needle" by navigating between Pelee Island and its Middle Ground Shoal (to the south) and Pelee Point with its Grub Reef on the (northern) Canadian mainland. This feat can be much more difficult than it would appear, even for today's relatively sophisticated ships, on stormy Lake Erie seas with high winds and steeply breaking waves. The difficulties presented to the early schooner captains who had to tack up this narrow channel by sail power alone were more grave.

The western point of entry is the Detroit River. Ships leaving Lake Erie must proceed up the river against a substantial current to Lake St. Clair, pass through that relatively small and shallow body of water, and then ascend the St. Clair River to Lake Huron. Modern commercial vessels have little difficulty moving up the river against this current. For the early sailors, and even the turn of the century steamships, the current in the Detroit river was more formidable. More than one schooner captain was forced to turn back and wait for a weather change in order to make "way" up the Detroit. By the middle 1800s a new industry had developed in which tug boats would tow schooners up the Detroit and St. Clair Rivers.

A favorite yacht club barroom tale told by modern sailors is the difficulty presented to today's sophisticated sailboats as they attempt to ascend the Detroit River. Most modern sailing yachts are limited to speeds of 6 or 7 knots. Depending upon current and wind conditions, the river may flow south at 5 to 6 knots in some spots. The resultant speed made good over the bottom is, therefore, sometimes as little as 1 or 2 nautical miles per hour. For both rivers the most difficult spots are the bridges spanning the exits to the open lakes (St. Clair and Huron). The relatively short trip up the rivers can be quite arduous.

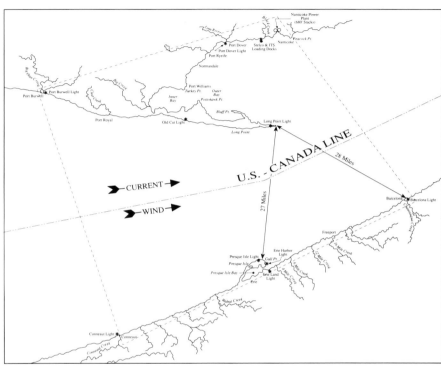

Figure 3-2
The Quadrangle.

Aerial view of loading docks at Stelco Steel.

THE LAKE ERIE QUADRANGLE

So finally, we come to a description of the Lake Erie Quadrangle (Figure 3-2). The physical area of the Quadrangle is defined by two north-south lines drawn across the lake. The first connects Conneaut, on the U.S. shore, with Port Burwell on the north side. The second (almost parallel line) is from Barcelona on the south coast to Peacock Point, just east of Nanticoke, Ontario.

There are a number of landmarks and minor landing sites within the Quadrangle of little consequence to the overall view of Lake Erie. But, these landmarks are important in setting the stage for the stories which follow. To build a foundation for subsequent chapters, we will describe the shorelines in detail beginning with the north shore. As in earlier descriptions, we will proceed from east to west.

The first point of interest on the Canadian side is Peacock Point. A jutting sand spit—this point of land protrudes almost a mile from the mainland and marks an area of navigational difficulty. From Peacock Point west to Port Dover, there are a number of dangerous shoal areas with rocky bottom structures. Unlike much of the eastern and most of the central and western basins, which are sandy bottomed, these shoals represent the same significant dangers to modern deep draft boaters (sailboats and commercial vessels) as they did in the old days. Before the advent of charts, these rocks took their toll on a number of wooden schooners.

Moving east, the port of Nanticoke was a sleepy fishing village for most of the early history of the north shore. In the early 1970s, however, the construction of an industrial park with Stelco Steel, The Nanticoke works of Ontario Hydro, an oil refinery and several secondary support industries, was completed. Today's Nanticoke area is a busy industrial port. Ontario Hydro built its own docks east of Nanticoke's old harbor. Just to the west, Stelco created a one mile pier to accommodate its delivery ships. The docks themselves have no natural charm. They are simply massive steel and concrete edifices protruding into the lake and connected to the industrial park by automatic conveyer systems.

The town of Port Dover is located about 10 miles from the Nanticoke docks. Dover is a unique and quaint village. There is a river entrance to the port, with a well-marked pier and deep draft capability. Immediately to the west of Dover are several miles of white cliffs. These cliffs were responsible for the name of the town (Dover England). Along the 12 mile run from Port Dover to Turkey Point, at the entrance to the Inner Bay, there are two landing areas of historic significance: Port Ryerse, and Normandale. Normandale was the sight of the first iron oven in Ontario, and was an important location during the early history of the province. Ryerse was once a more important port than Dover. During the era of the Old Cut in Long Point's Inner Bay, Ryerse was an important stop over station for schooners.

Port Dover: harbor entrance.

Turkey Point (like Peacock Point) is also a jutting sand spit. It marks the entrance to the important Inner Bay. Today's Turkey Point has become a thriving tourist area, featuring a provincial park, camping, and a large number of cottages. There is a large marina which can handle moderate draft vessels.

Immediately south of Turkey Point, is Pottohawk Point, the northern-most point of land along the north beaches of Long Point. Standing at Turkey Point on a clear day, it is possible to look south to Pottohawk some 5 miles away. Although it seems as though the waters between Turkey Point and Pottohawk would be easily navigable by large boats moving into or out of the Inner Bay, this is not the case. A shallow sand bar proceeds from Pottohawk toward Turkey Point. During late summer, there is often as little as one or two feet of water along the top of this submerged sand ridge. There are two navigable channels through the bar allowing vessels to enter the Inner Bay. More than a few boats, however, have either been unaware of the bar or have missed the channels and run aground.

Port Rowan.

Continuing along the north shore past Turkey Point to the Inner Bay, there is the port of St. Williams, which is followed by Port Rowan at the head of the Inner Bay. Rowan is another charming fishing village, and is home to a large recreational and charter fishing fleet. There is also some commercial Seine fishing in the Port Rowan area.

Erie's Harbor.
Photo by ART BECKER

Pottohawk Point.

Immediately south of Port Rowan (along the causeway built in 1928) is the cottage village of Long Point. Long Point is a summer community with a number of marinas and camping parks. The village guards the western end of Long Point (to its east) and adjoins the provincial park. This is the eastern-most point of public access to the great peninsula. To the west of Long Point, there is a series of truly spectacular sand dunes which were formed by the geological sand nourishment system which is responsible for the Point. Just west of the cottage community is the previous location of Port Royal, a thriving port of the mid–1800s that no longer exists. The shoreline then falls off to the north west until it reaches Port Burwell, a small fishing port and the western boundary of the quadrangle. From the vantage point of the water, the shoreline from Burwell (back east) to the tip of Long Point, represents a continuous 37 mile run of shoal waters and beach, with no port of sanctuary for even medium draft vessels. Only a beachable boat could stop along this expanse of shoreline.

On the U.S shore, the Quadrangle begins at Barcelona, a harbor which now services primarily recreational craft. Moving west toward Erie, there is a new marina just past the Pa. line called Safe Harbor. This operation can accept medium draft recreational vessels, but is of limited size. There are several launching points along the shore between Safe Harbor and Erie including the North East Yacht Club at Freeport Beach, and the launches at Shades Beach and Lawrence Park. Even for shallow draft vessels, however, the 27 mile expanse from Barcelona to Erie is a hostile shore in a storm.

The harbor at Erie continues to represent the finest natural refuge on the lake. From the outside entrance and Lampe Marina, a boater making way into Presque Isle Bay has access to a number of natural anchorages (Misery Bay, The Marina Basin) as well as a series of marinas and yacht clubs. Moving west from Erie, there are a few minor launch sights prior to the port of Conneaut. These include the Pa. Fish Commission access at Walnut Creek, which can accept shallow draft vessels, and the Avonia Beach launch just north of Fairview.

The glacial action which formed the lake created a sandy basin along the south shore of the lake. Thus, the waters along the U.S. side of the Quadrangle are primarily sandy bottomed, presenting far less difficulty to navigation over the years than the rocky shoals deposited by the glacier along the north shore.

DOING THE DETROIT

In the early 1980s Fr. Robert Levis, a priest and faculty member at Gannon University was ascending the Detroit River on a summer sailing vacation with his friend Fr. Robert Goodell on the 38 foot sailboat *Stella Maris*. They had begun the river portion of the trip late in the morning, and were concerned about completing the trip before dark. They were operating with only the engine and making 6 knots (through the water). As they passed Detroit, it was becoming apparent that they were not making much progress with respect to riverside landmarks.

Their plight was made increasingly obvious by freighters that were passing them in the same direction. As they approached the Ambassador Bridge at Detroit, a particularly fast moving section of the river, they could see that they were making painfully little progress. As the *Stella Maris*, in effect, sat still in the river, one freighter after another appeared astern, caught them and then passed to the north. Looking back, they saw one more in a series of freighters appear and decided that they would have to take some kind of action to make faster progress.

The Ambassador Bridge from the Detroit River.
Photo by JOHN MITCHELL

Keeping an eye on the latest ship, which was closing from astern, they raised the mainsail and then the headsail. This exercise took about 5 minutes. The sails raised their speed appreciably. They were now motor sailing and making better progress. But, they were no longer able to make a course directly up river. Sailing as close to the wind as possible, they were being driven toward the west bank of the river and the center of the navigable channel.

They decided that they could solve this dilemma by tacking to starboard and passing in front of the approaching freighter. Their estimates suggested that such a maneuver was feasible, so they came about and began the fateful tack to the east side of the river. They planned to pass in front of the freighter and then tack back under its stern to safety near the end of the river which was now almost in sight.

Unbeknownst to the two priests, the vessel which they were about to tack in front of was a Russian freighter with a U.S. harbor pilot aboard. The pilot was anxious to extend every courtesy to the Soviet Captain and his crew. As the 38 foot sailboat tacked, the priests began to realize that they had possibly "cut this one a bit too close." The sailboat was making better progress through the water, but the freighter was closing the distance between them rapidly. The crossing was going to be close but not dangerous. Suddenly, the freighter began sounding its horn in an intermittent signal which indicated danger. Puzzled by this apparent overreaction, they quickly raised a larger headsail and pushed the engine harder. The sailboat heeled over, picked up speed, and crossed well in front of the Russian freighter. The freighter continued its warning blasts, however, and altered course toward the right side of the river channel.

A quick review of the charts suggested that if the *Stella Maris* exited the marked channel to the right, she would be in danger of grounding. But the freighter relentlessly continued toward them sounding its horn. The two priests could see no alternative. They sailed out of the channel and to within several yards of the river bank as the Russian freighter passed by. Remarkably, they escaped running aground and tacked back out into the marked channel to the relative safety of a calmer stretch of river. In a short time, they were out of the river and into Lake St. Clair.

Aboard the freighter, the pilot had orders to impress his Russian associates with the hospitality of the U.S., which was anxious to improve international business along the lakes. After a final blast of the horn, he called the U.S. Coast Guard to complain, assuring his new Russian friends that these "crazy sailors" would be dealt with by U.S. authorities.

Back aboard the sailboat the two sailing comrades were congratulating themselves on their escape from a close call and on the completion of the river trip. As they set sail across Lake St. Clair, they heard sirens and looked back to see a Coast Guard Cutter approaching. The U.S. Cutter ordered the sails lowered and took the boat into custody. After much discussion and apology, the crew of the cutter relented and agreed that they would let the sailboat continue its journey. But first the Coast Guard would have to conduct a complete ship's inspection. The Coast Guard had to conduct their inspection back down river at their station docks. They took the sailboat in tow and returned to the head of the river, where the two priests were detained for several hours and given a reprimand. The next day, the up-river journey began for a second time. This time there would be no tacking in front of freighters.

Lake Erie Adventures

1. It's field trip time again. We suggest that you take time for a close inspetion of both shorelines of the Quadrangle.

2. On the North Shore you should begin at Nanticoke. Drive to the power plant (680 foot stacks) and go from there west into the town itself. Visit the dock area and eat at Hoover's. Follow the Old Lake Road behind Stelco and stop every little while to see the sights. You can actually traverse Lake Shore Drive (although the name changes) all the way to Port Rowan. Be sure to visit Dover, Ryerse, Normandale, Turkey Point, St. Williams and all the other points of interest on the way. (Incidently there is a wonderful bike route called the Talbot Trail.)

3. On the south shore begin at Barcelona and follow the lake road to Conneaut. Take time to walk the bay front at Erie visiting the South Pier to see the channel and working your way west. West of Erie you can visit the lake shore at a number of spots including Walnut Creek Access, Avonia Beach, Lake City Community Park, and various points along the Ohio shoreline east of Conneaut.

4. This is important! Visit the Lake Erie Islands in the western end. There are regular ferry services operating out of the Sandusky or Leamington areas. If you wish you can take a car or a bike with you. At Put-in Bay a trip to the top of Perry's Monument is a must. We also recommend Kelly's Island and Pelee Island for their unique charm. There are so many things to do in this area that you can easily spend several days there. It gets busy in mid-summer, though, so we prefer early spring or fall seasons.

COMMERCIAL AND MILITARY SAILING: THE SCHOONERS

*I*t would seem that a book about commercial vessels in Lake Erie should include two distinct periods, an age of sail followed by an era of steam propulsion. In actuality, sailing ships and steamers cohabited the lake for all of the 19th century. After the War of 1812, the numbers and types of commercial sailing vessels grew rapidly. Steamships appeared in the 1920s and 1930s and also increased dramatically. By the middle of the century, the numbers of both steamers and schooners were reaching their peak as the two types competed with each other.

Great Lake's schooners continued to operate successfully throughout the 1800s. As steamers grew in size and number, their routes were formalized and their schedules became predictable. Slowly the sailing ships, which depended upon the wind and could not easily predict departure or arrival times, began to fall into disfavor. Though this evolution took place during the second half of the 1800s, a viable market niche remained for the entrepreneur who could afford to build and operate a wind-powered schooner. While passenger traffic flocked toward steamers, and the steamer cargos evolved toward large container loads and predictable packet runs, the schooners continued carrying smaller loads and serving minor ports on an as-needed basis.

Commercial sailing continued through the 1800s and well into the 1900s. In fact, the last known sailing ship in regular service, the *J.T. Wing*, operated until the mid–1930s. For many years after, schooners which had been converted to barges remained in service as tows.

Lake Erie's sailing ships are best categorized by rig. Purists may argue the details, but the following simple classification system is offered: 1. **Sloop** ... single masted, fore and aft rigged. 2. **Schooner** ... two or more (up to five) masted, fore and aft rigged, and usually having a smaller mast forward. 3. **Brig** ... two masted, and square rigged. 4. **Bark** ... three or more masted, with square rigged masts except for the mizzen.

Bark

Brigs and barks are square rigged. Their masts carry yards (or horizontal booms) which hold sails that are trimmed from two lower corners. Sloops and schooners use fore and aft rigged masts, and triangular sails on booms which are trimmed from the lower aft corner. There was a common anomaly among square riggers on the Great Lakes which is troublesome for classification buffs. This was the use of fore and aft rigged mizzen (rear) masts on barks and brigs instead of square rigging. This Great Lakes innovation was an attempt to minimize sailing effort. The hybrid rigs are called barkentines and brigantines. Their fore and aft mizzen mast rigging required fewer sailors to operate and resulted in better windward (higher pointing on the wind) performance. Another odd rig developed on the lakes was the topsail schooner. This rig used a single square rigged yard on the main mast of a schooner. Under sail it looked remarkably like a brigantine rig.

THE GRIFFON

The first commercial sailing vessel on Lake Erie was the *Griffon*. The idea for this vessel was proposed by LaSalle as a money making scheme to support his explorations of the new world. LaSalle moved materials and shipbuilders from

Quebec across Lake Ontario and up the Niagara River. He portaged the falls, dragging all of his materials up-river to a spot near the opening to Lake Erie. There he constructed his ship, a bark, during the winter and spring of 1678-1679. LaSalle planned to use the *Griffon* to move furs from the upper lakes to Quebec.

The August 1679 maiden voyage of the *Griffon* marked the advent of sailing on Lake Erie. It was also a herald of events that would befall commercial sailing for the next 200 years. First, there was difficulty moving the *Griffon* out of the river. LaSalle had apparently miscalculated the strength of the current and almost failed to escape the Niagara. Once free and sailing the lake, LaSalle presumed that he was out of danger as he headed west for the Detroit River.

At the eastern boundary of the Lake Erie Quadrangle, the *Griffon* almost became the first disaster on Long Point. Sailing west in thick fog, LaSalle's navigator began to get lead-line soundings of less than 30 feet. He also thought that he could hear the sounds of breaking surf. He reported this to LaSalle who had been thinking that he was in the center of the lake and free of navigational problems. Fortunately, LaSalle remembered seeing a chart of Long Point which had been drawn by Galinee during his winter at Port Dover. He doubted that this point of land could extend into the lake to the location of the *Griffon*, which he judged to be 20 miles offshore. But he reduced sail and proceeded with caution. Suddenly, the fog lifted and all hands were able to see the tip of Long Point in their immediate path. They would surely have run aground if they had not slowed the ship's progress. LaSalle named the tip of the point "Cape St. Francis" as he continued his westward voyage.

Unfortunately, things did not go well for the *Griffon*. The ship encountered a fierce storm in Lake Huron, after ascending the Detroit river with great difficulty. By this time the crew began to question the wisdom of the venture. The 60 foot ship did eventually reach its destination in Green Bay, where it was loaded with furs. The *Griffon* and its increasingly disgruntled crew left for the return trip, but was never heard from again.

Two Masted Fishing Schooner

Brig

The fate of the *Griffon* is unknown. Marine archaeologists and historians have searched for her remains for centuries. One thing is apparent, however. The failure of the venture dissuaded the early settlers and voyageurs from continuing efforts toward commercial sailing. For the duration of the 1600s and most of the 1700s, commerce on Lake Erie was carried along the shores by canoe and bateaux.

THE EARLY YEARS

As towns grew along Lake Erie, there was a resurgence of interest in commercial sailing. It was obvious to the settlers of the region that trade between lakeshore towns offered the potential for profits. In the late 1700s and early 1800s, a small number of sailing vessels appeared on the lake and began to make trading runs between cities. To a large extent, ship building was amateurish. It took place at towns with creek inlets as natural harbors. Understandably, the builders of early vessels were timid about investing large amounts of capital in an unproven venture.

Most ships were developed for the purpose of trading with other towns along the lake. Often, they were built with a trade route or cargo in mind. The builders used native materials, which were plentiful along the lakes at the time. The favorite rigs were schooners and sloops. The vessels were relatively small, ranging from 30 to 50 feet. The first commercial sailing vessel launched in Lake Erie, during this period, was the schooner *Washington*.

Three-masted schooner from late 1800s.

The *Washington* was built at Freeport (North East, Pa.) in the outlet creek in 1797. A few years later, she was moved around Niagara Falls on wheels, renamed the *Lady Washington*, and put into service on Lake Ontario. At the turn of the century

(1800), there were five sailing vessels working Lake Erie. These included the *Good Intent*, the *Harlequin*, the *Otter* and the *Erie Packet*.

As the number of commercial sloops and schooners slowly grew during the pre-war period, there was a simultaneous build-up of military vessels on both sides of the lake. Some military shipbuilding had taken place at the time of the War of Independence, but the increasing frictions prior to the War of 1812 caused a resurgence of military vessels. Unlike the private businessmen who built relatively simple sloops and schooners, military builders used larger square rigged designs.

THE WAR OF 1812

As hostilities escalated, the natural harbor areas of Erie and Long Point became important strategic building blocks. Two important events took place within these areas marking the historical development of the respective towns forever. In Erie, a businessman and sailor, Daniel Dobbins was pressed into service to design and build a fleet of warships for the U.S. Navy in the city's harbor. Since the harbor was not yet well developed, and deep draft ships could not sail past the Peninsula, Dobbins reasoned that a fleet could be built in secrecy then floated out of the harbor to join the war effort the next year.

Dobbins, an Erie resident, had substantial commercial sailing experience. He was chosen for this task because he knew the area and its resources, and had both the skills and charisma to engineer and lead the project. For political reasons, however, his command was given to Commodore Oliver H. Perry just prior to the completion of the fleet. This change in command from a trusted and experienced local sailor was more than unsettling to the war effort. Eventually problems of command were settled and the Erie based fleet sailed to the western end of the lake where it engaged the British in the now famous "Battle of Lake Erie."

A more interesting but lesser-known battle took place in Port Dover in 1814. A five ship American sailing fleet with 800 men under the command of John Campbell sailed from Erie into the Outer Bay behind Long Point hoping to engage the British Fleet, which was said to be holed up near Port Dover. They also hoped to destroy all of the mills which were supplying food to the enemy forces. Not finding the British fleet, the Americans anchored, rowed to shore in Port Dover (then called Dover Mills) and burned the entire town. The men of Dover had left to fight with the militia, leaving women, children and elderly.

Campbell's men moved from building to building setting fire to everything and slaughtering the animals. Upon reaching the last building where a woman was cooking bread, the sailors stopped to eat the freshly baked bread. Because of the kindness of feeding Campbell's hungry men, the house was spared. Legend has it that the house still stands in the town of Port Dover. When the townspeople rebuilt Dover, they moved the town center east to the present-day site of the main harbor and renamed it "Port" Dover.

Returning to their ships, Campbell's fleet sailed up the shore from Dover toward the Inner Bay. They stopped again at Port Ryerse and Normandale, rowing to shore to burn the mills and houses. Continuing up the coast toward the Inner Bay and the Backus Mill, they were fooled into retreating by a tiny group of militia members who had stayed behind because of their advanced years. This clever handful of elderly men set up farm implements including sticks and hats along the cliffs near Turkey Point and then took turns appearing on the edges of the cliffs in British Redcoats. They would then run along the back of the cliff for several yards before reappearing at another location. Their frantic activity convinced Campbell that a large force was mustering to attack his forces. He promptly brought his fleet about and sailed back to America. (There are at least two other explanations for the failure of the American troops to burn Backus Mills, but this one seems to be the most plausible.)

After the war, the people of the area who had suffered personal losses brought suit against Campbell. In a judgement made in Buffalo, Campbell was officially reprimanded for his actions.

THE AGE OF SAIL

The years between the War of 1812 and the Civil War represented the golden age for sailing ships on the great lakes. Business prospered during the era and freight rates were quite lucrative. During the period, the favorite rig was the schooner. Sloops were also popular, and a number of enterprising merchants either built (or retrofitted old military) brigs and barks. For the early part of the period there was little serious competition from steam propelled ships. Even in the early days of steam, engine driven vessels were essentially schooners with engines. Until the late 1840s and early 1850s steamers remained unproven and had many mechanical problems. People "just didn't trust them."

The prototypical Lake Erie merchant sailing vessel was the two or three masted schooner. This type of vessel appeared in great number immediately after the War of 1812. Even in the face of the development of steamships, schooner activity continued to increase for the years prior to the civil war. The first schooners were predominantly two masted. They carried fore and aft rigged sails, which allowed them to perform much better on up-wind courses than contemporary ocean sailing square riggers. This was quite important, given the problem of sailing upwind in the narrow lake.

The schooners carried large bow sprits, which allowed them to fly a number of individual fore sails. This practice of having many small sails, which was

The New Dominion, a typical two master.
GREAT LAKES HISTORICAL SOCIETY

Glad Tidings – A two masted schooner.

unique relative to ocean going square riggers, created sailing flexibility. As the tricky Lake Erie winds shifted, it was easy to add or reduce sail area by changing the small and easily handled head sails. This technique was also utilized for gradually slowing the schooners as they entered harbors. One of the best features of the schooner rig was that it was easy to operate. It was much more difficult (labor intensive) to operate a square rigged vessel of similar size.

SHIP BUILDING

The early 1800s on Lake Erie were characterized by a thick virgin forest of hard and softwoods which extended, in most areas, almost to the shore. This was an important factor in the development of schooner trade. When it became obvious that there was money to be made by transporting goods and passengers between port cities along the lake, prospective ship builders began to construct vessels right at the lake shore using readily available forest materials.

Hardwoods, usually oak, were used to construct the frames. Often a tree could be felled so close to the proposed construction site that a skillful woodsman would drop the first timber (to make up the keel) right on the launch sight. Construction would begin from that point. Once the ribs and side framing were finished, the planking would be formed of soft wood. The most popular ship building sights in those years were places such as Freeport (where the *Washington* was launched in 1797), where there was a creek running into the lake and a nearby forest of hardwood and softwood.

Perhaps the premier sailing-ship building sight on all of the lakes was Port Burwell on the north west corner of the Quadrangle. Burwell was blessed with a natural harbor formed by a creek running into the lake and an extensive Carolinian forest offering choice building materials. The catalyst for the construction industry at Burwell was David M. Foster, a former indentured slave from New York State. Foster was a fugitive from love. He had run away with the daughter of the man that he was indentured to. To avoid the wrath of his "father in law," he went to sea on the Great Lakes in the early 1840s. As a sailor, he soon met and married a girl from Port Burwell where he moved in 1847. By the early 1860s, Foster had established the reputation of being the best schooner builder on the lakes.

Foster built schooners which were smallish, by 1800 standards, but his ships had a reputation for integrity, speed, and upwind performance. He was known to have built or refit 45 boats ranging from small schooners to steamboats. Like most builders, he named many of his ships after himself or members of his family. This included the *David M. Foster*, the *Annie M. Foster*, the *Adrianne*, the *Sarah Jane*, and the *Argo* (his children). The *D.M. Foster*, his namesake and pride and joy, was launched as a brigantine (foremast square rigged) in 1863, and converted to a barkentine via addition of a third mast several years later. The *D.M. Foster* completed a ground breaking ocean run from Toronto to Halifax in 1871. The *Foster* ultimately sunk in Oswego, New York in 1881 when she ran into a breakwater while trying to enter the harbor in a December storm. At the time, it was said that the sturdy craft, although already 18 years old, had many sailing seasons left in her.

Foster's early business practices were to build schooners and sail them himself under the flag of his Foster and Ryerse (William Ryerse of Port Ryerse) Company while he sought a buyer. Because of his growing fame, many of his vessels were ultimately purchased for service in other areas including South America and Europe. He was a lively and fun character whose favorite trick was to extol a ship's visitor with tales of the huge rats living in the bilges. Usually bare footed, he would then tweak the visitor's ankle or leg with his bare toes, simulating a rat bite. This fabled prank earned Foster the nickname "pincher toes."

On the U.S. side, there was originally some schooner building in the Erie area. This soon gave way to steamship construction, however. By the middle of the century, Conneaut, Ohio had emerged as the primary south shore center of sailboat construction.

David Foster.

The Stretch Schooner Era

As steamships grew in number, size, and reliability, schooner builders began to recognize the threat to their trade. Their first reaction was to improve their rigs and make their schooners perform better. This era (around the middle 1800s) saw the development of the topsail schooner, as well as experimentation with brigantine and barkentine rigs. Many ship builders hedged their bets by simultaneously building sailing and steam vessels.

Early steamship construction was essentially identical to schooner building. Until steamships began to be made of iron and steel, the traditional builders continued to dabble in both technologies. The late 1800s brought about rapid movement toward iron then steel construction, however, and this technological development soon created an inseparable chasm between the sailors and steamers. As steamships evolved their own unique designs, it became apparent to most builders that the technologies were so different that they had to choose one or the other.

A number of traditionalists hung on for years in the schooner building industry. They laughed at the heavy metal ships, saying that they were all doomed to sink since they were not made of wood. They also pointed out the dangers of steam engines, noting problems of explosions and fire. But the handwriting was on the wall for the schooner industry by the post-Civil War era.

In a last ditch effort to compete, schooner builders began to create a stretch version of the traditional schooner. Four, and five masted schooners began to appear offering the promise of cargo capacities almost as large as the biggest steamers. The largest of these was the *David Dowes*, a 265 foot five masted schooner launched in 1881. The *Dowes* visited Erie's harbor regularly with cargos of coal.

Problems persisted, however, and it was soon clear that there were three difficulties which sailing vessels simply could not overcome. The first was a technical limitation in the size of wooden sailing ships caused by construction technology. It was clear that 400 foot steel steamships would soon be built. Wooden schooners of that size would be impossible to engineer. Second, the large schooners were difficult to sail. More sailors were required to work the sails on the five masted behemoths. Steamships could be sailed with a small crew. Finally, steamships could move in and out of the developing harbors with ease. Sailing vessels, especially the larger ones, either had to anchor off shore or depend upon tug boats to move them in and out of harbors or up the Detroit River.

During the final decades of the 1800s and the early 1900s, a few hard nosed schooner operators continued. Their boats were paid for and therefore they were able to hang on past the limits of their natural era. Like any small businessman operating with fully depreciated assets, however, they and their boats grew older and gradually disappeared. They could not afford to replace the vessels, nor could they interest younger persons in taking over their operations.

THE RABBIT AND BARGE ERA

As the post-Civil War era commenced, there was an interesting application of the steam engine within the lakes. While much shipbuilding effort went into the creation of the large and efficient steamers, some entrepreneurs saw the opportunity to create specialized steam tugs. The 1830s began the rush for harbor development. All along the lakes, cities and towns were busily dredging the creeks which led to the lake. They wanted to create harbor oriented business districts with piers and other amenities. This left sailing ships high and dry. They were generally unable to sail into harbors, and thus had a hard time competing with steam ships.

Enterprising entrepreneurs soon came upon the idea of a steam tug, and, by the 1860s, there were a large number of these vessels plying the lakes. Most harbors had at least one tug operator whose business was to do all kinds of local work, including the towing of sailboats in and out of the harbor. Steam tugs were also commonly used by the late 1800s to tow sailboats up and down the Detroit River, thus making the ascent to the upper lake much easier.

George M. Case, foundered off Long Point in 1886.

As the late 1800s unfolded and abandoned schooners began to fill many harbors along the lakes, a new concept emerged. Steam tugs had already been used quite successfully to make long distance runs towing loads of floating lumber. These special duty long running tow tugs were called rabbits by captains on the lakes. During the late 1800s, entrepreneurs began to organize freight runs in which rabbits towed one or more schooners. In the early years of this practice, the schooners were towed with a sailor aboard whose job was to work the sails. The sails would be raised when the wind conditions were favorable to assist the tow tug in making way.

As the rabbit and tow era continued, there were two sequential developments. First, the numbers of tows increased. As engines became more powerful, it became possible to tow up to six large schooners. This development, however, made it increasingly difficult and dangerous for one or two sailors to work the sails on the tows. The rabbit crews began to experience difficulties with individual schooners sailing out of control in wind gusts, colliding with each other, or capsizing in heavy seas. It was also increasingly dangerous for the crews who were moving from schooner to schooner while under tow.

Ultimately, the masts were removed and the proud old schooners became wooden barges. The practice of towing wooden schooner-barges with tugs continued into the 1950s. Like the schooners, themselves, the barges were not replaced when they deteriorated, and they slowly passed from existence. Many a proud old schooner captain must have had a tear in his eye when he saw how his once beautiful schooner had been reduced to the role of wooden tow barge only to be chopped up for firewood and replaced by an ugly square metal barge when economies dictated.

Dave Stone standing on exposed schooner ribs on Long Point's south beach.

BURNING OUR MARINE HERITAGE

By the turn of the century most people began to regard the venerable schooners which were still inhabiting harbors as junk. As traditionalists struggled in vain, many cities adopted the practice of setting these majestic old ships on fire for the "spectacle" of it. Towns along the lakes would celebrate a 4th of July or Labor Day by dousing an old schooner with gasoline, floating it off shore and igniting it. As the mindless crowds applauded, the sailors shed tears of disbelief. It was one thing to have a ship go to the bottom in a storm but to burn it for fun was unthinkable!

The tradition actually began at Niagara Falls where several old timers were lit up and sent over the falls as tourist attractions. But most places where such an event occurred soon regretted what they had done which was to destroy tradition for all time.

In Toronto in 1934, the last such event took place with the burning of the *Lyman M. Davis* to celebrate the city's centennial. The proprietors of an amusement arcade on the lakeshore purchased the 61 year old vessel and made plans to burn her at midnight as a park promotion. Outraged citizens led by the vessel's old captain, John Williams conducted a campaign to save her. At the time, the *Lyman Davis* was judged to be the last schooner in structurally whole condition on all of the Great Lakes.

The fight was to no avail, however. At midnight on July 1, 1934 the old ship was loaded with fireworks, and towed from the Sunnyside Amusement Park to a spot about a mile out into Lake Ontario. Thousands of spectators lined the banks of the lakeshore that night to watch the ship burn. At first they were in a festive mood, like the "Romans cheering for the lions." But shortly after the ship began to flame, and the rockets started exploding from her hull, a dead silence fell over the entire crowd.

A *Toronto Star* reporter wrote: "Even the most thoughtless of the watchers began to sense, in the sinking of this vessel, something more than the destruction of an inanimate object." Indeed, this act represented the final conclusion to one of history's most important periods, the era of the Great Lakes schooner.

THE SCHOONER NEW CONNEAUT

In the fall of 1833, Captain Gilman Appleby was working on the construction and launch of a new steamboat (the *North American*) at Conneaut, Ohio. Captain Appleby had earned his fortune as part owner and master of a schooner called the *New Conneaut*. The launch of the steamer was behind schedule and

Appleby was anxious to get the new vessel into the water for a few runs before the season ended.

Meanwhile, his aunt, from Buffalo, had been vacationing in Erie and was anxious to return to her home before the end of autumn. Captain Appleby tried to persuade her to wait for the new steamer, but her impatience grew and she finally convinced him to allow her to book passage on the *New Conneaut*. The schooner left for Buffalo and sailed along the lake shore with no difficulties until a sudden squall hit the ship just off Erie. Unable to reduce sail in time, the little schooner rolled over on her side and filled with water.

The crew quickly scrambled on deck and launched a yawl. Just before abandoning the *New Conneaut*, which seemed about to sink, the crew tried to find Captain Appleby's aunt. Not able to raise her by calling, they presumed that she had drowned while trying to escape the cabin. They were concerned that the increasing winds and waves would ruin their chances to make shore, and quickly set off for land and safety. They landed ashore near the New York state line.

Captain Appleby, who was still in Conneaut working on the *North American*, heard of the tragedy and asked Captain Wilkins of the steamboat *Peacock*, which was heading east, to keep watch for either the *New Conneaut* or the body of his aunt. Wilkins found the half sunken hull of the *New Conneaut* with its mast still up laying sideways in the water some three days after the accident. He brought his ship along side and searched for the woman's body but could not find it. He sent word of his find to his friend Appleby. Two days later, a despondent Captain Appleby brought a salvage vessel along side to right the schooner and tow her to port. As the *New Conneaut* was winched to an upright position, the woman walked up the companionway stairs onto the deck and safety.

She had been trapped in waist-deep water and unable to swim for safety either when the crew was first abandoning ship or when the *Peacock* had come along side. She had spent five days in waist deep water eating only the few food stuffs which she had been able to find floating in the bilge water.

Exposed ribs on Long Point's south beach.

THE GRAVEYARD

As the age of commercial schooners came to an end on Lake Erie, there were two reported phenomena. First was the typical existence, within most harbors, of decaying old schooners lying at anchor or tied to secondary docks. Since most attention at the end of the century was being paid to the larger and more cost effective steamers, these old classics were thought of as harbor junk and allowed to rot. No one considered their historic significance. This was also because they were so commonplace.

The few old timers which had a bit of structural integrity left to them had long since been converted to barges. The remaining veterans were regarded as nuisances and met the ends of their days as victims of the saw or by being burned to their water lines to make room for more productive vessels.

The second interesting circumstance at the turn of the 20th century was the large number of abandoned and wrecked schooners on beaches. The Quadrangle and in particular, Long Point, developed a deserved reputation in the early 1900s for being a schooner scrap yard. This was particularly true of Long Point's south beaches, since they were so remote. Schooners which ran aground in that area were often judged to be unrecoverable because of the great distances to the nearest town. Also, by the later years of the 1800s, when schooners were giving way to steam, many owners whose vessels had gone aground on the beaches decided that it was not economically feasible to try to salvage them, and replaced them with new engine-driven vessels instead.

There were many such wrecks on the U.S. side as well, especially along the beaches between Conneaut and Presque Isle, but the numbers could not match those on Long Point. Sailors who passed the shores of Long Point during the early 1900s often told stories of beaches littered with wrecks and of the ghosts of the sailors who had "gone down" with these ships. Of course, most of the sailors of those vessels had actually walked the beaches to safety.

While the pine boards which comprised the hull planking of these early schooners soon deteriorated, the hardwood ribs and keels often buried themselves in the beach sand. During low water times, the sand dunes built up around the wrecks burying them. Gradually, the scrap yard disappeared below the beaches and became an anchoring structure for Long Point's beaches. In some cases, the schooner ribs began to act as a natural part of the beach ecology, and a dune line was formed with vegetation growing over the old wreck structure. Some of these wreck inspired ridge lines allowed beach structure to develop between them and the shore, giving the impression that they had somehow been inland shipwrecks. Even today, from time to time a schooner wreck is discovered along Long Point's beaches after a fall storm's shifting sand or high waters.

Lake Erie Adventures

1. Visit the Brig Niagara in Erie. Take a tour and try to learn as much as you can about it.

2. In Port Dover, you can take the historic walk and learn about the burning of the town by Campbell. Pick up a brochure at the harbor museum.

3. There are a number of historical placards along the Canadian side of the Niagara River between the Peace Bridge and Niagara on the Lake. Take a slow drive down the river. Stop and visit each historical sight and learn about the War of 1812. As you do this, imagine the building of the *Griffon* and the strategic problems of moving materials from Montreal.

4. Go to a tall ships celebration the next time you can and or when you travel try to stop to see historic sailing vessels. Mystic, Connecticut, as well as New York City's South Street Seaport are among the best exhibits.

ENGINE DRIVEN SHIPS: THE LAKERS

*T*he birth of the steamship heralded the beginning of an entirely new era on the lakes. By the 1840s and 1850s the steamship had become a major transportation presence, and both freight packages and passengers had come to depend upon newly predictable steamer runs to meet the needs of a rapidly developing society.

In earlier days, the use of schooners for either freight or transportation had been a difficult process at best. For the most part, schooner operators were a "salty" lot and quite off-putting to ordinary citizens. The merchants who were forced to deal with schooner captains found them to be difficult, unclear about schedules and rates, and generally cantankerous. They often lacked regular offices and business hours, and rarely kept regular shipping schedules. Instead, they left with the wind and arrived at destinations (when possible) depending upon wind direction and velocity.

To arrange shipping or book passage, a person had to physically go to the docks and find a schooner captain. This alone could be a challenge. From that point on, the process was a bit like bargaining at a European market. Once aboard, passengers often found their trips quite uncomfortable, due to spartan accommodations and difficult weather.

The Western World:
A classic 1850s sidewheel steamer.
GREAT LAKES HISTORICAL SOCIETY

There were also dangers for both passengers and cargo. Hundreds of schooners were lost during the 19th century (as will be discussed in chapter 8). This created an air of mystery and danger for passengers and shippers alike. But there were no railroads or highways to the west. The railroads did not connect Buffalo with Toledo and points west until the mid-1850s. And, from Buffalo along the south shore of Lake Erie, there were gulches, gorges and vast expanses of swamp, making a land passage to the west extremely arduous. Therefore people and supplies which were moving west found the schooners, and then the steamers, the best possible form of transport.

This was the business environment which stimulated the growth of steamships. There was no other reasonable way to go west. Schooners were unreliable, dangerous and difficult. Yet, Lake Erie represented a connection to the rapidly developing industrial cities of America's mid-section. It was the water gateway to the west. Steamships offered significantly larger and more efficient means of freight transport. They promised reliability and predictability, since they did not depend upon the wind or have to tack against it. They could travel directly to and from destinations. For passengers, the steamship offered a comfortable and safe passage. Staterooms, fine dining, orchestras and other amenities were available for first and second class travelers by 1850. By the mid-1850s, there were regularly scheduled passenger and freight services between Buffalo and the western ports, including those on the upper lakes. Unlike schooners, the steamers had little difficulty driving up the Detroit and St. Clair Rivers and into the northern and western lakes. The steamers quickly connected Buffalo and points east with Erie, Cleveland, Toledo, Detroit, Milwaukee, Chicago and other ports.

By the middle of the 19th century, there was more vessel traffic on Lake Erie than any other place in the world, including the oceans. Ship captains and sailors from the world's oceans somewhat reluctantly gravitated to the lakes as the industry grew wildly. At the same time, there was a rush among the port cities of the lake to develop harbors which would stimulate the growth of local business.

THE WALK IN THE WATER

While the basic concept of steam driven ships had been experimented with over many decades, steamships did not appear in America until the work of Fulton on the Hudson River. Shortly thereafter, Fulton's technology was brought to Lake Erie in the form of the first steam ship, the *Walk In The Water*. This historic 135 foot vessel first slid into Lake Erie's waters in 1818, marking the beginning of a new era in shipping.

The *Walk In The Water*, a name derived from an Indian description of Fulton's first steam vessel, looked quite like a brig rigged sailing vessel with a side paddle wheel and a central smokestack. It was rigged (as most early steam vessels were) with a functioning set of sails on two masts and often used a combination of sail and steam power. The maiden voyage of the *Walk In The Water* was from her home port of Black Rock (near Buffalo) to Dunkirk and then Erie, where she took on wood to fire her boilers and discharged passengers. The "steamship," as she was popularly known, made a regular run along the south shore of the lake to Detroit and back, every 10 days. She carried package freight and passengers, who were berthed in either a men's or women's bunk room. The small ship ran as close to shore as possible. She either discharged or took on passengers and freight by anchoring and rowing a dory to shore. Except for the natural harbor at Erie, there were no developed ports in those days. The "steamship's" crew developed a tradition of rowing passengers to and from shore. Women and children were carried through the surf to beaches. If the weather was rough, and stops could not be made along shore at ports such as Dunkirk, Conneaut or Ashtabula; passengers and freight continued to Detroit and (hopefully) were dropped off on the return trip. Regularly scheduled stops for the *Walk In The Water* included Erie, Grand River, Cleveland, Sandusky and Detroit. Other stops were made on an as-needed basis.

The steamship continued in regular service for four seasons, netting her owners handsome profits and motivating others to consider building steamships. Passengers raved about the beautiful and convenient trips up and down the lake. By 1821, the ship was almost always filled to capacity. Many wealthy people took the ride as a form of entertainment. Meanwhile, small cities up and down the lakes were motivated to begin major programs of harbor development. It had become apparent that cities with protected harbors would attract regular steamship visits and the business which accompanied them.

The *Walk In The Water* came to an unfortunate end in November 1821. She left Black Rock for a regular trip up the lake. A few hours later, a severe gale began to blow from the west. The captain put her sails up and tried to run the ship out to sea. As the waves built he decided to try to anchor in the limited protection just east of Dunkirk instead. During the evening, however, the anchors tore loose and the ship drifted out of control and landed ashore. The passengers were all saved. But the beating that the wooden vessel took on the open beaches from gale force winds and waves totally destroyed her hull.

As testament to the engine's integrity, salvors removed it for use in another vessel. The engine was taken to a site in Buffalo (not far from the wreck) where it became the power plant for Lake Erie's second steamer, the *Superior*, which was launched in 1822. Interestingly, a great controversy arose over where to build the second steamer. The citizens of Black Rock were quite miffed when the *Superior* was built in Buffalo. Subsequent to the launch, the *Superior* moved to the newly developing harbor at Buffalo. Black Rock ceased to be the important eastern port of entry that it had once been.

THE EARLY DAYS

As entrepreneurs from the lakes began to hear of the success of the *Walk In The Water*, there was a rush to get into the steamer business. Naturally, the first builders of steamships were the traditional schooner people. Captains and owners alike began building a fleet of wooden schooners which carried stream engines and paddle wheels. The earliest technology was to use a single engine that was connected to sidewheels to drive the vessel through the water. The steam engines were driven by hardwood and achieved reasonable efficiency. As the forest close to the lake was thinned out, however, and captains began to experience great variation in the quality and dryness of wood, coal was substituted as a fuel. Coal was more space efficient, and also much more dependable.

In the early years, when wood was the primary fuel source, ship captains quite logically insisted on carrying a sailing rig. The sails were utilized to assist the engine when winds were favorable. If the ship's boiler went out, the wood supply was exhausted, or a storm developed, the sails could also be used for emergency power.

By the 1840s, it was evident that steamships were not a fad. Owners had established regular routes. Their ships had proven to be dependable with respect to scheduling and safety. Both passengers and shippers were clamoring to increase business. The railroads had not yet connected Buffalo to the west. So, in effect, the steamers became a transit monopoly.

A combination of the general reliability of the engines, and the efficiency of coal as a fuel, led to the most important period of development in steaming. A group of builders made a radical departure from the tradition of mounting a steam engine on a schooner. Instead, they designed and launched a series of palatial vessels designed as steamships rather than retro-fitted schooners. The first of this type, the *Great Western*, was launched in 1839. Skeptics argued that its superstructure housing staterooms would make it top heavy and unseaworthy. After a few seasons, however, the ship proved its reliability and became a prototype for the period which was to follow.

THE GOLDEN AGE

The late 1840s saw the launching of several grand victorian styled steamers. These ships were 250 to 300 feet long (huge by comparison with schooners). They carried enormous engines and were fast, making scheduled runs from Buffalo to Detroit in 20 hours or less. They had the power to ascend the Detroit River with ease. They were attractively designed, featuring opulent styling and were appealing to passengers.

Ships such as the *Atlantic* (1848), the *Mayflower* (1849), and the *Buckeye State* (1850) redefined steam travel. The traditional masts and sailing rigs were conspicuously missing. In their place was an ornate octagonal wheelhouse and an elevated superstructure to house first class passengers in private staterooms. Since there would be no heeling while under sail, decks were arranged to allow passenger access. Railings permitted patrons to stand on deck and admire the scenery.

As these wonderful and romantic ships entered or left harbors, flags and streamers were flown from the superstructure. Passengers lined the decks for these occasions and often the ship's orchestras played grand marches. The sight of a steamer leaving or entering port evoked excitement and romance for all. Townspeople took picnic lunches to the shore to wait for such an event. Every child dreamed of taking a steamship ride! A steamship landing had almost the social significance of a parade. On board there were both first and second class accommodations; including fine dining, entertainment, and dancing. There was usually a men's smoking and spirits room, where business and other matters could be discussed. During their time, these lake trips rivaled (and pioneered) the contemporary "Love Boat" vision of an ocean cruise. Below decks there was plenty of room both for freight and steerage accommodations. Typically, there were two large bunk rooms: one for men and another for women. These would often be filled with several hundred immigrant passengers heading for new lives in America's west.

The owners made handsome profits. First class passengers often took trips as a recreational diversion, so price was not an issue. In steerage, hundreds of immigrants who needed transportation to the emerging western states happily crowded aboard and paid a fee for passage. And, for the first time ever, package freight could predictably be delivered up and down the lakes. The freight prices, alone, made the steamship business very lucrative.

By the mid 1850s, however, two fatal flaws were exposed. First there were, indeed, dangers in steamboating. Several accidents had occurred, including the sinking of the *Atlantic* off Long Point (see the Epilogue), and the burning of the Erie-based Reed Shipping Company's *City of Erie*. Passengers and shippers, who originally had boundless optimism about lake shipping and travel began to have second thoughts. But the ultimate "dagger to the heart" of shipping, was the northern climate. No matter how efficient, opulent, and safe the steamers might become, weather was an insurmountable constraint.

While the late summer months proved wonderful passages, the rest of the year was a different story. Spring and fall were often unpleasant and sometimes frightening. Cold, wind, and rain, often conspired to make a trip absolutely miserable. Then, for several months each year, ice made ship travel absolutely impossible. The railroads began to squeeze steamships out of the package freight and passenger service market. By the late 1850s, reliable passenger and freight hauling railroads had connected both the U.S. and Canadian sides of the lake to the west. The age of the grand sidewheel steamer was fast coming to an end.

OTHER SHIPPING DEVELOPMENTS

Prior to the Civil War, a number of developments effected the Great Lakes shipping business in both positive and negative ways. Some of the most important included:

1841   Propeller driven ships appeared. The first propeller driven steamship, the *Vandalia*, was launched on the lakes. At first, skeptics doubted that a ship could be driven from the stern, and the early "propellers" (as they were called) were slow by comparison with sidewheelers. In a short time, however, they proved themselves to be highly efficient, and by 1862 the number of propellers had surpassed the number of sidewheelers.

1843   Iron ship building began with the launch of the *Michigan* (later renamed the *Wolverine)* at Erie. The *Michigan* was a revenue cutter used for patrolling the lakes and defending U.S. shores (against Canada?). She was a barkentine rigged sidewheeler, and could make 12 knots under power. All of the early iron ships were government vessels.

1844   The Erie Extension Canal opened linking the port of Erie with Pittsburgh.

1850 Dual engines emerged. Marine engineers began to design and produce ships with two engines, thus reducing the dangers of fire and explosion, and increasing reliability.

1851 Regular schedules evolved for steamers. There were sidewheelers and 20 propellers making regular runs to Buffalo and Chicago.

1852 Railroad competition began. Rail lines were completed from New York City and Montreal to Toledo, Detroit and Windsor. This was the beginning of a depression in shipping that lasted until after the Civil War.

1854 Barks, brigs, and sidewheelers began to pass out of existence. Almost all new vessels launched were either schooners or propellers.

THE STEAM BARGE

As the Civil War ended, a revolution was slowly beginning in Great Lakes transport. The great victorian sidewheelers had outlived their usefulness. Passengers and package freight had shifted to the railroads. Construction technology had also changed dramatically. It was clear that the future of shipping would lie in steel construction and propeller driven hulls.

Shippers shifted their interests to the delivery of bulk cargoes such as ore and grain to ports throughout all of the five Great Lakes. As shipping on the Great Lakes was being redefined, it became apparent that the largest possible cargo capacity would lead to shipping economies. It was also clear that ship size would be limited only by the locks between the lakes, since the new (steel) building technologies removed obstacles to building large ships.

The steam barge emerged to take advantage of the technology shift. Its basic design was to provide the prototype for modern ships, including the super freighters of the 1970s. The fundamental design characteristic was an essentially square cross section in a ship whose dimensions were just slightly smaller than the smallest canal way lock.

Typical package/passenger steamer of the 1890s.

The first steam barges were built to the dimensions of the canals of the 1860s. They were 140 feet long, with beams of 26 feet and drafts of 9 feet. While these little freighters were much smaller than the victorian sidewheelers, their operation taught some important and lasting lessons. First, builders learned that focusing ship design on the single purpose of bulk cargo hauling created economies of scale. The steam barges were slow but economical, due to their powerful high torque engines. Unlike the sidewheelers, which primarily worked Lake Erie, the steam barges were designed to move through all of the lakes. Steam barges also helped to demonstrate the limiting nature of canal locks thus stimulating interest in increasing canal size capacities.

The post-Civil War economy provided renewed impetus for shipping. Business grew rapidly, and there was plenty of freight for both the railroads and the steamships. In fact, a number of railroad companies hedged their business positions by acquiring shipping firms. The success of the steam barge had paved the way for future shipping. Gradually, post-war attention turned to the task of moving raw materials such as coal, iron ore, lumber and grain up and down the lakes. In a continuing sequential process which was to last for 100 years (through the opening of the Poe Locks at Sault Ste. Marie in 1970), first the canals and their locks grew, and then the sizes of ships increased proportionately. As this happened, the faithful little steam barges were slowly replaced by giant ore carriers.

As the country's construction needs escalated, there was a huge growth in the demand for lumber. A number of the old steam barges were converted to lumber tugs, and worked the lakes hauling giant fields of floating logs. In the decades following the Civil War, the thick forest which had once reached to the lake shore had been chopped down, moved to the water's edge, organized into tows and hauled by steam barge to big city lumber mills. The Inner Bay area of Port Rowan was a favorite place for this activity because of its thick forests and sheltered waters, in which the lumber could be floated. The lumber towing tugs were to inspire the design of both the steam fish tug (see chapter 10) and the rabbits which hauled schooners (chapter 4).

The most important events of the post-Civil War period are listed below:

1862   The 200 foot iron clad propeller *Merchant* was launched in Buffalo marking the beginning of the use of metal ship building in a non-military ship.

1866   A new ship building boom era started, 71 new vessels were launched.

1867   The tug boat business also flourished. There were five tugs working Lake Erie either towing schooners up the Detroit, or moving them in and out of harbors.

1868   A record number—331— of lives were lost on the lakes.

1871   Erie Extension Canal went bankrupt and closed. This was a severe blow to the growth of Erie's port.

1882   The first iron hulled freighter was launched. The *Onoko* was 287 feet long, carried a schooner rig, and pioneered the now familiar profile of wheelhouse up front, flat deck, and engine with engineering in the rear.

1886   The first steel hulled freighter, the *Spokane* was launched.

1886   The number of steamships on the lakes surpassed the number of sailing vessels.

1887   The Welland Canal was expanded for the first time.

1889   The whaleback (pig type) hull was introduced by Alexander McDougal. This design was rounded much like the shape of a modern submarine for ease in handling Lake Erie's square waves.

1890   A record year for launching new boats was noted. The economic boom resulted in 236 new vessels.

The Lakewood (1901), a classic turn of the century steamer, once the flagship of the Erie Sand Steamship Fleet.
ERIE SAND STEAMSHIP

1898   The largest boat ever launched was put into service. The *Samuel Morse*, at 476 feet, paved the way for ship design over the next few years.

1908   The first self unloader was launched. The 286 foot *Wyandotte* with a beam of 45 feet, became the prototype for grain and ore carriers with her efficient self unloading gear.

1913   "Dark Sunday," the greatest recorded storm in the history of great lakes shipping occurred on November 9. During the first hour, temperatures at Erie fell by 36 degrees. The winds, which peaked at

88 miles per hour, averaged 49 miles per hour over a 60 hour period, and 22 inches of snow fell. On all of the lakes, 251 persons and 71 ships were lost, including 17 vessels and 6 lives on Lake Erie.

1916　"The Black Friday" storm of October 20 occurred. This was said to be the worst all time storm on Lake Erie. Four ships, including the *Whaleback Colgate*, were lost.

1924　The first lake freighters with diesel engines were launched. The *Henry Ford II* and the *Benson Ford*, 598 foot sister ships were the first to use diesel power. These ships provided the prototype for freighters until after the second world war.

1932　The Welland Canal expanded to its current dimensions.

1946　Radar was first installed on a lake freighter, the *E.J. Block*.

1948　New freighters were built in the mid 600 foot range.

1959　The St. Lawrence Seaway opened, admitting shipping (salty's) from the oceans.

1967　All new vessels launched had either diesel engines or oil fired steam turbines. The remaining coal burning steamers would eventually be retro-fitted or scrapped.

1970　The Poe Locks opened to Lake Superior, allowing vessel sizes to 1100 feet with beams of 105'. This was the advent of the era of the super-laker and created what is called the "Poe Class," lakers which can only pass through the Poe Locks.

1972　The *Stewart J. Cort* was launched at Erie marking the advent of the super-laker period. A total of 28 of these monsters were subsequently put into service over the next 10 years.

1973　The *William R. Roesch*, a non super-laker, was launched. Its design featured a bare bow with wheelhouse and all cabins in the stern, allowing a smaller crew and providing a new prototype.

1981　Shipbuilding came to a halt with the launch of the 1000 foot super-laker, the *Columbia Star*.

*Railroad Ferry Marquette & Bessemer #2,
lost in the Quadrangle, 1909.*
GREAT LAKES HISTORICAL SOCIETY

RAILROAD FERRIES

The merger of railroad and steamship interests by a number of companies after the Civil War led to the development of a new form of transit. A category of ship called the car (or transport) ferry appeared in the late 1860s, and grew in popularity in the 1880s and 1890s. There were two styles of railroad ferries. First was the short term river ferry, which worked places like the Niagara and Detroit rivers. It trundled rail cars between trunk lines, thus avoiding either a long ride around the lake or the creation of bridges and tunnels.

By the 1880s, the efficiency of this kind of operation had led to the creation of a deep draft lake crossing cousin of the river ferry. Its duties were to load railroad cars on shipboard tracks, then transport them across the center of the lake. Most were built of steel and had formidable ice crushing capabilities. They were able to operate for most, if not all, of the season on the central lake basin. Some car ferries took passengers on their regular runs. The ferries became known as reliable forms of cross lake transport for business people.

Railroad ferries on Lake Erie were primarily engaged in coal transport. Coal was delivered to U.S. shipyards by train from Pennsylvania, West Virginia, and Ohio. It was loaded on ferries in Conneaut, Ashtabula and Sandusky, then shipped to Canadian and western ports. Conneaut, on the western border of the Quadrangle, was a major shipping port with regular cross lake runs to Port Burwell, and Port Dover. These runs created significant navigational dangers for turn of the century ship captains, who lacked radar and other navigational tools.

By 1900, railroad ferries, such as the *Marquette and Bessemer* (lost in the Quadrangle), were 350 feet long, with beams of 50 to 55 feet. They were capable of carrying 30 loaded coal cars, and making round trips across central Lake Erie in 9 hours, including loading and unloading. It was the efficiency of the car ferries which kept the Ontario government from developing the highway infrastructure along the north side of Lake Erie in the years before the world wars.

THE GREAT INDUSTRIAL AGE

From 1890 through 1960, the lakes became a conveyor belt for the greatest industrial boom in the history of the civilized world. The steel industry, the automotive business, and appliance manufacturing sprang into existence almost overnight. The lakes were used to provide deliveries of iron ore and coal to fuel these businesses. Hamilton, Buffalo, Cleveland, and Gary emerged as steel manufacturing centers. Detroit became the epicenter of the automobile industry. Port towns thrived. Detroit, for example, grew from a population of just over 100,000 to almost a million between 1900 and 1925.

The steel mills along the lakes became sponges, absorbing all of the coal that could be delivered from the fields of Pennsylvania, Illinois and Appalachia, as well as iron ore from Lake Superior ranges such as Mesabi and Gogebic. On the lakes, this translated into a tremendous volume of ore carrier traffic. Shipping companies developed efficiencies in carrier systems, cargos, and routes to take advantage of the continuous volume. For much of the period, ore carriers moved west with loads of coal, cement, or iron ore and returned with cargos of grain from western ports. In the east, large cities such as Erie had systems of piers which included coal docks in close proximity with grain elevators.

Industrial growth continued through the world wars and business increased on the lakes. Unlike the Civil War period, when shipping slowed, the wars brought a rush of traffic in war materials. Gradually, the ore carriers grew larger and more specialized. Sizes accelerated from the 200 foot range at the turn of the century to the middle 600 foot range after World War II. To improve efficiency at the dock, almost all of the large ships had become self unloading by the 1940s.

A little-known Erie connection to the shipping business of the time was the automobile transport company of Timothy McCarthy. McCarthy was born on Erie's lower east side and grew up on the water front. As a youngster, he took a job on the docks loading and unloading. He soon rose to a supervisory position, and began to envision entrepreneurial projects. In 1935, after meeting Captain William Nicholson (Nicholson-Erie-Dover Ferry Line) he began to consider the automobile transport business. Nicholson had gotten into this business at a very bad time, just prior to the depression. When his contracts to move cars for the auto companies went sour, Nicholson moved his boats (the *Keystone* and the *Dover*) to Erie for a few years and attempted to operate a ferry service to Port Dover.

McCarthy recognized the wisdom of Nicholson's original business idea. He was also quick to understand that as soon as the depression years ended, the automobile delivery business would pick up again. He purchased a small fleet of automobile transport vessels at attractive depression level prices and moved to Detroit, where he successfully entered the delivery business.

Prior to World War II, it looked as though lake transport might become the primary method for the delivery of new cars. McCarthy had contracts to deliver automobiles up and down the lakes and into the New York City area as well. But the war presented a business interruption which ultimately redefined the auto industry. Meanwhile, McCarthy's ships had been fitted out to deliver war materials across the Atlantic, and his business never quite regained its former position. By the 1950s, when auto production was picking up again, the big three had decided on either railroad or over-the-road delivery, leaving the McCarthy lines to haul Hudsons, Kaisers and Studebakers. McCarthy died in 1961 and his heirs liquidated a few years later.

THE SECOND AGE OF THE PASSENGER SHIPS

Even though the classic victorian steam-ships had passed from existence, passenger travel never really ended on the lake. Entrepreneurs in every port of reasonable size launched excursion or special interest run ships of a more modest size. The romantic allure of steamboating continued through the 19th century, but passengers were now interested in a summer cruise around the harbor or a short sight seeing trip rather than transportation. Excursion boats operated with great success in Buffalo, Erie, Port Dover, Cleveland, Sandusky, the Lake Erie Island area, and Toledo.

By the 1890s, the country was in the midst of another major economic growth period. Shipping on the lakes was at a new peak level, and

The excursion ferry Lawrence about 1929.
GREAT LAKES HISTORICAL SOCIETY

entrepreneurs were looking for new ventures. Sensing an optimistic return to pre-Civil War steamboating days, the Northern Steamship Company commissioned and launched two opulent passenger steamers. At 386 feet in length with multiple deck levels, both the *North West* and the *Northland* looked, for all purposes, like modern ocean cruise ships of the 1990s.

The twin ships of the Northern line helped to launch a new era of passenger travel. The excitement of the 2000 plus passengers carried on each trip soon spread, and it became increasingly difficult to book passage. The combination of the opulence of the ships with the sheer beauty of their northern lake itinerary motivated hundreds of thousands of tourists to book passage. By the turn of the century, a dozen additional liners were plying the Great Lakes. In 1900, two million passengers exited the port of Chicago on cruises.

Erie-Dover ferry line at Port Dover pier, 1928.

Photo by DONALD BUSCOMBE

The crowning vessel of the new passenger liner period was the *Theodore Roosevelt*, of the Indiana Transport Company. At 289 feet with a 46 foot beam, the *Roosevelt* represented the culmination of passenger ship design. Her keel to bridge dimensions of 52 feet gave the illusion of a colossal office building on the water. Wide promenade decks and gracefully appointed staterooms allowed her to carry 3500 passengers per trip in a style which had not been experienced since the pre-Civil War boom times. Passengers thrilled to summer excursion cruises which plied all of the lakes,

The *Philip R Clarke* was built in 1952 at 647 ft, lengthened to 767 ft in 1974. Note the traditional profile with wheelhouse forward.
Photo by JOHN MITCHELL

including the beautiful and mysterious Lake Superior. The liners developed a reputation for style and affordability. They soon became the magical vacation dream for an entire continent. People traveled great distances to book summer cruises to far away mysterious lands such as upper Michigan.

During the same period, many large cities, such as Detroit and Cleveland, began to see the evolution of "day liners." Somewhat smaller than the 300 footers, the day liners were still able to carry large crowds, since they did not feature overnight accommodations. Instead, they focused on either 4 to 12 hour excursion trips, or short runs between cities. En route, however, these day liners offered many of the amenities of the great liners, and often showed greater profits. Day liners of the 1000 to 2000 passenger class operated from Detroit, Toledo, Cleveland, Lake St. Clair, Port Huron, and the Thousand Islands. The *Greyhound*, for example, made two round trips daily (June through September) between Toledo and Detroit, stopping at Sugar Island Park in the Detroit River. Although she was only 250 feet long, she could carry 3500 passengers.

World War I seemed to bring an end to the renewed passenger era on the lakes. Many of the lake liners were pressed into service during the war, and somehow never returned. The years after the war were punctuated by economic

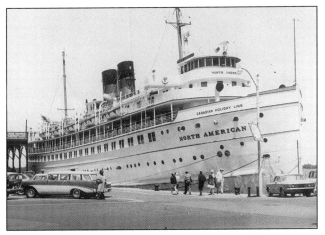

Photo of North American at the Public Dock.

difficulties. By the conclusion of World War II, roadway development and the automobile, in combination with grizzly war images from the north Atlantic, altered the North American image of water travel as a form of recreation. The love affair with television had begun, and, at least for a time, most forgot about the inland passenger liners. One by one, the grand old liners passed from existence and were taken to scrap yards.

Both Erie and Port Dover were the recipients of liners of various sizes over the years. In fact, there once was daily passenger service between the two ports. During the late 1920s and early 1930s, the Nicholson-Erie-Dover Ferry Line made regular runs between the two ports carrying passengers and cars. In 1929, 100,000 persons were carried from Erie to Dover (and back). Another 25,000 passengers traveled from Port Dover to Erie (and back). On August 23, 1929, the *Keystone* was heading for Erie. At 3:00 p.m., just south of Long Point, her engine seized up. The *Keystone* sounded her distress whistle until two fish tugs came to her assistance, attached tow lines and slowly towed the ferry back to Port Dover.

The *Keystone* was repaired over the winter and joined by a sister ship in an expanded ferry route the next season. For the next few years, there was twice daily service on the weekends and daily service during the week between the two ports. On the weekend runs, the two ferries would pass each other near Long Point as passengers waved and steam whistles signaled the meeting. For Erie and Port Dover, the early 1930s represented the salad days of the twin city relationship, and many residents from both towns developed lasting cross-lake friendships which were to continue and grow over the years.

Other passenger ships visited both Port Dover and Erie over the years. In fact, a number of cruise liners made regular stops in Erie. By the time of the passenger liners days, Erie had lost its once deserved reputation as the greatest lake port and fallen well behind many of its neighbor ports in growth and development. As a result, most of the passenger liners were not regularly docked in Erie.

Liners continued to make stops at Erie's Anchor Docks through the 1950s, taking passengers to Chicago and other western ports. Perhaps the symbolic end of the passenger liner era in Erie was the short tenure of the *North American*, which was purchased and brought to town in the mid 1960s.

The *North American* and her sister ship, the *South American*, were classic examples of early 20th century passenger liners. At 291 feet, they were representative of the glory days of steaming. Both had been built by the Great Lakes Engineering Works in 1914 and had served admirably up and down the Great Lakes systems. But, both were past their prime and the venture which brought the North American to Erie was clearly a risky one. For a few years, this once proud passenger liner was berthed at the public dock, offering excursion trips of various lengths with dining and dancing. Unfortunately for her owners, the *North American* venture failed. She was towed away from Erie's Harbor in 1967 to be refitted for new duties on the Atlantic Ocean. Sadly, the *North American* capsized and sunk in the Gulf of St. Lawrence during the tow.

CURRENT SHIPPING ON THE LAKES

Perhaps the best way to portray the history of steaming on the lakes, in context with sailing (see chapter 4), is to present some summary statistics. Table 5-1 contains the total numbers of vessels registered on the lakes, by type, for select years between 1800 and 1992. It shows the transition from sail to steam, the evolution from sidewheelers to propellers, and the growth and decline of the industry. Reporting systems and statistical reference points changed over the years, and there were periods during which no reliable data were available, but Table 5-1 still clearly marks the trends.

Since the opening of the St. Lawrence Seaway in 1959, ocean going trade ("Saltys") have been added to the traffic on the lakes. In fact, in recent years, in

The 689 foot J. W. McGiffin built in 1972.
Photo by JOHN MITCHELL

The James Burker (Built 1976), A 1004 foot self unloader, shows the modern Super Laker profile with the wheelhouse and Engineering Aft.
Photo by JOHN MITCHELL

terms of simple ship count, salt water vessels have accounted for approximately one third of the total passages in the seaway system. The current U.S. Great Lake's bulk fleet has fallen to only 57 vessels. In addition there are 6 registered cement and 3 tanker vessels. The Canadian fleet (while making almost three times as many transits as the U.S. fleet) is falling almost as rapidly and there are no plans to add new ships in the near future. The newer lake freighters are huge by comparison with ocean going vessels, and highly specialized. In the U.S. fleet, 29 (of the 57 registered) fall into the Poe Class or super laker category and have established trade routes in which they carry iron ore, stone, cement or coal. In the iron ore trade for example, tonnage hit an all time low (since the depression) of 43 million tons in 1982, after peaking at 95 million tons in 1974. As of 1992, iron ore tonnage had climbed back to 67 million tons, but that total is not growing. Seaway statistics from 1992 list the following major cargos in order of tonnage: Iron Ore, Coal, Limestone, Gypsum, and Grain. Minor cargos (also in order of tonnage) include: Cement, Liquid Bulk, Potash, Salt, and Sand. A total of 230,366 passengers utilized the seaway system in 1992.

Meanwhile, the industry is at a virtual standstill, with crews growing older year by year. In 1992, the average age of crew members was 50. A young man can no longer get a job "on the water" easily and make a good living. In Alpena, Michigan, at the 1993 meeting of the Lake Carriers Association, president George Ryan told the assembled membership that their industry was dying. Half the U.S. fleet has been cut up for scrap in the past decade. The number of registered bulk carriers in U.S. fleets fell from 599 in 1942, to 266 in 1950, 160 in 1965, 116 in

Year	Schooners/ Sloops	Brigs/ Barks	Sail	Sidewheelers	Propellers	NonSail	Total
1800	9	11	20				20
1825	39	21	60	60			
1832	79	28	107	9		9	116
1836	183	34	217	45		45	262
1846	340	67	407	67	26	93	500
1850	648	98	746	95	45	140	886
1863	1340	285	1625	135	258	393	2018
1869	904	225	1129	121	247	368	1487
1942							1299
1950							637
1965							363
1982							291
1985							247
1992							139

Table 5-1
Registered Vessels By Type for Select Years.

1982 and 57 in 1992. The days in which an ambitious young person could proceed from deck hand to captain in a few years are gone forever. In Port Colborne, Walter Gonyou, president of the Canadian Mariners Union echoed the same sentiment in August of 1993. Ten years ago, according to Gonyou, CMU represented more than 600 sailors, but the number has fallen to 320. And to make matters worse, more than 60% of those sailors were out of work during the summer of 1993. In part, this trend is clearly due to the efficiency of the modern fleet of 1000 footers (one of these replaces 4 or 5 of the ships built in the 1940s). But, it is also an artifact of the domestic and world economies. The representatives of the Great Lakes shipping interests are hoping just to hold steady against the impending decline!

The Olympic Melody, an ocean going ship, steaming up the Detroit River.
Photo by JOHN MITCHELL

Lake Erie Adventures

1. Visit Erie's Public Dock and walk around. Note the shipping activity on the docks at the foot of Sassafras Street, home of the Erie Sand Steamship Company. If you are persistent you will see the 620 foot *Richard Reiss* unloading at the dock. Stop and watch. It will help you understand the overall process. You will also see the 299 foot sand sucker *J. S. St. John* working out of this dock on a regular basis. Try to catch it unloading. Take a boat ride on the *Little Toot!*

2. The 1897 Steamer *Niagara* is tied to the end of the Erie Steamship Co's dock. This vessel (which was shortened by 24 feet in 1926) is a floating museum piece, a visual reminder of shipping at the turn of the century.

3. In the winter it is useful to visit the Erie Marine repair docks at the foot of Holland Street. Most winters will find several lakers tied up for repair. In recent years there have been super-lakers (of the 1000 foot type) at the Erie Marine docks.

4. Conneaut is a busy commercial harbor specializing in coal. Take a trip to the harbor and a hike around the commercial areas. While you are there treat yourself to lunch or supper at the restaurant on the waterfront.

5. The Great Lakes Historical Museum at Vermilion, Ohio has a fine exhibit on lakers including video tapes of trips through the lakes.

6. The very best place to watch shipping is the Detroit River where both lakers and saltys are compressed into one narrow area. The best viewing place is Windsor, Ontario along the banks of the river. Take a picnic and a camera.

7. Contact the Great Lakes Carriers Association in Cleveland for their list of inexpensive videos and other materials.

8. Book passage on a laker and go for a ride. This is the ultimate way to experience steamships on the lakes.

PIRATES, MAYHEM AND THE LONG POINT COMPANY

*T*oday's Long Point is a typical sand spit peninsula. It juts southeasterly from the mainland of the north coast from a point some 12 miles east of Port Burwell. Along its south beaches (approximately 12 miles from its base) it makes a gradual curving hook to the east, so that the final leg (of some 10 miles) bends to the northeast terminating in a sandy point and a continuous sandbar. If one were to walk the south beach of Long Point, the total distance would be approximately 25 miles. The aerial view of the point (Figure 6-1) shows the bend of the beach, as the point gradually bows away from the mainland and turns east. It also shows the strip of sandy beach leading along the south shore and the lighthouse.

The drawing of Long Point (Figure 6-2) depicts the primary areas and geological structures as they currently exist. At the extreme western boundary of Long Point, there is a causeway connecting the cottage community of Long Point to Port Rowan. At the end of this road, cars must either turn west (right) along the severely eroded Hastings Beach cottage area, or east toward the Provincial Park. The 3 mile roadway to Long Point's provincial park passes through the center of the cottage community of some 900 residences. The provincial park, itself, is

Figure 6-1
Aerial view of Long Point.

Photo courtesy of JOHN KINDURYS
STUDIO ONE PHOTOGRAPHY,
SIMCOE, ONTARIO, CANADA

divided into two sections, with private cottages between them. The eastern-most park section borders upon the private property of the Long Point Company.

If one were to walk the south beach from the provincial park and past the Canadian Wildlife Services management area, eventually a barrier gate would be encountered identifying the private property of the Long Point Company and forbidding trespass. This first 5 miles of beach ends at the south edge of Courtright Ridge and protects some of the most interesting features of Long Point, including the Inner Bay and the Company's shooting marshes.

The next stretch of beach (almost 20 miles) belongs to the Canadian Wildlife Service and is patrolled on a regular basis to protect against trespassing. The land at the end of the point is shared by the Department of Transport and Communications (Lighthouse) and The Ministry of Natural Resources.

THE INNER BAY AND CUTS

Even though today's Inner Bay area is relatively shallow, this stretch of water was of great navigational importance during the 1800s. In those days, the waters of the Inner Bay area were 15 to 25 feet deep, and navigable by schooners and early freighters. The shore of the Inner Bay (in particular Turkey Point) was the site of considerable forestry activity. The relatively calm waters of the bay were ideal for organizing log transport barges.

Along the road to the provincial park, there is a placard denoting the "Carrying Place." This was a part of the Iroquoian system of portages. The early travelers (including the Indian-led voyageurs) would not have ventured out into the lake to travel east or west. Instead, they would have paddled to the sight of today's causeway. They would have portaged their vessels into (or out of) the Inner Bay, continuing their travel along the relative safety of shore.

In the early 1800s, small channels occasionally worked their way through the sands between the Inner Bay and the lake, during periods of relatively high water. By the late 1820s, the increase in schooner trade along Long Point led to an interest in building and maintaining a permanent navigable channel. In 1833, a sudden storm erupted while an engineering survey was being conducted. The storm did the construction work automatically. In early November, a gale resulted in a 390 foot wide channel being cut through the neck of the Point. Lieutenant John Haris reported the results of the storm to the federal government. He proposed that work commence to construct and maintain piers at the site of this natural excavation. This first maintained channel at the cut was completed in 1836, and marked with a lightship by the year 1840.

Unfortunately, nature did not favor the location of this cut. Almost as soon as nature created the channel, it began to eat away at it. There were reports during the first year of construction that the channel was beginning to fill in. There was also continual damage to the piers, which were built out into the lake to

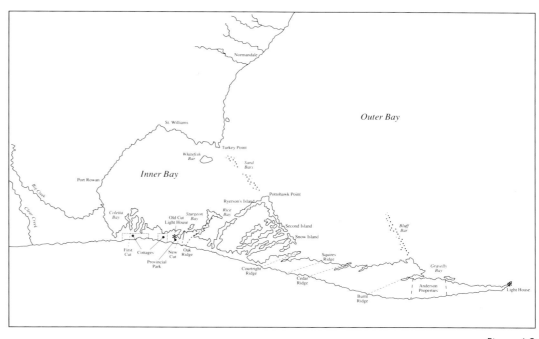

Figure 6-2
Drawing of Long Point.

Boat houses near Hastings Cut.

Cottages along bayside cut near Long Point.

protect the channel. The cut eventually silted in with weeds. By 1895, it was almost filled in completely and was soon abandoned by larger vessels.

During the mid 1860s, a new cut appeared to the west of the original channel. At first, everyone ignored this second cut. As the first one filled in, though, nature seemed to be opening up the newer one. By 1870, the new cut had widened to almost 800 yards and was 20 feet deep. So many vessels began using the new cut that, in 1879, a lighthouse was built just to the east of it, marking the navigation of the new cut.

The north beach portion of the Old Cut disappeared entirely during a fall storm in 1906. Some duck hunters who had built a cottage next to this cut had left their punt tied to a piling, and floating in the Old Cut waters one night. After an evening of gale forced winds from the west, they woke to find their punt just where they had left it. But it was sitting on sand rather than in water. In one evening, the forces of nature had filled in the cut.

The second cut was abandoned, and lighthouse services discontinued by 1916. Lake traffic was reduced. Shoaling on the lake side of the cut had made the risk of running aground increasingly dangerous. The Inner Bay, itself, had begun to silt in and was becoming too shallow for large vessels. Since the early 1900s, Long Point has generally remained a peninsula. The cuts, while still existing on the bay (north) side of Long Point, have remained filled in on the lake, or south side. There have been a few high water years during which relatively small trickles of water have broken through the head lands. In the mid 1980s extreme high water created a new half mile wide cut approximately 2 miles east of the Provincial Park. This cut, which was navigable by small boats, created a major threat to the Long Point Company and its shooting marshes. A combination of conservation efforts by the Company and falling water levels have eliminated this new cut and today's Long Point is a true peninsula once more.

THE RIDGES

Moving east from the base of Long Point, there are a number of major ridge lines ranging at 45 degree angles from the south beaches, across the sand spit to the bay side beaches. The ridges generally move in wave (bow) shapes from south to north. Structurally, each succeeding ridge line anchors the marsh, pond, and sandy beach areas behind and to the west of it.

The first of these is called Oak Ridge, and guards the critical Long Point Company marsh areas immediately to its west. Oak Ridge forms the western boundary of Umbrella Pond. Just to the east of this pond area, which is guarded by Snow Island, is Courtright's Ridge. The Courtright Ridge line anchors the eastern banks of Umbrella Pond, and marks the beginning of the continuous Long Point peninsula structure. About a half mile west is another major ridge line, called Squire's Ridge. These two ridge lines are followed, as one moves eastward along the point, by a series of smaller but structurally similar ridges which generally terminate in inlets on the north beach.

The existing Long Point Company compound is located on the eastern-most beach areas of the marshes, which are protected by Oak, Courtright and Squire's Ridges. It was located in this spot, facing the Inner Bay and Port Rowan, for ease of access both to Rowan and the marshlands which are contained by the ridge line geology.

The second major ridge structure on Long Point is Burnt Ridge. This line runs parallel to Squires Ridge, and is located approximately eight miles to the east. Burnt Ridge angles across the sands of Long Point, and hooks back to the west to form Bluff Bar in the Outer Bay area. The south beach area along this ridge contains some absolutely spectacular sand dunes, some of which rise as much as 50 feet from the depressions next to them. The north side of Burnt Ridge anchors the Bluffs Club, which evolved from the Long Point Company. It also provides the east bank of Bluff Pond, which is a major inlet from the waters of the Outer Bay.

Squire's Ridge.

Burnt Ridge.

There are several ridge lines between Squire's Ridge and Burnt Ridge. The primary ridge lines moving east include Helmer's, Cedar Creek, Bouck's, Little Creek, and Townsend which is adjacent to Burnt Ridge.

From the eastern edge of Burnt Ridge to the tip of the point, the land flattens out until the very tip of the point takes on the low profile of a sand bar and beach. Buildings and activities along the north beaches toward the end of the point include the Lighthouse on the tip, a number of Canadian Wildlife Service outposts and research stations located along the north shore, and the "Anderson" cottages (more on these later) at Gravely Bay.

SETTLEMENT NEAR LONG POINT

The first Europeans to lay claim to the Long Point area were the Sulpician missionary voyageurs Galinee and Dollier. They paddled down the Grand River and followed the lakeshore to today's Port Dover in 1669, representing France. They established a wintering sight about a mile inland, after following (today's) Patterson's Creek and spent time exploring and drawing charts of Long Point. It was a recollection of Galinee's handwritten chart of Long Point that alerted LaSalle to the location of the tip of the point, and helped avert a disastrous grounding on the first voyage of the *Griffon*.

Although the missionaries wrote wonderful descriptions of their wintering place, the area was slow to attract settlers because of its remote location. The first serious wave of settlers were UEL's following the American War of Independence. Governor General Simcoe offered substantial plots of farm land to those Americans who still felt an allegiance to England. In a relatively short time after the formation of the United States, settlements began to grow along the shore behind Long Point, from Port Dover to Port Rowan. Most of these were anchored by mills. In fact, the original name of Port Dover was "Dover Mills." By the War of 1812, there were towns at Dover, Ryerse, Normandale, St. Williams and Port Rowan.

From the time that LaSalle and the *Griffon* narrowly avoided disaster by running aground on its tip, Long Point began to develop a sinister reputation. The spit of sand was both inhospitable to year round living, and remote. Most knew it only by reputation. From a sailor's perspective, it stuck out into the middle of the lake and presented a frightening navigational hazard. For the shore bound, it was a place of mystery, filled with wildlife and beauty. Prior to the development of the causeway leading from Rowan to the base of Long Point, it could only be reached by boat. For the early settlers, there was plenty to do on the homesteads, and they had little interest in exploring the land masses of Long Point.

Typical section of shoreline on Long Point's North Beach.

The first systematic problems on the Point began because of the channel (or cut) which connected the lake to the Inner Bay near the western base of Long Point. There were lots of reasons for sailors to use this channel during the early 1800s. First among these was seeking shelter from storms by getting out of the open lake to lie at anchor in the Inner Bay. A second reason was to take a short cut along the north shore, avoiding the relatively hostile open waters of the lake. For the early schooner captains, who had to tack up or down the lake, the shortcut saved many difficult hours of upwind work. It had the added comfort of allowing the sailors to proceed in the relatively calm waters of the Inner and Outer Bays.

BLACKBIRDING

As the population grew along the north shore behind Long Point, locals began to see opportunities to augment their farming activities. At first, the most popular techniques were hunting and trapping. The men of the area would leave their families at home and set up temporary quarters on Long Point. These were not elaborate residences. They were simple shacks providing shelter, a place to sleep, and storage for equipment and supplies.

Old Cut lighthouse as it looks today.

As the numbers of these entrepreneurs grew, they began to communicate with each other, forming informal groups for the purpose of supporting and assisting each other. By the mid-1800s, some loosely knit groups found a new way to make easy money: blackbirding. This special type of pirating (also called wrecking) was easily accomplished from land on Long Point. When they saw a ship headed for the cut (and into the Inner Bay) at night, the blackbirds erected a false light on shore, tricking sailors into thinking that they had arrived at the entrance to the channel. Most blackbirding was done during stormy evenings when visibility was impaired and ship's crews were overly anxious to reach the safety of the Inner Bay.

Schooner captains, anxious to retreat from the stormy lake, would steer their vessels toward the false light, thinking that they were approaching the cut. Closing upon the beach, however, their ships ran aground and foundered hopelessly in the sand and surf. The crew usually realized that they had been tricked by blackbirds. Fearing for their lives, they made their way to shore and fled toward Port Rowan or Port Burwell for safety. Meanwhile, the pirates helped themselves to the cargo. By the time authorities from London or Simcoe were notified, the wreckers had stripped the ship and hidden its cargo away in caches on Long Point.

Most of the victims of blackbird attacks were American ships and crews. This ultimately resulted in complaints from American businessmen to the U.S. government. In turn, the United States complained to England and Upper Canada. But Long Point was far removed from the centers of Ontario civilization (Toronto, London and Windsor), and effectively out of the control of Canadian authorities. The Long Point area remained a troublesome frontier area for much of the 19th century.

POACHING

The fundamental ongoing economic activity for the adventurers of Long Point's early days, however, was not wrecking. It was the harvest of the plentiful game which was drawn to the area. There are stories told about how abundant muskrat, beaver, elk, wolves, deer, ducks, geese and fish were during the early days. Game was supposedly so abundant that anyone could successfully make a living by hunting, fishing and trapping. The early adventurers harvested as much as they could carry without regard to gaming seasons or preservation. There are pictures and stories from the mid 1800s of "market hunters" bringing thousands of ducks to Port Rowan for sale.

The notion of hunting, trapping and fishing conservation did not set well with these individuals, and gradually their activities became increasingly alarming. A growing number of interested sports hunters began to worry that Long Point would soon become a barren wasteland, devoid of fish and game. By the time Canada was being formed in the early 1860s (as an independent constitutional monarchy) there was a general perception, on both sides of the lake, that Long Point had become a lawless wilderness and was believed to be a threat to shipping and the balance of wildlife. The lands of the Point were said to be populated by desperados who participated in a variety of destructive activities, including blackbirding. There were outcries on both sides of the lake for someone to control the area and to put an end to these dangerous activities. In addition to these primary problems, lumbering was being carried on without regard for the natural environment, and there were stories of taverns and bordellos on the Point.

It was within the context of this political and economic environment that the seeds of the original Long Point Company were sewn. A group of relatively wealthy sportsmen/businessmen made a deal with the newly forming government of Canada to purchase the entirety of Long Point and to bring the region under control. The government had offered the majority of the lands on Long Point for sale in the late 1850s, but there were no takers. The newly organized "company" persuaded the government to reoffer the lands for sale, and purchased them for $8,540 on May 4, 1866. The members of the newly formed company were primarily Canadians from Hamilton and St. Catherines who had established sport hunting shanties on the point. By the 1860s, sports hunters like the new company

Gravely Bay and the Anderson cottages.

Allan Ridge, named after the detective who was killed.

members generally conducted their activities on the western end of the point. The locals (engaged in somewhat less "scrupulous" industries) were largely active on the eastern end.

As the bylaws of the company were drawn up in 1866 the group began to conspire on ways to gain full control of Long Point. They hoped to end all activities which seemed unacceptable to the members. The basic conflict which soon emerged was between the wealthy out-of-town sportsmen, who were seeking control, and locals who were trying to augment their living. Naturally, the first order of business was to gain physical control of the land itself.

THE ANDERSON PROPERTIES

Some of the lands on Long Point were already in the possession of private individuals. Those closest to the company's established base of operations near the western end were gradually subsumed by the company. Typically, the company would buy the privately owned lands from individual owners in return for lifetime hunting and fishing privileges. But, there was a lumberman on the eastern end of the point named Walter Anderson who refused to sell and thus began a three decade war with the company.

First there were property squabbles. Then, the company began to accuse Anderson of allowing his local friends to poach on their property by entering from the Anderson lands. The company charged that Anderson and his friends were shooting deer and fowl faster than they could re-establish them. To gain local leverage, in 1890 Anderson divided his 88 acre property into a large number of small plots, and either sold or leased them (for 999 years) to locals. This maneuver made Anderson a local hero. It had the added effect of insuring legal access to Long Point for a large number of non-company people. In an infamous scheme to infiltrate and gather evidence against the "Anderson Gang," the company hired a private detective named B.B. Allan. Allan purchased a share in the Anderson property under an assumed name and traveled to Long Point to spy on the poachers.

He is known to have arrived at Gravely Bay near the Anderson property but he failed to return to the cottages after hunting with two Anderson shareholders. His body was found later by members of the Long Point Company with his head shot off.

The Anderson lands (as well as the adjacent crown lands), which are located within a few miles of the tip of the point, continue to have a few private cabins on them. They can be seen along the north shore just west of the lighthouse. As the owners of the cottages on the crown lands pass away, the lands, and the cottages on them, revert to the Canadian Wildlife Service.

THE LONG POINT COMPANY

The company (called the "Millionaires Club" by locals) began its operations in 1866. They have been in continuous control of Long Point since that time. Their iron-handed management has resulted in two important developments. First is the continuance of the area as a virtual wilderness which has been inaccessible to tourism and development. Second is the continuous judicious management of wildlife, especially ducks and geese. These factors are responsible for the ongoing role of Long Point as a major flyway for migrating birds of all species, and for the currently pristine conditions of the lands.

The physical setting of today's "millionaires club" is the western most beach structure behind Oak Ridge, which faces the Inner Bay. The distinctive row of red cottages can be seen from the Inner Bay, and includes a separate sleeping cabin for each member. There is a common dining hall building and a number of other structures. Members are ferried to the cottages from Port Rowan by boat or sea plane. Over the years, the membership roster increased to twenty. The composition has also shifted, and now has a distinctly American flavor. The compound is in the constant care of one or more "keepers," who continue the maintenance, and organize cooking and hunting duties when members come for shooting.

Long Point Company warning sign.

The Long Point Company.

A classic tradition of the Long Point Company is the punting system for moving members and guests to shooting locations within the marsh. The keepers organize a system of "punters," or locals who function as shooting guides. Each punter guides a member to a productive shooting location by means of a small open boat called a shooter's "punt." Today's punters come from all walks of life including physicians and other professionals. The punter packs guns, ammunition and the day's lunch, which is prepared in the dining hall. He then poles the member away from the cottages and into the marshes. There are families in the area who have served as punters for four and five generations.

A list of the members and guests of the Long Point Company reads like a "who's who" of recent history. The Cabots, Lodges, Morgan's, Winthrop's, McLaughlin's, McKenzies, and Hathaway's have all been shareholding members. Famous guests who have signed the register at the clubhouse include artist Louis Fuertis, England's Prince George, Governor General Michner, Queen Victoria's son Edward, and President Theodore Roosevelt.

Long Point Company's shooting marshes.

OTHER CLUBS AND DEVELOPMENTS

From the beginning, there were boundary disputes, pressures from locals to allow additional shooting clubs, and other land encroachments. The Rice Bay Club, for example, was founded by squatters who cleverly manipulated their way onto Company land between the cottages and the base of Long Point. Although the original members of the Rice Bay Club were probably poachers looking for a way to encroach Company controlled lands, an amicable relationship developed and continues to this day.

The Bluffs Club, which can be seen along the north beaches at Bluff Bar, was originally leased to friends of the Long Point Company in 1919. Records suggest that the members of the Company looked to the Bluffs Club and its keeper to guard against encroachment from the Anderson Gang. Today's Bluffs Club is in good repair, after a devastating storm almost obliterated the cabins in 1975. Its current membership doesn't quite rival the Long Point Company in prestige. It does, however, include the Johnson family (of Johnson Wax fame) and a number of other prominent Canadians.

Interior shot of a member's cottage – Long Point Company.

The Bluffs Club in 1920.

When the Old Cut lighthouse ceased to operate, interest began to grow in the development of the lands adjacent to the Company and to the west of the cut. In 1921, Ontario established a provincial park immediately adjacent to the Old Cut. The province then built a causeway connecting Port Rowan to the Old Cut area, which brought significant development to the area at the base of Long Point. In 1928, another plot of 140 acres of land was wrestled from the control of the company. It became an addition to the provincial park.

Meanwhile, land which had been expropriated by the crown for use with the lighthouse and old cut operations was sold privately to a developer. The developer began to create cottages just west of company property. In 1944, another block of some 140 acres was privately deeded by the company to its head keeper, who also began to develop cottage sights. The cottage development near the area of the old cut became the present day community of Long Point.

Most recently, the Long Point Company has begun deeding all of the lands which are not adjacent or critical to the continuation of their shooting operations to the public domain. Notably, the lands to the east of Squire's Ridge (with the exception of the Bluffs Club) have now reverted to the Canadian Wildlife Service for management, control, and protection as a wilderness. This plot will eventually include all of the Anderson properties, as the current owners pass on. In 1980, a public ceremony was held at the Provincial Park and the last of the Company's non-shooting holdings were donated to the Ministry of Natural Resources.

THE JERSEY CITY

The night of November 25, 1860 was a cold and blustery one for the keeper of the Long Point Light. Harry Clark had spent 25 years on the tip of Long Point, but that evening became a night to remember. Clark was in the midst of preparing to close up for the year. The navigational season was coming to an end and he was looking forward to winter on land and the upcoming holidays. As he busied himself that evening with outdoor maintenance, he was surprised to see a ship on the eastern horizon. He watched it as darkness fell, and became somewhat concerned because of the deteriorating weather. The winds had risen to more than 30 knots from the southwest, and there were high seas running on the lake side of the Point.

As he watched the ship's approach, Clark thought that it might give up the idea of pounding its way upwind and duck behind the Point for shelter. As darkness fell, he was surprised to see the ship pass the tip of the Point to the south and continue its westerly course. The waves were rolling by that time, but the ship was a steamer and seemed to be making slow but steady progress. Clark presumed that the captain was in no difficulty, and continued his preparations.

Aboard the *Jersey City*, things were not so cozy. The 182 foot steamer was only five years old and the captain and crew knew her to be strong and fast. But the trip from Buffalo had become increasingly difficult that day. They were bound for Toledo with two passengers and a below deck cargo of flour and pork. There were problems, however, with a deckload of cattle. The cattle were becoming increasingly agitated by the growing waves. As the *Jersey City* neared Long Point, the crew hoped that the captain would seek shelter and anchor for the evening. The captain, however, acting in behalf of the ship's owner, opted to continue for Toledo. He reasoned that if the winds kept up, it would be too difficult to anchor behind the point. He thought that he could angle away from the waves and along the Canadian shore for a few more hours and then steer to port, running with wind and waves at the rear quarter for Toledo. He was also counting on the wind to shift to the northwest which would provide increasing shelter from the north shore.

The Bluffs Club present day.

Desolate south beach of Long Point.

As the *Jersey City* clawed its way along the south beaches of Long Point, the shoal waters and the tremendous waves which they have traditionally generated during storms, began to take their toll on the ship. The pounding on her wooden hull caused the seams to start opening. The engineers reported that she was taking on too much water. A decision was made to bring her around and run downwind for shelter behind the point. The turning maneuver did not go well. As the *Jersey City* began its turn, a 30 footer washed over the ship, destroying the decks and taking a passenger and many of the cattle overboard. There was absolute bedlam on deck. The remaining cattle stumbled about out of control. The ship rolled severely as several more monster waves pounded the deck. A few moments later, her fires went out and she foundered.

The *Jersey City* slowly and ponderously turned eastward and began to drift along the beaches toward the tip of the point. By this time, a blizzard was raging. Visibility was almost zero. The crew had become unruly, thinking that the captain had made a grave error in not seeking shelter on the first pass by the Point. The captain, the engineers, and wheelsman worked franticly to try and steer the sinking hulk toward the beaches of Long Point. They did not know how far they were from the tip, but they realized that their only hope was to run the *Jersey City* aground on the beaches before she drifted past the point and into deeper waters.

After an hour of drifting, the ship ground to a halt on a bar some 400 yards from the south beach. By this time, the weather had further deteriorated. The winds were shrieking. A driving wet snow was falling at such a rate that visibility was almost zero. The *Jersey City* seemed to be in danger of breaking up, or worse yet, floating off the bar and sinking in deeper water. The captain ordered the lifeboats launched and as the crew set off for shore they lost one member in the boiling surf. The captain and his cadre of the wheelsman, two engineers, and the remaining passenger launched a second lifeboat and made it to shore.

On the beach all hands were wet, frozen, and frightened. The captain decided that they should walk east along the beaches to the lighthouse. He reasoned that they were closer to the tip than to the base of the point. He thought that they would have the best chance of finding the lighthouse and help if they walked the beaches with the wind at their backs. The crew was not particularly happy with the captain's decision-making up to that Point. They decided to go in different directions, including overland, away from the beaches and toward the shelter of the Outer Bay side of Long Point.

Around 11:00 p.m., Harry Clark was aroused by sounds of people at the door of his keeper's house. He arose to find a frostbitten party of five including the captain, the wheelsman, two engineers, and passenger. They had made their way some two miles down the beach to the lighthouse, and were saved. Clark put on heavy clothing and walked the south beaches in the blizzard looking for other survivors. Finding none, he returned to minister to the needs of the captain's frozen party.

The next morning, when the winds had calmed, Clark walked the beaches again to see how the *Jersey City* was doing. He began to find frozen bodies near the stricken vessel. Apparently, some of the crew had given up walking to the west and returned to the sight of the ship, where they died of exposure. Over the remaining months, other bodies were found in various positions within the inland portions of Long Point. One crew member was found frozen to a tree in late spring. With the exception of the captain's party of five, every member of the crew died of exposure that night on the unforgiving beaches of Long Point.

View of Long Point's interior.

Lake Erie Adventures

1. It's field trip time! Visit the Long Point area. For our U.S. readers this means a trip to the other side of the lake and probably an overnight. Be sure to drive the lake road from Nanticoke then Port Dover to Port Rowan. Stop at every vista and you will be able to see Long Point. Visit the beach at Turkey Point, and the piers at Dover and Rowan. We recommend fall and spring for the best view and the least congestion.

2. Take binoculars and enjoy the vistas from three important vantage points; the hilltop over the government marina in Dover, the clubhouse at the Turkey Point Golf Course, and the overlook on the lake road just east of Port Rowan.

3. Drive the causeway from Port Rowan to Long Point and look around. Visit the provincial park and walk the south beaches of the point.

4. As you drive the causeway and then the road to the provincial park stop and look at the seine netting operations, the walking path on the marsh side of the road and finally the Old Cut Lighthouse near the Provincial Park. Explore the roadways on the north side of the road leading to the Provincial Park. Here you will find the cuts leading into the Inner Bay.

5. Visit the Backus Conservation Area in Port Rowan. They have the best exhibit on Long Point and the Long Point Company.

6. If you camp, there are Provincial Parks at Turkey Point and Long Point. If not, there are accommodations in Port Dover but they are generally filled during the summer season so make reservations. We recommend either the Erie Beach Hotel or the Brant Inn in Port Dover.

7. Port Rowan celebrates a Tomato Festival the first weekend of September. The event includes Punter's contests and other aspects of Long Point's history.

PRESQUE ISLE:
FROM WILDERNESS TO STATE PARK

*D*evelopment near Erie began earlier than on the Canadian side of the lake. This was due to the strategic importance of Erie's location. The exploratory quests of the voyageurs were both west and south. Western exploration was considered speculative since there was no clear understanding of distances from the Great Lakes to the Pacific. And as explorations continued, it became increasingly clear to the French that the westward trek might be unreasonably long.

Southern exploration was a different matter. Distances to the Gulf of Mexico (for trade with the Spanish) were well known. As the French continued their excursions, they became convinced that a southern route along the Allegheny, Ohio, and Mississippi Rivers would be the gateway to commercial success. In the push south, Erie was seen as a key location. Proximity to the French Creek basin (near today's Waterford) and access to the Allegheny River made Erie the keystone in the French plan to build a new world. This was why, in their vision of 13 strategically located forts, the French planned and built three forts near Presque Isle and one at LeBoeuf. They anticipated trade from all over the lakes

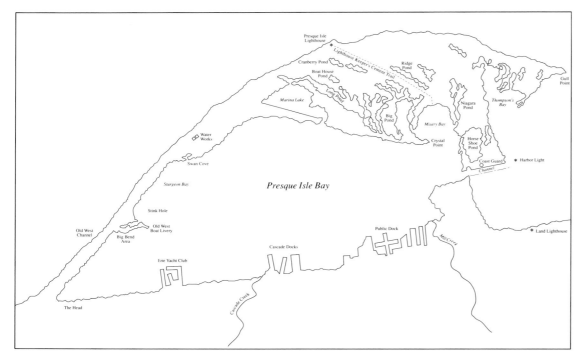

Overall chart of Presque Isle including points of interest.

moving to Erie, being transported via the Iroquois portage to Lake LeBoeuf and French Creek, and ultimately moving all the way to the Gulf of Mexico.

Erie's three forts were located (1) at the tip of the Peninsula, (2) on the western arm of Presque Isle and (3) on the mainland near Mill Creek. All were established between 1720 and 1759. After the French lost to the British, (French and Indian War) they burned the forts down as they abandoned them. The British built a stockade at the western Peninsula site. They built a blockhouse on the ruins of the French fort by Mill Creek. In 1763, these were captured and burned by Indians. But, the Americans regained control by 1790 and added a fort to protect the harbor near Crystal Point (Misery Bay).

Even without forts, the pioneers of Erie continued to think of the Peninsula as the guardian of a harbor gateway to the south. It would not be until the steamboats and then the Civil War era that Erie's business community would fully appreciate the potential for trade with the western Great Lakes' ports.

THE DEVELOPMENT OF THE TOWN OF ERIE

Erie's pioneering settler was Col. Seth Reed, a physician from Uxbridge, Mass. Reed came to Erie after hearing of its beauty and its strategic trading location. Reed and some of his family traveled from Buffalo on a boat owned by John

Talmadge, who was planning to begin regular trade runs between Buffalo and Erie. The Reeds landed on the Peninsula in July of 1795 and camped there. Meanwhile, a garrison of militia near Mill Creek with a surveyor named Thomas Rees saw the Reed's fire and worried that hostile Indians were about to attack their encampment. Scouts were sent to the Peninsula only to learn that the camp fire belonged to the Reed family. Rees became friendly with Col. Reed and convinced him to cross the bay and settle near the mouth of Mill Creek. Reed built Erie's first house in this area. The next year, after Reed's wife and other children had joined them, he built a hotel at the same sight. In 1797, Reed moved south to Kearsarge, leaving his son Rufus in charge of the hotel.

Within a few years, Rufus had entered the trading post business and was dealing in furs. Soon he was building boats which he used to haul supplies up the lakes to trade for furs, which were returned to Erie's trading post. Rufus was primarily interested in the trading business, and saw the schooner and bateaux as tools for moving goods along the lake. His son Charles, however, who was educated in the east as a lawyer, loved ships of all types. After joining his father in business, he specialized in the manufacture of steamboats, becoming the premier boat builder on the lakes. Rufus died in 1846, leaving his fortune to Charles, his only son.

Charles died at the age of 69 in 1871 in his home at Sixth and Peach Streets. This house, the "Reed Mansion" is still standing, and was built by the employees of the shipyards. It opened in 1846. For much of the 19th century, the Reed name was synonymous with shipping on the lakes.

At the time that the Reed family arrived, there was already military and commercial activity in the bay, because of the fort on Presque Isle, and the beginnings of salt shipping. The city was seasonally inhabited by wagoners who used teams of horses to transport goods and materials along the old Indian portage to Fort LeBoeuf. The most common commodity in those days was salt, which was shipped by bateaux from Buffalo, transferred to wagons, and drawn overland to French Creek. From there, it was floated down the Allegheny to Pittsburgh.

As the town developed, almost all of its economic activity could be linked to the lake and the harbor. In 1796, Eliphalet Beebe came to Erie looking for a site to build a shipyard. Beebe was the lake's first commercial sailing ship builder. He had hoped to establish a business within the confines of Presque Isle Bay. Finding Reed and others on the east end of the bay, Beebe scouted the west end for a suitable sight, but abandoned this idea. He reported that there were bogs near the head of the bay which would make the waters unsuitable for navigation, that the arm of the Peninsula seemed too narrow to afford lasting protection from the elements, and that the prevailing south-westerlies would make sailing in and out of the head of the bay difficult.

Instead, Beebe moved his shipping operation to Freeport, where he launched his first ship, the *Washington*, in 1797 for the Pennsylvania Population Company. Beebe was convinced that the North East location, strategically located on the Buffalo side of Erie, would stand him in good stead as business between the two ports accelerated. In 1799, he launched a second ship, called the *Harlequin*, in the same location. The *Harlequin* was captained by Daniel Dobbins, a swash-buckling young man (23 years old) who had moved to Erie to enter the sailing business. In 1799, the Reeds launched the first sailing ship within Erie's harbor, the *Good Intent*. During the next few years several other sailing ships appeared along Erie's Bayfront including the *Wilkerson*, launched in 1801 by the Reeds, and the Mary which was launched by Thomas Wilson in 1805 near the mouth of the Cascade Creek.

By the early 1800s, Dobbins was well known to all of Erie's ship builders and had become partners with several of them in ship design, building and ownership. In those days, the epicenters of ship building were at the mouths of Mill Creek on the east side of town, and Cascade Creek, to the west. The War of 1812 was an incredible inconvenience to Dobbins, who was well on his way to becoming a wealthy man and a pillar of Erie's business community. At the beginning of the hostilities, Dobbins (with Rufus Reed), aboard his merchant schooner the *Salina*, was captured by the British at Mackinac. He was pardoned to return to his home, but his ship was confiscated.

Irritated by the British seizure of the *Salina*, he masterminded a plan to build the U.S. fleet within the protection of Presque Isle Bay at the foot of Cascade Street, and subsequently "sold" this strategy to the naval authorities in Washington. Once the fleet had been built, Presque Isle began to serve as a Naval Base. A blockhouse was built at Misery Bay in 1813 and remained in use until 1825. At the conclusion of the War of 1812, the naval ships were sunk at Misery Bay (a common practice to preserve wooden ships), in hopes of raising them for service at a later date.

Dobbins received a commission in the navy in 1813, which he held until 1826, when he was asked to go to sea to return the body of Perry for burial. He was recommissioned in 1845 in the Revenue Service and subsequently served as the captain of the revenue cutter *Erie*. He died in Erie in 1856.

THE TIME BETWEEN THE WARS

After the War of 1812, commercial activity in the harbor virtually exploded. A number of schooner builders began operations along the bay front. Docks appeared near the east side access of Mill Creek, along Cascade Creek, and also near the newly forming center of town at State Street. Word was spreading up the lake about the new steamship. The *Walk In The Water* was being built at Buffalo. Shipping interests in Erie and beyond were watching that development quite carefully. In 1824, a few years after the apparent success of Buffalo's steamship, Rufus Reed, Daniel Dobbins and five others formed the Erie and Chautauqua Steamboat Company. They began the development of their first steamship, the *William Penn*, which was launched in 1826.

The federal government declared Erie a U.S. Port, established a Federal Revenue Cutter Station on Presque Isle, and signaled its intent to administrate the Peninsula. The first revenue cutter to be stationed at the Peninsula was the *Benjamin Rush* in 1827. The *Benjamin Rush* was followed by the *Erie* in 1833, and then the iron steamers *Dallas* in 1846, and *J.S. Black* in 1857.

In 1824, the Army Corps of Engineers was commissioned to survey the harbor and the Peninsula. They intended to stabilize the weakening west arm of Presque Isle, and to improve the harbor entrance. Prior to that time, there were two parallel sand bars guarding the east (today's) entrance to the bay. More than one visiting ship (including the *Walk In The Water* on her maiden run) had gone aground trying to approach Erie. Dobbins used his considerable influence in Washington to gain a series of harbor improvement appropriations which were aimed at the creation of a viable commercial channel with fixed pier structures and a lighthouse. In 1824, a three year project was commenced which led to the creation of today's commercial harbor entrance.

The east harbor improvement project had a hiatus in the late 1820s and early 1830s. A series of severe winter storms over that period broke through the west arm of the Peninsula and ultimately resulted in the development of a channel similar to the cut at Long Point. By 1835, this west channel had reached a width of a mile and a depth of 10 to 15 feet. It was regularly utilized by commercial vessels. For the engineers working on the harbor, it gave pause to the overall direction of their project goals, which had been to establish an east channel and then to shore up the west arm. They began to reconsider this strategy and, under much protest, changed direction. They decided, instead, to build and maintain a west channel instead of shoring up the arm of the Peninsula. Appropriations began in 1836 for the development of the west harbor entrance, but controversy from commercial interests who could see no future in shipping to the west soon overwhelmed the project. Funding was terminated after 1840. From 1840 until 1864, the Peninsula remained an island. This fact had a profound influence upon the development of Presque Isle.

In the early 1800s, the population of Erie was primarily located east of Cascade Creek. Thus, even the hearty souls who ventured west to establish "frontier" homesteads were repelled by the Peninsula. The island portion of

Presque Isle was difficult to reach. Only the hearty ventured west to the area called "The Head," which ranged from the foot of today's Sommerheim Drive to the base of the Peninsula. The Head, or Massassauga Point as it was also called, consisted of the land ranging from the base of Presque Isle to the channel which separated it from the main island.

In 1833, an iron bog was discovered in the western end of the bay at The Head. Almost immediately, a commercial operation evolved to mine the ore. Pig iron was shoveled into flat bottomed boats, then floated down the bay where a smelting furnace was built to become Erie's first industry. For much of the pre-Civil War period, this industrial activity, along with the channel barrier to Presque Isle, dissuaded both recreational and homesteading activities. In 1834, a furnace at Conneaut made a deal with the owners of the iron bog to ship ore from. The Head. Two schooners were built for this business: the Jack Downing and the Olive Branch. These were wintered at The Head by being drawn up as far as possible on the beach.

By the 1830s, Erie had taken its place as a major shipbuilding community. This created intense pressure for the federal government to continue to improve and maintain the harbor. Between 1823 and 1894, the government spent $827,000 on harbor improvements. By 1840, the Reeds had built three major steamships including the *Pennsylvania* (1832), the *Thomas Jefferson* (1835), and the *Missouri* (1837). They also owned and operated the Erie which was built in the Colt and Jackson shipyard at the foot of French Street in 1837.

The first Iron Ship was launched at Erie in 1844. The *Michigan*, a U.S. Naval ship (not a revenue cutter), was prefabricated in Pittsburgh and assembled at the docks in Erie. This historic ship, which was later renamed the *Wolverine*, stood guard over Erie for many decades. She saw military action twice on Lake Erie. During the Civil War, she prevented a confederate attack against a prison encampment in Ohio, and later she stopped the Fenian Revolt on the eastern end of the lake.

The Wolverine steaming out of Erie's Harbor about 1910.

Photo by PAT SHOUP

In 1833, Rufus Reed used his considerable influence to get himself appointed Superintendent of the Peninsula. At that time, the land mass was assumed to be under the jurisdiction of the City of Erie. Reed's interests were clearly directed toward protecting the harbor and its shipping. His actions, however, were in the best interest of the lands, as he made rules against settling, logging, burning or picking cranberries. In those days, the Peninsula was well known for its abundant wild cranberries. Reed worried that the wanton harvest of the berries, whose delicate plants were an important anchoring structure for the sand marshes, might threaten the integrity of the entire Peninsula.

To placate the townspeople, one day was set aside for an annual cranberry harvest. The first Tuesday of October was declared "Cranberry Day." On this day, townspeople were allowed to go to the Peninsula and pick the berries. For many years Cranberry Day was a festive local holiday. People would cross the bay in droves the night before and camp. Unfortunately, the annual harvest became such a festive event that the cranberry plants were over picked and have all but disappeared from Presque Isle.

THE ERIE EXTENSION CANAL

The most important harbor activities of the 1840s and 1850s were clearly those related to the creation of the Erie Extension Canal. During the 1830's and 1840's, there was a race among Lake Erie's north shore cities to build canal connections to Pittsburgh and the Ohio River. Erie's shipping community, including Dobbins and Reed, knew that if they did not have a canal way, shipping from the east would bypass Erie and go to towns in Ohio that had canal access routes. This was before the railroad connected Buffalo with the west. It seemed logical to businessmen up and down the lakes that canals would provide the best trade access to the south and the west.

In 1844, Erie's Extension Canal (Rufus Reed was president of the canal company and Charles Reed was treasurer) opened. Its terminus near the foot of today's Peach Street was the west slip or canal basin (as it was called then). The canal rose 100 feet through 15 locks between the bay front and West 26th street. It exited town near today's 26th and Zuck Road, then turned almost due south, where it ran parallel with the Ohio state line to Conneaut Lake. It was water from Conneaut Lake which filled the canal way from there to Erie. At Conneaut Lake, it forked into two directions giving shippers the opportunity either to connect with Meadville along the eastern run, or New Castle on the western artery. The Meadville branch joined the Allegheny River at Franklin and continued to Pittsburgh. The west branch used the Beaver River to connect with Pittsburgh.

The Erie Extension Canal officially opened on December 5, 1844 with the arrival of the *R.S. Reed*, a passenger boat, and the *Queen of the West*, a coal barge. The canal system was in immediate competition with two others; one at Ashtabula and another which began in Cleveland. Both of these also connected with Pittsburgh and the Ohio River system.

By the late 1840s, Erie's harbor was a beehive of activity. On average, there were three steamers and as many as 10 schooner arrivals per week. And, there was a fury of activity associated with loading and unloading canal packet boats. The shipping community was optimistic in their projections that Erie would soon capture the bulk of the immigrant transport business from Buffalo, as hundreds of Europeans were transferred to canal boats and sent south each week.

Unfortunately, the forces which ultimately conspired to destroy the steamship business ate away at profits along the canal system. The railroads connected Buffalo with the west in 1853 and represented the first blow. Later, a railroad line was completed to Pittsburgh, making the hassle of canal boat travel obsolete. By the beginning of the Civil War, the economic destiny of the Erie Extension Canal looked increasingly grim.

The Reeds, perceiving the destiny of the Canal, quietly sold their shares in the canal company and bought into the railroad business. They developed railroad yards near Erie's bay front. This sealed Erie's shipping destiny, as local shipping interests were ultimately to control the bay front and the railroads. This created the impetus for the growth of the docks and shipping over the next 100 years.

THE POST-CIVIL WAR PERIOD

In 1864, the destiny of the Peninsula and harbor was permanently changed when Col. T.J. Cram, from the Army Corps of Engineers, surveyed the Peninsula. He declared that the silting action of the west channel had become so extreme that the strategy of maintaining two channels was impractical. Several years of low water had all but filled in the channel between The Head and the island portion of Presque Isle. Cram decided to return to the original plan of building a protective break wall along the west arm of the peninsula, and maintaining a channel at the east end of the bay.

The U.S. Revenue Service returned to active operation in the same year. Earlier revenue cutters had been pressed into service for the Civil War, leaving Erie's harbor with only the Michigan as protection. In 1864, the *U.S.S. Perry* was launched and stationed at the Peninsula. The Perry was a familiar sight to visitors at Presque Isle until 1886, when she was replaced with a newer, faster *U.S.S. Perry II*.

The second cutter served the Presque Isle station until 1893, when the Revenue Service was combined with the Lifesaving Service to form the Coast Guard (see chapter 9).

Meanwhile, economic times were prosperous and the population of the city had begun to grow. In those days, it looked as though Erie would ultimately be larger than Cleveland, Buffalo, or Pittsburgh because of its harbor location. Business in the harbor district grew tremendously after the Civil War. In 1860 there were only 38 registered commercial ships. By 1885, the number had grown to 95. The mission of the federal government at the Peninsula was to protect the harbor and its growing trade.

By the turn of the century, the bay front was a first class shipping center with railway access, two major grain elevators (at the Anchor Line Docks) and a 50 tug fishing fleet. The Anchor line offered bulk shipping, package freight, passenger liner service and a tug boat fleet.

Over the next decades (with the west channel gone) commercial activity began to move from the mainland onto the "isolated" Peninsula. Much of this was commercial fishing, which had spread both from the east channel and The Head. At The Head there were a number of commercial fisheries, including the pound netting operations of the Post and Durfee Company.

Much of the economic activity on the Peninsula was located at Misery Bay, within rowboat access of the city via the channel. By the late 1870s, there was an ice house located at this point. In 1874, a pound netting operation which specialized in sturgeon was established near Misery

Revenue cutter S.S. Perry steaming through Erie's channel about 1909.

The Presque Isle lighthouse.

Bay by Slocum and Meyers. They also erected a caviar factory on the southwest corner of Misery Bay at Sturgeon Point. Sturgeon were so plentiful in the late 1800s that a section of the bay along Presque Isle was named Sturgeon Bay, and the arm which protected Misery Bay from the rest of Presque Isle Bay was named Sturgeon Point. The sturgeon processors would extract the eggs for caviar, then salt and bury the split carcasses in sand dunes along the north beaches. After a few weeks, the sun dried meat would be extracted from the carcasses and sold. The remains of the carcasses were dumped in the bay near today's Swan Cove, resulting in that relatively deep section of water being called "Stink Hole."

During this period, the Peninsula began its long career as a summer tourist haven. The Head was becoming a popular picnic and bathing area, though there were no easy ways to get there. In 1868, Captain James Hunter introduced the first steam tug to Erie. He used this tug as an excursion boat to take picnickers from the downtown or Cascade dock areas to The Head and back on an hourly basis. Soon, there were other tugs as well as schooners and row boats ferrying people to the Peninsula for picnicking, hiking, swimming, and fishing. A summer day on Presque Isle could provide adventure, fun, and a nice string of fish as a bonus.

The excursion boat business continued in Erie for many years. By 1880, there were four steam yachts engaged in the tourist business: the *Massassauga*, the *Lena Knobloch*, the *Emma Sutton* and the *J.H. Welch*. Of these, the *Massassauga* was the largest carrying 225 passengers. These ships carried picnickers and other excursioners to the Head and its elegant Massassauga Hotel or to the Peninsula's beaches and picnic grounds.

CONTROL OF THE PENINSULA

As the popularity of the Peninsula grew, the controversy over who really owned and controlled its land escalated. The federal government laid claim on the grounds that the land mass was critical to national defense. They had already spent substantial funds maintaining the harbor and developing lighthouses (see chapter 9). The Federal Government argued that only they could properly maintain the lands. The state, after struggling to control the triangle section of state land, was interested in owning as much land as possible. They were also vitally interested in access to the Lake. Finally the city, itself, had long considered the Peninsula to be its own. The city had in fact taken over its administration earlier, when it appointed Rufus Reed to run the park.

Political forces at the state and federal level pointed to Cranberry Day, the encroachment of commercial activity, and the excessive fishing and hunting which was being carried out on the park. These activities conflicted with the city's stated goal of maintaining the park as a preserve and clouded the city's ability to administrate a remote park area. By the late 1860s and early 1870s, the Misery Bay area was becoming a small commercial center. At that one general location, there was a pound netting operation, the caviar plant, a boat livery which specialized in ferrying persons back and forth to the mainland, an ice house, the sunken brig Niagara, which was becoming quite a tourist attraction, and other seasonal activities.

Pointing to the recent disappearance of the channel which guarded the west end of the Peninsula from incursion, political forces argued that it was only a matter of time until the park would become commercialized and settled. The final struggle for ownership began in the late 1860s, when for a brief time the park was turned over to the federal agency which ran the Soldiers and Sailors Home. In the few years of its control, several unpopular administrative decisions were orchestrated. The most disastrous was a mandate to cut down all of the red cedar trees on Presque Isle for use as fence posts. While lumbering operations were typical of private shore front properties, the increasing recreational use of the Peninsula heightened public objections. Ultimately, control was politically wrestled away from the federal Soldiers and Sailors agency.

In 1871, the state and federal governments reached a compromise (which squeezed the city out of ownership). Both agencies passed legislation granting ownership and physical control for the purpose of administration and conservation to the State of Pennsylvania. Eminent domain with respect to national defense, harbor maintenance and lighthouse keeping remained with the federal government.

Cottages at Fern Cliff near the west end of Presque Isle Bay.
Photo by CHERYL FREW

By 1890, it had become clear that the Peninsula was a recreational paradise. Its most popular areas included:

1. The Head … was reachable by excursion boat, and originally featured dining and lodging at two places: the Lone Fisherman's Inn and the Tracy Point Hotel at the foot of Sommerheim Drive. W.L. Scott owned the head and by 1875 he had completed a road connecting the Peninsula with the mainland. In early 1880, Scott built a grand hotel, the Massassauga, but it burned down after the 1882 season.

2. The Lifesaving Station … at the channel was another favorite. Citizens were ferried across the channel with picnics. They either walked the short distance to Thompson's Bay and its beaches or hiked along the lighthouse keeper's cement path to the mysterious north beaches.

3. Boathouse Pond … could be reached by excursion schooners. This area (home of today's Presque Isle Marina) was a popular picnic and bathing area.

4. Horseshoe Pond … which was connected by excursion ferry or could be hiked to from the Lifesaving Station was another favorite.

5. Big Bend … where the western arm of the Peninsula first begins to widen (later the home of the West Boat Livery) was a popular destination from the west.

By the turn of the century, there was increasing political pressure to make Presque Isle into a park for the city of Erie and its tourists. Visitors to the Peninsula were charmed by its raw beauty. Most realized that if it was not soon made into an official park, commercial activity would take over and ultimately ruin its natural beauty.

JOE ROOT

The Peninsula's best-known resident at the time was Joe Root, a character whose persona was an important part of the allure of the Peninsula for many years. Joe was a regular winter resident of the county poor house. Each spring, however, he would leave his room at the poor house and move to Presque Isle. Over his 20 odd years as a Peninsula summer resident, Joe built a number of shacks from drift-wood, packing crates, and other scrounged materials. At any given time, Joe had several domiciles. He would (quite logically) alternate his use of these depending upon wind and weather. He moved inland during cold windy weather and toward shore when it was hot.

Joe had a number of ways to make a living. He fished, picked fruit, and gathered eggs. But he was most famous for his sudden appearances at picnics. Shortly after a family had spread their blanket and begun the process of preparing a holiday feast, Joe would appear as if by magic. While parents were often put off by his appearance, children immediately loved him. He would captivate them, telling stories of his friends the jeebies (little people who lived with him on the peninsula). Joe's appearance was quite odd. He wore 4 or 5 pairs of pants, a vest, and a top hat. His scraggly long hair, bushy moustache and buck teeth immediately signaled children that, while Joe was a "big" person, he was somehow different from parents and other adults.

A ventriloquist, Joe would take his hat off and talk into it, delighting children when the creatures inside spoke back. After a few minutes of this, Joe almost always earned himself an invitation to the picnic (at the urging of the kids). Joe was often the recipient of the leftovers when the family departed. By the early 1900s, he was a legend. Families packed extra food hoping that they would be fortunate enough to see him.

Joe would also show up at the fish processing operations near Misery Bay and hitch boat rides to town. The fishermen loved him almost as much as the kids,

The Niagara after its 1913 restoration.
Photo by PAT SHOUP

The north beach at Presque Isle.

and would drag him along to waterfront pubs where Joe was always the grateful recipient of free drinks. Once blessed with a few brews, Joe would carry on for hours explaining to the patrons of Erie's taverns his dreams to begin a business on Presque Isle. His two favorite ideas were the "Balloon Farm" and the "Feather Factory." At first, both ideas seemed a bit crazy, but there was always a haunting germ of wisdom in each of Joe's ideas!

The balloon farm was based on Joe's observation of prevailing westerly winds. Joe hoped to plant rubber trees on the Peninsula, and then fabricate giant balloons, which could be used to lift and transport passengers to Buffalo along the prevailing winds. As Joe would reveal this plan, pub patrons would break into peals of laughter, until they pressed him for specifics. Then, well constructed details were presented, causing many to wonder if Joe was a lunatic or a genius.

The feather farm may have been Joe's best business concept. Joe Root realized the Indian heritage of the area. He was also well aware of the growing interest in Indian head dresses, feathers, and other items. Joe planned to utilize the plentiful bird population of Presque Isle as a feather producing bonanza. He planned to find and clean the feathers, then make them into all kinds of souvenirs.

As the 100 year anniversary of the Battle of Lake Erie approached, there was a move afoot to raise and refit the Niagara and turn the Peninsula into an official park. Locals began to wonder about the possibility that Joe Root might claim squatter's rights to Presque Isle. In a manipulation which was shrouded in secrecy, Joe was moved out of the poorhouse in the winter of 1910, before he could return to his beloved summer home on Presque Isle. He was incarcerated at Warren State Hospital, where he was diagnosed as mentally ill and held until he died in 1912, after a bout with severe depression.

Old timers say that Joe Root was "crazy like a fox." Perhaps he should be listed among the Quadrangle's human tragedies, falling victim to the evolution of progress. Children who visited the Peninsula over the next years missed their magical friend and his stories of Presque Isle's jeebies and goblins.

Shipping and Shipbuilding In The Harbor

When the canal went bankrupt and the Reeds moved into the railroading business, Erie's shipping future changed dramatically. The great shipyards of the 20th century evolved west of Erie, as the epicenter of great lakes shipping gradually moved toward the center of the great lakes. Still, Erie's harbor remained active through the war years. As a famous "safe harbor." The bay became a wintering place for steamships. Gradually, Erie built a reputation as a first class refitting and repair area.

Prior to World War II, Cascade Street was a major artery reaching to the bay front and the ship repair docks of Perry Shipbuilding. In those years and through the 1950s, dozens of ships would anchor for the winter in the protected west end of the bay off the Cascade docks. Shipping company employees would do winter maintenance while the ships were at anchor. If necessary, individual ships would be brought to the docks for extensive refit and repair. There was a ship's provisioning grocer and general store called Beckman's at Fourth and Cascade which used to hitch up teams of horses and haul coal and supplies across the frozen bay to the frozen-in ships prior to departure in the spring. Beckman's store and its carriage house can still be seen (under a different name) today.

During the war, the Perry Shipyard (then called Erie Concrete and Steel) developed and built several Naval utility boats whose function was to do harbor maintenance and delivery. These versatile "Yard Freighters" also had torpedo capabilities. A total of 34 of these 132 footers were built in Erie during the 1940s. The Perry Shipyard remained in operation doing repair work until the mid 1980s.

At the center of town, several builders were engaged in fish tug, pleasure boat, and excursion boat building from the late 1800s. The Paasch yard was a renowned builder of fish tugs and sailboats from 1867 until 1979. The Nolan yard built several tugs, and was actively building excursion boats into the 1980s. In 1992, Nolan's launched a houseboat for the misery bay houseboat community. During prohibition, Paasch developed a reputation for building armored speedboats which could easily outrun the Erie Station Coast Guard Cutter.

The Stewart J. Cort.

The Richard Reiss, 620' unloader built in 1934,
flagship of the Erie Sand Steamship Company.
ERIE SAND STEAMSHIP COMPANY

In the late 1960s, Litton Industries moved to Erie and established a ship-building facility at the foot of Holland Street. In a few short years, during the height of the jumbo shipbuilding era, Litton's Erie yard distinguished itself by launching the *Stewart J. Cort*, which was a 1000 foot jumbo in 1972. They launched the 1000 foot *Presque Isle* (which it still operates out of its Erie offices) a few years later. By the mid 1970s, however, shipbuilding had ground to a halt on the lakes. The Litton yard collapsed. What had seemed to be a major new industry in Erie had suddenly ceased to exist. In the late 1980s, Erie Marine Enterprises moved into the old Litton facilities and began what seems to be a highly successful maintenance and refit business.

The last vestiges of shipping can be seen at the Codan Yards on the Channel and the Erie Sand Steamship docks at the foot of Sassafras. Codan (Erie International Marine Terminal) is a full service shipper with bulk and package goods loading capabilities. Everything from iron ore to General Electric Locomotives has been loaded at the Codan yards. The Erie Sand Steamship Company still operates a fleet of self unloaders and sand suckers, some of which are painted in the company's distinct green with orange trim. Erie Steamship clearly operates a historic fleet. Their ship the *Niagara*, which was launched in 1897, has been designated as a future floating museum and is lying at the north end of the Erie Sand and Gravel docks waiting for a restoration effort. The *Niagara*, which was shortened 24 feet to her present size in 1926, converted to a sand sucker in 1927, and to a self unloader in 1959, was the oldest commercial vessel in use on the lakes before she was decommissioned in the mid 1980s. The 299 foot *J.S. St. John* (launched in 1945), Erie Steamships' local sand sucker can be seen entering and leaving the harbor on an almost daily basis throughout the year.

The *Lakewood* (1903), the company's former flagship has recently been sold for scrap and is lying at anchor in the Detroit River. Their new flagship is the 620.5 foot *Richard Reiss*. This 1943 steamer visits the harbor regularly to unload at the Erie Sand Docks.

THE EVOLUTION OF THE PARK

The early 1900s saw a cascade of events which led to the creation of today's state park as something other than a harbor barrier. A trolley service was completed, allowing easy access to Waldameer (which was owned by the trolley company). Access to Waldameer was much easier than travel to The Head. Scott's operations at the west end of the bay fell into disuse. Then, there were problems with the city's drinking water, which had been taken directly out of the bay since the 1860s. By the early 1900s, after the channel which sent

Aerial view of Presque Isle.

cleansing lake waters through the bay had closed up, there was growing concern for the quality of the bay water. These problems were highlighted by a typhoid epidemic in 1901. Local officials began a campaign against swimming in the bay. Gradually, the population began to favor the waters of the lake for swimming.

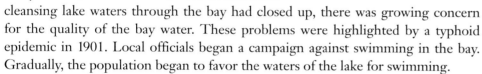

In 1904, the City Water Commission hastily began work to extend water intake pipes into the lake. They accomplished this by running lines under the park at the area now known as "Water Works." By 1908, the water department had extended their intake pipes across the Peninsula and commandeered a section of the middle of Presque Isle for their water works. In the early 1900s, the city added a settling basin, a pump house, a commissioner's house and other buildings.

In the years prior to 1913, there was an effort to raise and restore the Brig *Niagara* from her muddy grave sight in Misery Bay. The ship was completely refitted and floated in time for the 100 year celebration of the War of 1812. She went on tour for the next few years, being escorted and towed by the *Wolverine* and

The 1897 Steamship Niagara waits at the foot of Sassafras.

Hull of the Niagara about 1912 before restoration.
Photo by PAT SHOUP

subsequently moved to the Erie waterfront where she sat as a monument and tourist attraction in various states of decomposition until her most recent refit in 1991.

Stimulated by both the newfound interest in the Peninsula which was caused by the raising of the *Niagara* as well as the city's incursion onto the center of the park, the state intensified its efforts to gain absolute control of the Peninsula. Arguing that the issue of national defense at Presque Isle was no longer important, and that they (better than the city) could preserve the park, they finally succeeded in 1921. In a complex political "deal," Presque Isle State Park was created under Act 436 and signed into effect by Governor Fisher on May 27. The city was given control (but not ownership) of the lands known as Waterworks Park, and the U.S. Government was granted control of lands surrounding the lighthouse, Coast Guard Station and channel.

In 1925 a paved road was developed along the north beaches allowing visitors easy access by automobile and beginning the tradition of car travel to see the park and its surrounding waters. In 1926 Perry Monument was completed and opened to the public. By 1939 two boat liveries, a Police Barracks, a first aid house and a water main had been completed. The pre-World War II Peninsula had become a modern public park.

In 1956 a massive effort to protect the beaches and redesign usages on the park began. Sand was dredged from the interior of the park creating today's Marina Lake and moved to the west arm of the Peninsula. High water in the early 1950's had often cut across the narrowing arm of the Peninsula causing concern that it might revert to its mid-1800s island configuration. As a part of this massive restructuring, the west arm was widened, trees were planted and an improved roadway system was built allowing two lanes of traffic both entering and leaving the park. By this time summer tourism had increased and it was argued that better roadway capacity would put an end to the traffic jams of the late 1940s and early 1950s. In those days a summer storm would find thousands of cars struggling to leave the park while water flooded the roadway on the west arm.

As part of this project, the city gave up control of the Water Works area, in return for which the state traded its long owned water lots on Erie's bay front and land at the Canal Basin (west slip area). This area was ultimately utilized to house the Presque Isle Yacht Club, which had originally controlled the inlet which became the Presque Isle Marina. The state park marina was completed in 1962 and is located in the newly dredged Marina Lake. This operation, located at the west end of the interior lagoon system, was interconnected by the dredging operations so that canoes and other small boats could travel between Misery Bay and the Marina Lake.

Horseshoe Pond houseboat community.

As the park developed, it became apparent that a number of locals had established houseboat residences in Misery Bay and other waters of the park. A variety of floating dwellings had evolved, and the owners were not interested in abandoning them for the sake of the park. However, legislation had been passed in 1937 giving park officials jurisdiction over all waters within 500 feet of shore. So, the park gained control of the many houseboats and placed them in Horseshoe Pond. Negotiations with the owners of the houseboats resulted in a deal – the park allowed 24 sights to be maintained under strict regulations and guidance. Today's houseboat community is one of the unique aspects of the park. Hidden from the mainstream traffic on the tip of the park, the 24 sights remain a testament to the way things used to be.

From the 1960s to the present time, a few additional projects of note were completed on the park. By this time, however, public scrutiny, with respect to park stewardship, had dramatically increased and almost every project became the target of significant controversy. The most contentious was the installation of sand mound toilet systems to increase the sanitary capacity of the park. It was (and is) argued that these systems are inappropriate for a sand spit peninsula and contribute to groundwater pollution. Slightly less contentious was the completion of the all-purpose trail allowing hiking and biking access along the bay side of the park. Critics argued that the trail cut through sensitive areas, endangering plant and animal life and bringing crowds of people to a natural area.

Today's most visible controversy surrounds the 1989-1992 construction of beach protecting rubble mound break waters along the lake side. The Corps of Engineers argued that this project would dramatically reduce beach erosion, lessening the volume of replacement sand which had to be brought to the park each year. Critics complain that the rubble mounds are ugly and create pockets of stagnant, polluted water.

FUTURE MANAGEMENT OF THE PARK

Pennsylvania's state parks, including Presque Isle, have a dual mission. On one hand, their role is to promote and encourage recreation. On the other, they are to preserve and protect the natural environment. Perhaps more so than on any other park in the state, these objectives have been in historical conflict at Presque Isle. Almost every decision, if viewed from the vantage point of hindsight, has increased recreational usage but threatened the natural environment.

The roadway system, for example, was designed to allow motorists to tour and enjoy the park. All of the park's beauty became visible from automobiles. And, in fact, there may be no more beautiful drive than the 13 mile loop around the Peninsula. But, the architects of this project could never have envisioned the status of the automobile from their vantage point in the early 1920s. How could they have anticipated the hundreds of thousands of cars traveling the Peninsula by the 1990s? So on the positive side, millions of motorists are able to ride around the Peninsula seeing wildlife, flora, and fauna. But, what is the impact of their hydrocarbon spewing machines crossing a delicate sand spit peninsula?

Would it be possible, after all these years, to prohibit or even to limit vehicular traffic? How do park officials balance these needs? How can they meet the demands of the tourist based economy, (which depends upon the Peninsula), and interest groups such as boaters, duck hunters, and fishermen who hope to continue using the park in their own specialized ways, while stewarding the environmental needs of the park? Is such a complex mission theoretically or politically possible?

The recent Gull Point controversy exemplifies this question. Control of the Gull Point area, like other conflicts over the years, is another in a series of impossible balancing acts between interest groups and the two competing aspects of Presque Isle's mission. In other such balancing acts the results have always been less than perfect. The all purpose trail, for example, opened the bay side of the Peninsula to hundreds of thousands of hikers, bikers and skaters, vastly improving the park's ability to facilitate outdoor recreation. Critics, on the other hand, point to the thousands of people who now tramp all over the formerly little used bay side areas of the park, threatening animal and plant life.

The decision to open the lagoons created a similar controversy. Connecting Misery Bay to the Marina Lake allowed thousands of boaters to make tours through the Peninsula's inland waters, encouraging water based sightseeing. At the same time, the incursion of boats and their gasoline engines did irreparable damage to the plants and the water. In addition, the opening of the two formerly disconnected pond systems to each other allowed the invasion of plant forms between the two areas. The natural balance of the interior waterways was forever altered by an effort to promote usage.

On Gull Point, the eastern tip of the Peninsula, the latest community controversy rages on. For years this area, like Pottahawk Point on the Canadian side, has been the prime choice for a lake side anchorage. Summer weekends would find hundreds of boaters anchored near the point, enjoying the beauty of the Peninsula's isolated tip, while lying in the shelter of the land (protected from prevailing westerly winds). In recent years, boaters have taken to pulling up on shore, spreading blankets and picnicking on the beaches.

Part of Presque Isle's beautiful roadway system.

Misery Bay.

Environmentalists find this practice upsetting for several reasons. First, there is the general threat caused by the presence of humans on a critical beach front which is needed by birds. Even episodic human use is potentially disastrous to some birds, especially the migrating species trying desperately to conserve energy near the usually secluded point. Secondly, the odd boater has sometimes done significant environmental damage through such careless actions as setting fires by gathering and burning all available beach structure and driftwood, digging holes, and tromping on the delicate beach plant structure.

After many years of carefully trying to balance the interests of the park, the boaters, and environmentalists, Presque Isle State Park published a 1993 Management Plan in which it detailed compromise steps for solving the Gull Point problems by limiting boater access. In a preliminary "town meeting" held in late 1992, an angry crowd packed its way into a Gannon University lecture hall to express various displeasures with the proposed plan. To be fair, the plan was a good first attempt, but there were several inherent weaknesses. Interest groups from different sides of the issues took over the meeting, demonstrating their displeasure with the actions spelled out by the anticipated proposal.

There will probably never be a "best" plan for managing the park. Just as human induced changes on Presque Isle are almost understood, nature or external environmental factors shift. Zebra mussels, for example, may have a greater impact upon the park than any man made programs to date. Meanwhile, the conflict between public access and the preservation of nature will surely be ongoing, as will the pressure to maintain the 80 million dollars per year of tourism attributed to the park. Still, there may be some consolation in recalling the good fortune of events which kept the peninsula from becoming inhabited and commercialized in the 1800's. If it were not for the west channel, the early administration of Rufus Reed, and the remoteness of the park, Presque Isle might be just one more suburban housing development.

Lake Erie Adventures

1. Visit and tour Presque Isle. Spend a whole day and walk each area of interest. Stop at the park office for a map.

2. On Presque Isle, be sure to visit the House Boat Area, the Coast Guard Station and Channel, Misery Bay, the West Livery Area and all of the other historic sights.

3. Ask about interpretive programs and take a guided hike to Gull Point.

4. Drive around the park late at night and experience its beauty after dark along with a panorama of city lights. We recommend departing just before the park closes on a week night.

5. Park at the foot of Liberty Street and walk the bluffs over the Bay. Continue your walk up Plum and west on Second street, then go south on Cascade to Fourth street and Beckman's. At Second and Cascade you can still see the old path of the street to the Cascade Docks (now condominiums)

6. Take the free boat ride at the Presque Isle Lagoon Area and learn about the interior of the peninsula.

Shipwrecks in The Lake Erie Quadrangle

*H*aving laid historical and technical foundations, we begin the task of listing and detailing the Lake Erie Quadrangle's shipwrecks. To help visualize the events surrounding them, we'll start with a discussion of the primary factors which have made this portion of Lake Erie so dangerous. Admittedly, Lake Erie's shipwrecks did not result in as much loss of life as wrecks in the oceans. This is primarily due to the fact that so many of the wrecks in the Quadrangle occurred as a result of desperate captains deliberately beaching their vessels. Often (but not always) groundings resulted in cargo losses, while lives were saved.

In reviewing records of shipwrecks within the Quadrangle, there seem to be thirteen clearly distinguishable reasons for the almost unbelievably high number of losses within this small area.

1. The Unreliability of Early Vessels ... The ships plying early Lake Erie were not safe compared to their contemporary ocean going cousins, or to modern vessels. The lake schooners of the early 1800s were often built by amateur builders

who had more entrepreneurial than nautical-engineering skills. Many were recreations from distant or second hand recollections of persons who had seen ocean sailing ships. They were built from native materials, which were not always the most appropriate. Then they were nursed along in service long after their useful (safe) lives had expired. Many (notably the shallow draft scow schooners which were developed uniquely within the lakes) did not perform well upwind. As the wind velocity rose and captains found themselves needing to "beat to weather," these ships became a navigational liability. A number of accounts of shipwrecks describe ships driven onto a beach. Captains were unable to sail away from shore because they could not go upwind. The first steamers utilized crude versions of today's engines which literally "burned" fuels such as coal or wood. There was a continuous danger of these wooden ships catching fire or exploding. If water invaded the ship and flooded the boilers, the engines stopped. A number of steamers had their "fires go out" within range of safety, only to drift helplessly out to sea and perish.

2. Traffic Volume … Lake Erie acted as a combination of today's current highway systems, airports, and train stations during the middle years of the last century. Both freight and passenger traffic depended on Lake Erie to move west or east. Lake Erie was the home of the greatest industrial cities of North America, and the gateway to the rest. Buffalo, Detroit, Chicago, Cleveland and Milwaukee were all connected by routes which passed through the Lake Erie Quadrangle.

3. Lack of Shipboard Navigational Lights … There were no rules requiring running lights aboard ships until 1853. While passenger ships were sometimes "lit up like Christmas trees" at night, the schooners that tacked up and down the lake operated without running lights. In poor weather, the steamers were usually unlit and even harder to see. There are many tales of crusty old captains who demanded absolute darkness aboard, reasoning that this would help them to see other ships.

4. Lack of Navigational Aids … Lighthouses did not begin to appear on the Great Lakes until the middle 1800s. Even then, they were not always reliable and some captains refused to trust them. Advances such as radio, radar, weather forecasting, and depth sounding were not even imagined in the 1800s.

5. The Unknown North Shore … For most of the early 1800s, captains on Lake Erie avoided the north shore, and especially the Long Point area. By this time, the point had begun to develop a sinister reputation. Consequently, most ships tried to give it a "wide berth." As a result, there were few, if any, accurate charts of the waters around Long Point. When a storm or other circumstance arose requiring a ship to navi-

Riding out a gale behind Long Point.

gate this area, its captain had little or no information by which to guide his ship. It was not until 1848 that Captain Alexander McNeilledge, of Port Dover, produced a coastal pilot of the North Shore. This was the only navigational document in common use until the 1874 publication of Barnet's *"Coast Pilot For The Great Lakes."*

6. Crossing Patterns … There were a number of traffic crossing patterns within the Quadrangle. In addition to the predictable crossings of steamers and propellers, which were running straight up and down the lake, there were a number of railroad ferries running north and south through the area. Added to this was the traffic from relatively minor mid-lake ports such as Burwell, Dunkirk, Ashtabula and Conneaut. In effect, these vessels had to cross traffic, as they

The Majestic, sunk 1907.

attempted to move out into the up or down bound shipping lanes and the potential for collision increased geometrically. The existence of sailing ships, which continued well into the 20th century, further compounded the danger of collision. Schooners were required to tack as they moved up and down the lake, thus reducing the possibility that anyone could predict where a ship might be encountered, or the direction in which it might be sailing. Finally, there were the growing commercial fishing fleets at Erie, Conneaut, Nanticoke, Port Burwell and Port Dover. Prior to the relatively recent establishment of upbound and downbound tracks to guide commercial freighters, navigating without a collision was more a matter of skill and luck than science.

7. Regular Storms and Poor Weather Forecasting … The shallowness of Lake Erie makes it prone to rapid change due to storms and their winds. Since one or two extra trips could make significant difference in profit margins for shippers, there was a temptation to make "just one more run." Consequently, the shipping season was often extended well beyond the bounds of safety. The captains who were having financial difficulties were often the most guilty of tempting fate with a final late season run, plus piloting vessels in extreme need of repair (or sailing well past their useful lives). These factors, in combination with the relatively unsophisticated level of forecasting, often resulted in catastrophe. Unanticipated late season (November and December) storms sometimes caught ships off guard and the weaker vessels were unable to make the safety of port. A disproportionate number of disasters occurred during the months of November and December.

8. Long Point and Erie as Magnets … It is somewhat ironic that many of the ships which were lost near Erie or Long Point were, in fact, heading for these destinations. Their captains were (either making for port in Erie, an important destination, or running for shelter either in Presque Isle Bay or behind Long Point). These destinations were the only potential shelters in the center of the lake thus any ship seeking shelter in the middle of the lake would head to one of the two refuges. By the late 1800s, when charts had been developed for the north shore, it was known that there were two good anchorages behind Long Point. One was in the Inner Bay by Port Rowan, and was accessed via the "cut." The other was in the protected water behind the tip of Long Point. The bottom structure was good for anchoring in both of these areas, and the depths were relatively shallow, allowing for easy playing out and retrieval of anchor line. The harbor at Erie was also a fine anchorage. During violent storms on the lake, vessels would head toward either Long Point or Erie. Captains reasoned that if the storm worsened, they would be able to seek shelter. Inevitably many of these vessels ran into difficulty en route and sank.

9. Blackbirding … The extent to which blackbirding (wrecking) was responsible for losses to shipping near Long Point is not clear. Some historians venture the opinion that the losses were tremendous. Records of the Long Point Company in 1871 proudly declare to the Government of Canada that the company had finally gained control of the "wreckers," who had been plundering shipping on the south beaches. In any event, it is clear that blackbirding (see chapter 6) accounted for many losses to shipping in the 1840s, 50s and 60s, and that many captains began to steer clear for that reason.

10. Running Along or For Shore … Anyone who has witnessed the fury of a Lake Erie storm can relate to the apparently irrational practice of heading a vessel toward shore in a fierce blow. Fearsome gales influenced more than a few captains to risk their boats by leaving the center of the lake in favor of one of the

shorelines. Somehow, being able to see shore held the comfort of apparent safety for captain and crew. In reality, running close to shore is much more difficult for ship and crew than sailing the center of the lake. The increased pitch of near shore waves, coupled with the natural inclination of waves to twist toward a beach, caused the vessels (especially the early schooners) to run a great risk of going aground on the beaches. They were caught in waves and current and unable to claw their way off shore. In more than a few instances, captains who could see that their ships were sinking, or that their crew was at the point of exhaustion, steered vessels onto the beaches and aground in last ditch hopes of saving lives.

11. Fog … The lake creates a unique micro-climate along its shores because of its rather constant and slow-to-change water temperatures. In the fall and winter, the existence of the lake tends to warm surrounding land masses. During spring and early summer, however, the combination of relatively cold lake water with warm air creates conditions which are conducive to fog. The areas around Long Point and Presque Isle, in particular, are often affected by heavy fogs which can create major navigational problems.

12. Freak Storms … Even with the best of weather prediction technology, the lake whips advancing weather systems into unpredictable frenzies from time to time. There have always been, and will probably continue to be, incredible storms on the lake featuring the deadly combination of very high winds over sustained time periods. For the ship caught running for shore in one of these maelstroms, results can be disastrous. Such storms as the August 13, 1955 hurricane (Connie), the November 10, 1975 storm which claimed the *Edmund Fitzgerald*, and the infamous Black Friday storm of 1916 are but a few examples.

13. Geography … Last, but not least, is the sheer geographic presence of the two sand spits. In effect the two spits which are only 27 miles apart create a current vortex in the central portion of the lake which is otherwise almost 50 miles wide. The current flow naturally accelerates as the 50 mile wide "river" of eastward flowing water hits this relatively narrow watergate. During storm conditions this effect creates wild currents and monstrous surf near Long Point and Presque Isle.

SHIPWRECKS IN THE QUADRANGLE

The Adcliff Hall, sunk 1936.
GREAT LAKES HISTORICAL SOCIETY

As we begin the list, we feel compel-led to offer a caution. Much of the research on Great Lakes shipwrecks is incomplete at best. Many of the ships which were lost disappeared with no trace. Crews were not able to give accounts of exact locations. In other cases, accounts vary with respect to location. Thus, the materials which follow are somewhat difficult to document. We have done our best, however, to uncover the historical records of reported disasters and to list them in an accurate way.

Some ships were subsequently raised and returned to service. There are even vessels that went down two or more times. In other cases, new vessels were launched and given old names. In order to create a visual representation of shipwrecks within the Quadrangle, we have developed Table 8-1. It is arranged chronologically and includes names, types of ships, the cause of the loss, the general area of the disaster (U.S. or Canadian), and an approximation of the specific location. On the Erie side of the Quadrangle, there are four designated loss areas

(1) "W," representing the western region from Conneaut to the Ohio Line;
(2) "M" or middle, the area from there to the New York Line;
(3) "E," or the eastern region to Barcelona;
(4) "H," within the Erie Harbor.

On the Canadian side, the six specific wreck areas include

(1) "U," the Burwell to Long Point area;
(2) "C," the area near the old cut;
(3) "L," the area from the old cut east along the south beaches of Long Point;
(4) "T," the area near and behind the tip of the Point;
(5) "B," the bay areas behind Long Point; and
(6) "N," the areas to the east of Long Point and off Nanticoke.

Table 8-1 details the history of shipwrecks within the Quadrangle more eloquently than words. An overview reveals the trends as well as the chronology. In the 1800s, for example, the number of disasters systematically increased. This was due to the growth of shipping. For much of the 19th century, the number of shipwrecks was directly proportional to the volume of traffic. There were slow years for disasters and there were "big" years. These were traceable to either temporary reductions in trade (during the Civil War, for example), or weather. One or two severe storms during a season could account for a doubling or tripling of lake disasters.

The table also tells an interesting tale of the changes in shipping over the years. It is clear that the most popular vessel in the early years was the schooner. It is similarly obvious that the number of brigs and barks declined as the 19th century progressed. Then the brigs and barks all but disappeared. The disaster list also points to the evolution of steam propulsion, showing the transition from sidewheelers to propellers. In later years, the list highlights the dangers to commercial fishermen.

By the early 1900s, the number of disasters began to fall as a result of advances in technology. By the 1950s and 1960s, a traditional sinking had become quite rare.

There are 429 ships listed in Table 8-1. Each has a story that the captains, crews and passengers could have shared. Sadly, many of the stories have passed away with these men and their ships. While several of these tales are available in the literature, and some of those are told here, we can only imagine the rest.

THE LONG POINT MYSTIQUE

Sailors passing Long Point at the turn of the century reported that the south beaches were littered with shipwrecks. The remote location of the beaches, especially those which were close to the tip of the Point, prevented attempts at refloating vessels. Many of them would surely have been salvaged if they had foundered or gone aground on the U.S. shore. The remoteness of the location and the fearsome sight of the tremendous numbers of schooner wrecks enhanced the reputation of Long Point as "The graveyard of the lakes."

Even though the Long Point Company had long since brought the lands under general control and ended blackbirding, there were lingering concerns about dangers on the Point. The Anderson Properties were still out of control of the Company and located toward the remote tip. This continued to cause concerns for sailors who were operating vessels near Long Point. Many remembered the murder of the private detective who tried to infiltrate the gangs on Long Point. Other tales of danger continued to spice the reputation of the Point.

The Elphicke, sunk 1913.
GREAT LAKES HISTORICAL SOCIETY

The great number of schooner wrecks also caused a geological phenomena along the south beaches. As the schooner structures, with their hardwood keels and ribs, settled into the sand, they began to anchor sections of the beach and create newly formed dune ridges. During a high water storm, for example, a wreck might be lifted and floated either off shore or well up onto the beach. These wooden structures began to collect sand and vegetation as they slowly disappeared below the surface of a newly sculpted beach or ridge line.

As recently as the summer of 1992, changes in water levels and/or inland erosion revealed buried schooner ribs. Along the south beach, for example, there are currently two well preserved examples of complete schooner keels, with rib and planking structure attached. These appeared at the water's edge after storms and high water. In both cases, the schooners had been buried within 10 or 20 feet of the beach edge, and erosion from a temporary water level increase exposed them. There are surely more to be unearthed after being buried for a century in the graveyard of the Great Lakes.

THE WHALEBACK JAMES B. COLGATE

In October of 1916, the greatest storm ever to strike Lake Erie came to blows with the supposedly unsinkable ship, the whaleback. Alexander McDougal had designed this type especially to deal with the waves on Lake Erie and the whaleback, which was introduced in 1889, had served well. The *Colgate* was thought to be one of its best representatives.

The whaleback did not have a high bow or a square superstructure. Instead, its design featured cigar shaped topsides attached to a relatively flat bottom, and a substantial keel. In the years since the design's introduction, captains had come to think of whalebacks as indestructible, since waves and winds did not seem to effect them as they did traditional ship designs. Whaleback hulls had been produced for barges, freighters, and even passenger liners.

At 12:15 a.m. on Friday, October 20, Captain Walter Grashaw pulled the *Colgate* away from the Buffalo breakwater and headed for his date with destiny. The winds and waves were already hammering at the outer harbor wall, but Grashaw believed his ship to be invincible. He paid little attention to weather. Compared with some of his earlier assignments, the *Colgate* was indeed a tank. She was 24 years old, but she did not show her age. Her crews had grown confident in her abilities, and she acquired a reputation as the toughest ship on the lakes.

The Whaleback J.B. Colgate, lost in the Great Storm of 1916.
GREAT LAKES HISTORICAL SOCIETY

The *Colgate* was heading for the end of the lake and the Detroit River. She was bound for Lake Superior with a full load of coal. As she began the first leg of her trip toward Long Point and the Quadrangle, the full fury of Lake Erie's most violent storm in history began to build. Grashaw soon realized the force of the winds and waves. He noticed that even though he had been out some 7 hours and dawn was breaking, he was not yet at Long Point. Still, he trusted his ship and presumed that the winds would calm.

By 8:00 a.m., the early morning light revealed the extent of the Black Friday storm on which Captain Grashaw was riding. The winds were steady at 70 to 80 miles per hour, and gusting to almost 100. The waves were the largest that he had seen in 20 years at sea. He considered pulling up behind Long Point for shelter as he closed on the tip that morning, but the waters back there were wild with breaking surf. Grashaw realized that there would be no way to set an anchor in such a maelstrom. Instead, he pressed on down the south side of Long Point, making painfully slow progress against mounting seas.

As Grashaw and his crew of 26 kept their vigil along the north edge of the Quadrangle, three other ships were similarly trapped on the open waters of Lake Erie. The schooner *D.L. Filer*, the lumber tug *M.F. Butters*, and the steamer *Meridia* were all fighting for their lives. By dawn of the next day, each of these ships had disappeared with most of their crew.

As darkness fell Friday, the *Colgate* was still struggling along the south beaches of Long Point. The crew had donned life jackets. The realization that the ship was in grave danger had set in. The *Colgate* was taking on water, and the best hope was that darkness would bring a calming of the winds. Instead, the icy black night fanned the hurricane force winds. At 7:00 p.m., the *Colgate* began to list. At 8:00 p.m., Grashaw took a major personal risk by climbing onto the exposed bridge to train the ships search lights on the cargo hatches. His worst suspicions were confirmed. Even as he worked the powerful searchlight, the hatch covers were separating from the deck. As he watched in horror from his vantage point above the deck, the *Colgate* rolled badly to starboard and slowly buried her bow below the water's surface.

Grashaw realized that he and his crew were doomed. Even with life jackets, there would be no hope for survival in such seas. It would be only a matter of time until each floating body, including his own, would lose consciousness and die from drowning or exposure. But, as the water lifted him from his position on the bridge and his life preserver floated him to the top of the next wave, he felt a strange bump. As luck would have it, he had floated right into the *Colgate's* 9 foot life raft which had been launched by three of the crew. The men helped Grashaw aboard. He held on with them for dear life. It was 8:30 p.m., the wind was howling, and the seas were running at 30 to 40 feet. The water was ice cold. He knew that there was little chance of survival in such a small raft.

The tiny raft capsized two times during the night. Grashaw was the only man able to crawl back aboard after the second time. By late Saturday, as the storm finally abated, Captain Grashaw lay semiconscious, floating some 5 miles off the western end of Long Point's beaches. Sunday morning, some 36 hours after Grashaw had taken to the raft, the railroad ferry *Marquette and Bessemer #2* spotted the raft and picked him up. The Black Friday storm had proven its mastery over any ship, even the esteemed whaleback. Grashaw's entire crew, the *Colgate*, and three other ships had been lost. Lake Erie had proven once more that she had no master.

Lake Erie Adventures

1. Find a copy of Dave Stone's "Ghost Ships of Long Point" shipwreck chart and study it. Buy and read his first book, *"Long Point Last Port of Call."*

2. Visit the Great Lakes Historical Society Museum in Vermillion, Ohio. If you like this book, the Vermillion Museum will be a real treat. In addition to shipwreck information they have many other exhibits of interest. Plan an entire day there if possible.

3. Read some books about Great Lakes shipping. In particular we recommend the three book series by Dana Bowen. These and other books on lake lore are available from Freshwater Press in Cleveland, Ohio.

4. Wait for a storm in October or November and take a trip to the lake front. Go somewhere were you can walk to the water's edge (the Peninsula on the U.S. side or the beach at Port Dover will do). Pull on your hat and jacket and go for a walk for 30 minutes or so. When you get back to the warm dry car you will have a new appreciation for this chapter.

5. Visit Port Rowan's Backus Conservation Center and see Dave Stone's "Shipwrecks of Long Point Exhibit."

Table 8-1
Canadian and U.S. Disasters

Date	Name	Type	Disaster	Location General	Specific
1797	Detroit	Sloop	Sunk	USA	M
1799	Annette	Sloop	Sunk	CAN	L
1814	HMS Mohawk	Brig	Sunk	CAN	L
1817	Nautilus	Sloop	Foundered	USA	M
1818	Young Phoenix	Schooner	Sunk	CAN	C
1820	Eagle	Sloop	Foundered	CAN	L
	Owen	Schooner	Aground	CAN	C
1825	General Huntington	Schooner	Grounding	USA	M
	Good Intent	Schooner	Grounding	USA	E
1826	Brighton	Sloop	Sunk	USA	H
1827	Columbus	Schooner	Grounding	USA	E
	Ann	Schooner	Sunk	CAN	L
	Young Farmer	Schooner	Sunk	CAN	T
1829	Conneaut	Schooner	Sunk	USA	M
1830	William Penn	Steamboat	Collision	USA	E
	Pioneer	Steamboat	Collision	USA	
1831	Peacock	Steamboat	Wrecked	USA	H
	Marshall	Schooner	Wrecked	USA	M
1832	Lord Nelson	Schooner	Aground	USA	E
1833	New Connecticut	Schooner	Foundered	USA	M
	Utica	Schooner	Capsized	USA	M
1834	Lady of the Lake	Schooner	Foundered	USA	M
1835	Free Trader	Schooner	Aground	USA	E
	North America	Steamboat	Aground	USA	M
	Wm. Peacock	Steamboat	Aground	USA	M
	Columbus	Steamboat	Aground	USA	M

Date	Ship Name	Type	Disaster	Location General	Specific
1836	United States	Steamboat	Aground	USA	M
	Young Lion	Schooner	Sunk	USA	M
	Utica	Steamboat	Aground	USA	M
1838	George Washington	Steamboat	Fire	USA	E
	Benjamin Barton	Schooner	Sunk	USA	M
	Sandusky	Schooner	Aground	USA	M
	Colonel Benton	Schooner	Aground	USA	E
	Eagle	Schooner	Aground	USA	M
	Saratoga	Schooner	Sunk	USA	W
	S.B. Ruggles	Schooner	Aground	USA	M
	Odd Fellow	Steamer	Sunk	CAN	T
1840	Iowa	Schooner	Sunk	CAN	E
	Celeste	Schooner	Aground	CAN	E
1841	Savannah	Schooner	Sunk	USA	W
1842	Chicago	Steamboat	Sunk	USA	M
	Buckage	Schooner	Aground	CAN	W
	Dolphin	Schooner	Sunk	CAN	M
1843	Equator	Schooner	Sunk	USA	W
	J.G. King	Schooner	Sunk	USA	W
	New York	Schooner	Aground	CAN	U
1844	Potomac	Schooner	Aground	USA	M
	G.H. Walker	Schooner	Aground	USA	M
	Brandywine	Schooner	Aground	USA	M
	Grant	Schooner	Aground	USA	M
	Henry Clay	Steamer	Aground	USA	M
	Maria Hill	Schooner	Foundered	USA	M
	Wyandott	Schooner	Foundered	USA	M
	Marian	Schooner	Foundered	USA	M
	Georgianna	Schooner	Foundered	USA	M

Date	Ship Name	Type	Disaster	Location General	Specific
1844	Pacific	Schooner	Aground	USA	E
	Young Lion	Schooner	Sunk	USA	W
	Morning Star	Schooner	Foundered	USA	W
1845	T.W. Maurice	Brig	Aground	USA	W
	John Grant	Schooner	Capsized	USA	M
	Chapman	Schooner	Aground	CAN	T
	Texas	Schooner	Sunk	CAN	L
	Kent	Steamer	Sunk	CAN	C
1846	Swan	Schooner	Aground	USA	M
	Harwich	Schooner	Aground	USA	E
	Bayona	Schooner	Aground	USA	E
	H.H. Sizer	Brig	Aground	USA	M
	Alps	Schooner	Aground	USA	M
	J.F. Porter	Schooner	Collision	USA	W
	Helen Strong	Steamboat	Aground	USA	E
	Chesapeake	Steamboat	Collision	USA	W
1847	J.C. Dawn	Schooner	Capsized	USA	W
	Francis Mills	Schooner	Sunk	USA	M
	C.J. Danlie	Schooner	Foundered	USA	W
	Monteith	Brig	Sunk	USA	M
	Adair	Schooner	Capsized	USA	E
1848	Porter	Schooner	Sunk	USA	W
	Indiana	Steamboat	Sunk	USA	W
	Rainbow	Scow	Burned	USA	E
	Sandusky	Brig	Sunk	CAN	T
	Uncle Tom	Schooner	Aground	CAN	L
	Edw. Jessey	Schooner	Sunk	CAN	L
	Hero	Sloop	Sunk	CAN	C
	Constitution	Bark	Foundered	CAN	L

Date	Ship Name	Type	Disaster	Location General	Specific
1848	Brittania	Schooner	Aground	CAN	B
	Martha Freeme	Schooner	Aground	CAN	U
1850	Lexington	Steamboat	Sunk	USA	W
1851	D.D. Bogart	Schooner	Foundered	USA	M
	California	Schooner	Foundered	USA	E
	Whip	Schooner	Aground	USA	M
	Ellen Stuart	Schooner	Aground	CAN	C
	Rialto	Scow	Foundered	CAN	L
	Prince Albert	Schooner	Aground	CAN	T
	Flying Dutchman	Schooner	Aground	CAN	L
	Sarah & Cornelia	Schooner	Aground	CAN	T
	Billow	Schooner	Sunk	CAN	B
	M. Coo	Schooner	Sunk	CAN	L
	Chicago	Brig	Capsized	CAN	L
	Henry Clay	Propeller	Capsized	CAN	T
1852	Vermont	Schooner	Capsized	USA	M
	Rochester	Steamer	Sunk	USA	H
	R.C. Snead	Schooner	Sunk	USA	E
	Oneida	Steamboat	Sunk	USA	E
	Buffalo	Schooner	Sunk	CAN	L
	Sarah Eason	Schooner	Capsized	CAN	C
	Arkansas	Schooner	Foundered	CAN	L
	Rip Van Winkle	Schooner	Sunk	CAN	L
	New Haven	Schooner	Aground	CAN	T
	Atlantic	Steamer	Sunk	CAN	L
1853	Queen City	Steamboat	Sunk	USA	H
1854	Isabella	Schooner	Aground	USA	E
	Robert Wood	Schooner	Aground	USA	E
	Hudson	Schooner	Sunk	USA	W

Date	Ship Name	Type	Disaster	Location General	Specific
1854	Lewis Cass	Schooner	Sunk	USA	W
	Ashland	Brig	Sunk	CAN	L
	Conductor	Schooner	Aground	CAN	B
	Republic	Schooner	Aground	CAN	L
	Elizabeth	Schooner	Sunk	CAN	C
	A. Buckingham	Schooner	Sunk	CAN	L
	Trade Wind	Schooner	Aground	CAN	L
	Wm. Black	Schooner	Aground	CAN	U
	Saratoga	Steamer	Sunk	CAN	U
	Globe	Bark	Aground	CAN	U
	Forwarder	Schooner	Aground	CAN	U
	Suffolk	Schooner	Aground	CAN	U
1855	Charter Oak	Propeller	Sunk	USA	M
	Napoleon	Schooner	Sunk	USA	M
	Koefer	Propeller	Sunk	USA	M
	Wheaton	Schooner	Sunk	CAN	L
	North Star	Bark	Aground	CAN	C
	Emblem	Schooner	Sunk	CAN	L
	Halliwell	Bark	Sunk	CAN	T
	Virginia	Brig	Aground	CAN	L
	Travler	Schooner	Aground	CAN	U
	Josephine	Schooner	Sunk	CAN	U
1856	Golden Gate	Steamboat	Sunk	USA	M
	Ohio	Schooner	Foundered	USA	W
	Lord Elgin	Schooner	Sunk	CAN	C
	Ellen Gilmour	Brig	Aground	CAN	T
	Robert Bruce	Schooner	Sunk	CAN	U
1857	Sarah A. Green	Schooner	Sunk	USA	E
	Alice	Schooner	Sunk	CAN	T

Date	Ship Name	Type	Disaster	Location General	Specific
1857	Cataract	Schooner	Aground	CAN	C
	Dahlia	Schooner	Aground	CAN	U
	Everett	Schooner	Aground	CAN	U
	Louisiana	Steamer	Aground	CAN	U
1858	Watchman	Schooner	Aground	USA	E
	Java	Schooner	Foundered	USA	E
	Catchpole	Schooner	Sunk	CAN	L
	J.A. Hope	Schooner	Aground	CAN	U
1859	Ohio	Propeller	Exploded	CAN	L
1860	Washington Irving	Schooner	Sunk	USA	M
	Silas Wright	Schooner	Aground	USA	E
	St. Louis	Brig	Sunk	USA	M
	Dacotah	Steamer	Sunk	CAN	C
	Greenbush	Schooner	Sunk	CAN	L
	Jersey City	Steamer	Sunk	CAN	L
	Northerner	Bark	Aground	CAN	T
	J.G. Scott	Schooner	Sunk	CAN	U
1861	E.C. Williams	Schooner	Foundered	USA	M
	Akron	Propeller	Aground	CAN	L
1862	Fortune	Schooner	Lightning	USA	M
	Cadet	Schooner	Foundered	USA	M
	Chief Jstc. Marshall	Schooner	Aground	USA	E
	Post Boy	Schooner	Foundered	USA	E
	Pocahaantas	Propeller	Sunk	CAN	T
	Sam Amsden	Schooner	Sunk	CAN	L
	Bridget	Schooner	Aground	CAN	L
	Bay City	Schooner	Aground	CAN	U
	Northern Light	Bark	Aground	CAN	U
1863	Sarah E. Hudson	Schooner	Collision	USA	M

Date	Ship Name	Type	Disaster	Location General	Specific
1863	Kate Norton	Schooner	Foundered	USA	M
	Mary Jane	Bark	Aground	CAN	C
	Rebecca Foster	Schooner	Sunk	CAN	L
	Return	Schooner	Sunk	CAN	N
	George Davis	Schooner	Aground	CAN	U
1864	Star	Schooner	Aground	USA	W
	Scotia	Propeller	Collision	USA	E
	Ogdensberg	Propeller	Collision	USA	E
	George Moffatt	Steamboat	Sunk	USA	H
	Emma Jane	Schooner	Foundered	USA	M
	City of Buffalo	Steamer	Sunk	CAN	L
	Belle	Schooner	Sunk	CAN	L
	Jenny Lind	Schooner	Aground	CAN	T
	Amity	Steamer	Sunk	CAN	L
1865	W.O. Brown	Schooner	Collision	USA	M
	Frontinac	Schooner	Aground	CAN	U
1866	A. Holmes	Scow	Capsized	USA	M
	Arabian	Bark	Sunk	USA	M
	Lone Star	Scow	Aground	USA	W
	Alma	Schooner	Foundered	USA	M
	Darian	Schooner	Sunk	USA	E
	Elm City	Schooner	Burned	USA	M
	A. Bradley	Schooner	Sunk	CAN	T
	Junious	Schooner	Aground	CAN	C
	Merimac #2	Schooner	Aground	CAN	L
	Pacific	Scow	Aground	CAN	U
	Tom Wrong	Schooner	Aground	CAN	U
	Josephine	Bark	Sunk	CAN	U
	Notswer	Schooner	Sunk	CAN	U

Date	Ship Name	Type	Disaster	Location General	Specific
1867	Orkney Lass	Brig	Sunk	USA	M
	Sacramento	Schooner	Aground	USA	M
	Mary Elizabeth	Schooner	Foundered	USA	M
	Acme	Propeller	Sunk	USA	E
	General Worth	Brig	Foundered	USA	E
	Snowbird	Schooner	Foundered	USA	M
	Corinthian	Schooner	Sunk	CAN	L
	Isabella	Schooner	Sunk	CAN	T
1868	Maria F. Johnson	Schooner	Sunk	USA	M
1869	Governor Hunt	Schooner	Sunk	USA	M
	Falcon	Scow	Aground	USA	M
	Kate Gerlach	Tug	Burned	USA	M
	Florida	Schooner	Sunk	CAN	N
	Arcturus	Schooner	Aground	CAN	T
	Little Belle	Schooner	Sunk	CAN	C
1869	Zephyr	Schooner	Sunk	CAN	L
	J.C. Hill	Schooner	Aground	CAN	C
	Quick Step	Schooner	Sunk	CAN	L
	Annie Hanson	Barge	Sunk	CAN	T
1870	Henry Young	Scow	Aground	USA	M
	Indiana	Bark	Sunk	USA	M
	Ellen White	Schooner	Burned	USA	M
	Sir E. W. Head	Bark	Foundered	USA	M
	Elyria	Schooner	Aground	USA	M
	C.T. Richmond	Steamship	Foundered	USA	E
	Empire	Propeller	Sunk	CAN	T
	Mary Morton	Schooner	Sunk	CAN	L
	Medora	Schooner	Sunk	CAN	N
	Shierwasso	Barge	Sunk	CAN	L

Date	Ship Name	Type	Disaster	Location General	Specific
1870	W.G. Keith	Schooner	Sunk	CAN	T
	Glad Tidings	Schooner	Aground	CAN	L
	E.S.J. Bemis	Schooner	Sunk	CAN	T
	Missouri	Steamer	Sunk	CAN	U
	Britania	Schooner	Foundered	CAN	U
	Leviathon	Schooner	Foundered	CAN	U
	Juliet	Schooner	Sunk	CAN	U
1871	Resolute	Schooner	Sunk	USA	M
	Grace Murray	Schooner	Sunk	USA	M
	Juliette	Schooner	Sunk	USA	M
	Eli Bates	Schooner	Sunk	USA	W
	Myra	Schooner	Foundered	USA	M
	Evergreen City	Steamer	Aground	CAN	C
	P.C. Sherman	Bark	Aground	CAN	L
	Resolute	Schooner	Aground	CAN	L
	Saxon	Schooner	Sunk	CAN	C
	Jesse Anderson	Schooner	Sunk	CAN	C
	Burnside	Bark	Sunk	CAN	L
	George Able	Schooner	Foundered	CAN	U
1872	Rapid	Schooner	Capsized	USA	W
	Orion	Schooner	Sunk	USA	M
	Fenton	Schooner	Aground	CAN	C
	D.L. Crouch	Schooner	Sunk	CAN	N
	Baltic	Barge	Sunk	CAN	L
	Orion	Schooner	Sunk	CAN	C
	Gus	Schooner	Aground	CAN	L
	Forester	Schooner	Sunk	CAN	U
	Elliot	Barge	Sunk	CAN	U
	Foster	Barge	Sunk	CAN	U

Date	Ship Name	Type	Disaster	Location	
				General	Specific
1873	City of Detroit	Steamer	Sunk	USA	E
	Cesia	Schooner	Sunk	CAN	L
	Cape Horn	Schooner	Aground	CAN	C
	Adriatic	Barge	Sunk	CAN	T
1874	Wm. Hunter	Schooner	Sunk	USA	M
	Wild Rover	Schooner	Sunk	CAN	L
	Miami	Schooner	Aground	CAN	T
	Wanderer	Schooner	Sunk	CAN	N
	N.C. West	Schooner	Sunk	CAN	C
	C.W. Chamberlain	Schooner	Sunk	CAN	L
	Frances Palms	Schooner	Aground	CAN	T
1875	Juno	Scow	Sunk	USA	M
	Globe	Barge	Waterlogged	USA	E
	Persian	Schooner	Sunk	CAN	N
	Dan Marble	Schooner	Aground	CAN	C
	Grace Sherman	Schooner	Aground	CAN	U
	Gibson	Schooner	Aground	CAN	U
1876	Tillinghurst	Tug	Burned	USA	M
	Eveline	Schooner	Sunk	USA	M
	Beals	Schooner	Aground	USA	H
	Mocking Bird	Schooner	Sunk	CAN	L
	Hannaford	Barge	Sunk	CAN	T
	T.C. Street	Schooner	Capsized	CAN	L
1877	Lady Dufferin	Schooner	Sunk	USA	M
	Thomas Thompson	Tug	Sunk	USA	M
	Madiera	Schooner	Aground	CAN	T
	E.L. Turner	Schooner	Sunk	CAN	C
	P. Liza	Schooner	Aground	CAN	L
	Belle Cash	Brig	Sunk	CAN	L

Date	Ship Name	Type	Disaster	Location General	Specific
1877	British Lion	Schooner	Sunk	CAN	T
	Rising Star	Schooner	Sunk	CAN	L
	D.W. McCall	Schooner	Aground	CAN	U
1878	Correspondent	Schooner	Foundered	USA	E
	J.G. McGrath	Schooner	Foundered	CAN	T
	C. Jeffries	Schooner	Sunk	CAN	N
	Portage	Schooner	Sunk	CAN	L
	Asia	Schooner	Sunk	CAN	C
	H.I. Rathbun	Schooner	Aground	CAN	U
1879	Geo. E. Frost	Steamboat	Burned	USA	H
1880	Eldorodo	Schooner	Foundered	USA	M
	Wesley	Barge	Foundered	USA	M
	Bay City	Barge	Foundered	USA	M
	Aimee	Steamer	Sunk	USA	M
	George Mowbray	Schooner	Sunk	USA	M
	Zealand	Steamer	Sunk	CAN	L
	Dictator	Barge	Sunk	CAN	T
1881	Carlingsford	Schooner	Collision	USA	E
	Siberia	Schooner	Sunk	CAN	L
	E.P. Dorr	Schooner	Sunk	CAN	N
1882	Florida	Schooner	Sunk	USA	M
	St. Andrew	Schooner	Sunk	CAN	N
	James Scott	Schooner	Sunk	CAN	N
1883	Vulcan	Tug	Burned	USA	M
	Escanaba	Schooner	Foundered	USA	M
	J.R. Benson	Schooner	Foundered	USA	M
	Baldwin	Barge	Sunk	USA	M
	Edmund Fitzgerald	Schooner	Sunk	CAN	C
	Leadville	Schooner	Sunk	CAN	L

Date	Ship Name	Type	Disaster	Location General	Specific
1883	Mayflower	Propeller	Aground	CAN	L
	W. H. Vanderbilt	Propeller	Sunk	CAN	L
	Blazing Star	Schooner	Aground	CAN	T
1884	King Sisters	Schooner	Aground	USA	M
	Fortune	Schooner	Sunk	CAN	C
	New Dominion	Schooner	Sunk	CAN	L
1885	Highland Maid	Schooner	Capsized	USA	M
1886	Honora Carr	Schooner	Foundered	USA	M
	Belle Mitchell	Schooner	Sunk	USA	M
	G.M. Case	Schooner	Sunk	CAN	L
	Anora Carr	Schooner	Sunk	CAN	N
1887	Manzanilla	Schooner	Sunk	USA	M
	James F Joy	Schooner	Sunk	USA	W
	Resolute	Barge	Sunk	CAN	C
	C.O.D.	Schooner	Aground	CAN	U
1888	Anna P. Dore	Tug	Sunk	USA	E
	John Tibits	Steamer	Sunk	CAN	C
	P.C. Sherman	Bark	Aground	CAN	L
1889	Commerce	Steambarge	Sunk	USA	M
1890	Chenango	Propeller	Burned	USA	M
	Roanoke	Propeller	Burned	USA	M
	Tom Matham	Tug	Sunk	USA	M
	Huron	Schooner	Sunk	USA	M
	Verona	Schooner	Sunk	USA	W
	Two Fannies	Schooner	Sunk	USA	M
	Isaac May	Steamer	Burned	CAN	L
1891	W.L. Peck	Barge	Sunk	USA	M
	British Lion	Schooner	Foundered	USA	M
	Montcalm	Schooner	Sunk	CAN	T
	George Finney	Steamer	Foundered	CAN	T

Date	Ship Name	Type	Disaster	Location General	Specific
1892	General Burnside	Schooner	Sunk	USA	M
	Newbury	Steamer	Sunk	CAN	C
	Lone Star	Schooner	Aground	CAN	L
1893	Dean Richmond	Steamboat	Foundered	USA	E
	Wocoken	Steamboat	Sunk	USA	E
	Pelican	Schooner	Sunk	USA	W
	Continental	Dredge	Sunk	USA	W
	McDougall	Barge	Waterlogged	USA	M
	Riverside	Schooner	Sunk	USA	M
	Annie Laurie	Tug	Sunk	USA	M
1894	Colgate Hoyt	Whaleback	Sunk	CAN	L
1895	Roy	Tug	Sunk	USA	M
	Alzora	Schooner	Aground	CAN	L
1896	Bertha Winnie	Schooner	Capsized	USA	M
	Sweepstakes	Schooner	Sunk	USA	M
	J.R. Pelton	Schooner	Sunk	USA	M
	Wallula	Steamboat	Burned	USA	W
	H.S. Walbridge	Schooner	Aground	CAN	L
1897	L. Strickland	Steamer	Sunk	CAN	N
	Idaho	Propeller	Sunk	CAN	T
	L. Shikluna	Propeller	Sunk	CAN	L
1898	Keepsake	Schooner	Foundered	USA	M
	104	Barge	Sunk	USA	M
	McConnell	Propeller	Sunk	USA	M
	Niagara	Steamer	Sunk	CAN	L
1900	John B. Lyons	Freighter	Sunk	USA	W
	Charles Foster	Schnr/Barge	Sunk	USA	M
	Dundee	Schnr/Barge	Sunk	USA	W
	Lulu Beatrice	Schooner	Sunk	CAN	U

Date	Ship Name	Type	Disaster	Location General	Specific
1900	Barge #3	Barge	Sunk	CAN	U
	Barge #4	Barge	Sunk	CAN	U
1902	Owen	Steamer	Sunk	CAN	L
	S.J. Macy	Steamer	Sunk	CAN	U
1904	Shenango #1	Car Ferry	Burned	USA	W
	Mautinee	Schooner	Foundered	USA	E
1905	Chas. Burton	Schooner	Foundered	USA	E
	Siberia	Steamer	Sank	CAN	T
1906	George McCall	Schooner	Sunk	CAN	N
1907	Majestic	Steamer	Sunk	CAN	B
1908	Sir Van Straubenzie	Schooner	Sunk	CAN	N
	Pascal P. Pratt	Propeller	Sunk	CAN	T
1909	Marquette&Bes. #2	Car Ferry	Sunk	CAN	L
	Conneaut	Steamer	Sunk	CAN	L
1910	Dinah	Schooner	Sunk	CAN	L
1912	Rob Roy	Scnr/Barge	Sunk	USA	M
	S.K. Martin	Steamer	Sunk	USA	E
1913	C.W. Elphicke	Propeller	Sunk	CAN	T
1914	City of Rome	Steamer	Burned	USA	E
1915	Philip D. Armor	Barge	Aground	USA	M
	C.F. Mischler	Tug	Burned	USA	M
1916	Chas. Trinter	Tug	Sunk	USA	M
	Merida	Freighter	Sunk	USA	E
	J.B. Colgate	Whaleback	Sunk	CAN	T
1918	Tempest	Steamer	Sunk	USA	M
	Magnetic	Barge	Sunk	CAN	L
1920	Fleetwing	Ferry	Sunk	USA	W
1921	Lawrence	Steamer	Sunk	CAN	L
1922	Charles Reed	Tug	Burned	USA	M
	City of Dresden	Propeller	Sunk	CAN	C

Date	Ship Name	Type	Disaster	Location General	Specific
1923	Colonial	Steamer	Burned	USA	E
1925	Angler	Fish Tug	Sunk	CAN	T
1926	Howard Gerken	Dredge	Sunk	USA	M
	Adam Schuman	Barge	Foundered	USA	M
	Colonial	Steamer	Sunk	USA	E
1930	Smith	Tug	Sunk	CAN	L
1931	Hunter Wills	Fish Tug	Burned	USA	M
1932	J.J. Boland Jr.	Freighter	Sunk	USA	E
1933	Isolde	Steamer	Sunk	USA	M
1936	David Foster	Steambarge	Sunk	USA	M
	Adcliff Hall	Steamer	Sunk	CAN	L
1937	American Sailor	Barge	Sunk	USA	E
	Betty Hedger	Barge	Sunk	USA	E
	American Scout	Barge	Sunk	USA	E
	Lizzie Harvey	Barge	Sunk	USA	E
1939	Sunday Pat	Fish Tug	Sunk	USA	M
1940	F.A. Georger	Scnr/Barge	Sunk	USA	W
1943	Marjon S	Fish Tug	Explosion	CAN	U
1944	James Reed	Steamer	Sunk	CAN	T
1955	Ciscoe	Fish Tug	Aground	CAN	U
	Irac	Fish Tug	Sunk	CAN	B
1959	Brown Brothers	Fish Tug	Sunk	CAN	L
1967	Sandy Pat	Tug	Sunk	USA	M
1972	Gus	Sloop	Aground	CAN	B
1974	Aletha B	Fish Tug	Sunk	CAN	B
1975	Southside	Fish Tug	Aground	CAN	U
	J.M. Loader	Fish Tug	Burned	CAN	C
1984	Stanley Clipper	Fish Tug	Sunk	CAN	B
1985	Toya	Sloop	Aground	CAN	T
1991	Captain K	Fish Tug	Sunk	CAN	B

CHAPTER NINE

LIGHTHOUSES AND LIFESAVING

*I*n the early years there were no lighthouses or lifesaving stations. As entrepreneurs began commercial ventures with their homemade schooners, and the military patrolled the lakes, the governments of the U.S and Canada had little awareness of the fact that an inland maritime industry equal to that of the oceans was about to emerge within the Great Lakes. The treacherous nature of the lakes as well as the lack of sea room caused by their small size (compared to oceans) soon resulted in a growing number of disasters. This, in turn, led to lobbying in both the U.S. and Canada, for lighthouses and other aids to navigation.

Eventually both federal governments accepted responsibility for the creation and maintenance of a comprehensive system of lighthouses and lifesaving stations. Lighthouses were to be navigational markers designating either areas of danger such as the tip of Long Point, or entrances to harbors such as the channel at Erie. Lifesaving stations were to be manned posts, positioned in locations which were most likely to have marine disasters. These stations were to be "manned" at all times by persons and equipment which could be used to effect a shore-based rescue.

Erie's land lighthouse.

The first lighthouse on Lake Erie was constructed at Erie on the banks overlooking the channel entrance. It marked the (then unimproved) entrance to the bay. An equally important mission of this light was to warn westbound traffic of the Peninsula. This structure was opened in 1818. As additional lighthouses and lifesaving stations were planned, Lake Erie with its tremendous traffic volume, and the Quadrangle with its dangers to shipping were first priorities. There were more of these operations within the Quadrangle, than in any other portion of the Great Lakes.

By the middle of the 19th century the U.S. federal government had accepted responsibility for harbor development, lighthouses and lifesaving on the Great Lakes system. Canadian interests were slow to follow. This was primarily because Canada did not achieve independence until 1867 and approval had to be granted by England. Shortly thereafter, the Canadians, following the preliminary steps of the British Parliament, established a north shore system much like its American counterpart.

LIGHTHOUSES OF THE QUADRANGLE

Following is a chronological list of lighthouses within the Quadrangle. Most are still functioning. Those which have been discontinued are still standing. In the early days, all of the lighthouses were manned on a seasonal basis by "keepers." Lighthouse keepers worked for their respective federal governments and were paid room and board (they lived at the lighthouse sites) as well as a stipend. As the years wore on lighthouses were automated and the keepers disappeared. The U.S. was well ahead of Canada in this evolution. The last lighthouse to be automated, was the Long Point Light in 1989. Prior to this time the modern day keepers at Long Point, functioned just like the keepers of the 19th century. They lived 25 miles from civilization, received supplies by boat or helicopter, maintained the light, performed regular maintenance duties and made radio (and later telephone) reports of weather and traffic to the federal government.

Barcelona lighthouse.

Fully automated Long Point Lighthouse, 1993.

1. Erie Land Lighthouse (1818) ... The first lighthouse on the U. S. side of the lakes was built on the bluffs east of Erie, overlooking the channel. The original building was replaced in 1856, and rebuilt again in 1858. Although it was discontinued in 1880 the light was brought back into service in 1881 and continued until 1899. The building still stands and can be seen at the foot of Lighthouse Street on Erie's east side.

2. Barcelona Light (1829) ... The existence of natural gas at Barcelona (then called Portland Harbor) convinced the service to establish a light at the cliffs overlooking the creek inlet. The Barcelona light was the first to be fueled with natural gas. As the years passed, however, the gas ran out and it became apparent that Dunkirk would be a more important harbor. After fueling the Barcelona Light with whale oil for some 10 years it was discontinued near the middle of the century. The structure is now a private residence.

3. The Long Point Light (1830) ... In a November 1827 storm, four American ships went down on Long Point. The U.S. sent an emissary to the British Parliament and demanded a lighthouse, threatening to take over Long Point and build one themselves if no action was taken. Plans for the Long Point Light were finalized and approved in 1829. The original 50 foot structure was hurriedly erected and began operation in 1830. By 1835 it had become apparent that the surveyors had not taken beach erosion into account. The lighthouse was sinking and leaning badly. A replacement lighthouse was begun in the 1840s and began operation in 1842. The new structure was 75 feet high and remained in operation until 1916. It also fell victim to beach erosion heralding the dynamism of the sand structure at Long Point. The current lighthouse was built in 1915 and became operational the following year. The 102 foot structure was placed close to the center of the land mass at the tip of the Point to prevent erosion damage. This seemed like a good solution until the mid-1980s when high water threatened its structural integrity. In a colossal building project undertaken in the late 1980s, the structure was rebuilt, shored up by concrete pylons (reaching to bedrock) and fully automated.

4. Erie Harbor Light (1830) ... Originally called the beacon light, this structure was a 50 foot tall wood on concrete beacon with a fog horn, a whistle and a regular keeper. The light was hit by a schooner in 1857 and destroyed, then rebuilt in 1858 into the metal lighthouse which stands today at the north harbor entrance.

5. Port Dover Lighthouse (1832) ... A lighthouse marking the improved harbor entrance to Port Dover was constructed just following the building of the Long Point Light. Today's light is an automated beacon with a radio direction signal which stands at the end of the rebuilt harbor wall.

6. Conneaut Lighthouse (1835) ... The first light was built in 1835 but it was regarded as too short to be serviceable and rebuilt in 1875. By the 1880s the Lighthouse Service was trying to eliminate stations. When the Erie Land Light was reactivated in 1881 the Conneaut Light was discontinued causing considerable consternation since by that time the port of Conneaut was thriving after falling into disuse in the 1870s. Ultimately the Conneaut Light was reactivated and the Erie Land Lighthouse was discontinued.

7. Port Burwell Lighthouse (1840) ... In the second tier of construction along the north shore a lighthouse was constructed at the Burwell harbor. Given ship construction, and commerce at this port as well as the difficulty of entering the tiny harbor opening, Burwell was judged to be an important sight.

8. Presque Isle Light (1872) ... A lighthouse with adjoining keeper's house was built on the north shore of the Peninsula in 1872, and became operational the next year. Originally called the flash light, this is the structure which most Erie residents now think of as Erie's lighthouse.

9. Old Cut Light (1879) ... The increasing popularity of the channel (cut) into the Inner Bay as well as the government's construction and maintenance of piers at the site created a demand for a lighthouse at the base of Long Point. At first, the government, fearing that the cut could not be maintained, used a Lightship to mark the entrance. By 1879, however, they built and began operation

Port Burwell Lighthouse.

The Lyle Gun.

of a lighthouse. After the cut filled in during the early 1920s, this structure was abandoned and sold to a private party. The new owner eventually converted it to a cottage. The converted lighthouse can still be seen along the road leading to Long Point Provincial Park.

LIFESAVING

The federal governments of both countries also committed to a networked series of lifesaving stations which were to be concentrated in the most dangerous sections of the lakes. Naturally Long Point and Presque Isle were judged to be high priority locations. For citizens of the 19th century, lifesaving was a high art and a romantic form of heroism. Children of the late 1800s held lifesaving in much the same reverence that today's kids feel about superheroes on television.

Lifesaving stations were tall physical structures (akin to a firehouse) on the beach. The men who manned the stations were called surfmen, because their duties often involved launching a large rowing dory through beach surf, and rowing to a stricken ship. Lifesaving stations worked in concert with lighthouses to keep a constant watch for trouble. During storms, the surfmen took turns patrolling the beaches and keeping watch from the crow's nests of their stations for ships in distress. The equipment at a station would traditionally include flares, Lyle (launching) guns to send lines off shore to stricken vessels, and a breeches buoy for moving personnel to and from any boat which was in trouble near shore.

The captain of the house was called a coxswain. His duties included continuous training of personnel and steering the lifeboat as it went out on assignments. Lifesaving boats could either be launched from steel rails which led out of most stations and into the water or towed on large wheels to a disaster sight. Most of these rowing boats were 25 to 30 feet long with self righting capabilities, and air compartments which made them unsinkable. The continuous training at a station was always the object of public interest. Surfmen were trained (and received certificates) in rowing, firing the Lyle gun, operating the breeches buoy (for moving sailors off a stricken ship), morse code, and resuscitation.

The two stations within the Quadrangle included:

1. The Erie Station (1876) … Located some three miles west of the Beacon Lighthouse (at the channel), the first station was positioned close to the edge of the beach. The crew included a coxswain and six (later increased to seven) surfmen. The station used a system in which the lifeboat was rolled to the water's edge on wheels (rather than rails). The position at the northernmost curving beach extremity of the Peninsula soon proved to be impractical and the station was moved to the current location of the Coast Guard compound on the north pier of Erie's channel entrance in 1878. In 1915 the operations were merged with those of the revenue cutter service and formed the foundation for today's Coast Guard operations in Erie.

2. Long Point Station (1883) … The first beach station was positioned on the south beach just west of the Old Cut. When the channel began to silt up and fewer boats were having difficulties near the base of the Point it was decided to move the station closer to the tip of the Point. The new "east end" station opened in 1910. This location soon proved to be unacceptable, however, because of the extreme size of the surf at this point along the south beaches. In stormy weather when it was often necessary to launch a lifeboat, waves usually prohibited doing so. In 1912, the station was moved to the north beach facing the Outer Bay where launching was much easier. By the time the lifesaving station was discontinued in the late 1920s, it had been credited with saving almost 50 lives.

AMATEUR LIFESAVING

Over the years, more assistance has been rendered to sailors in difficulty by non-professionals than by the official representatives of government agencies. There is a long maritime tradition of sailors and shore dwellers, alike, coming to

The Dobbins lifesaving certificate awarded to surfmen.

The Erie Lifesaving Station.

The Long Point Lifesaving Station.

the assistance of boats in distress. On Long Point, for example, there is the fabled story of Abigail Becker who saved the crew of the *Conductor* on November 25, 1854. Abigail was one of the few women who regularly accompanied her husband to his trapping cabin along the south beach of Long Point. Abigail was alone with her children waiting for her husband to return from Port Rowan that day. On her morning walk to the beach to get water for breakfast, she spotted the wreck of a schooner which had run aground trying to find the Old Cut the night before.

The ship had rolled badly in the surf. It was leaning hard and awash. The captain and crew had climbed the rigging and spent the night exposed to freezing winds and snow. Abigail gathered her children on the beach and convinced the men to swim for the safety of the beach. One by one they attempted the swim, at her behest. Most floundered because of the surf and their weakened condition, but Abigail waded or swam out into the surf to save them. She took the exhausted and frozen crew to her cabin where she warmed and fed them.

For her efforts, Abigail Becker has become known as the heroine of Long Point. She received a number of honors including a gold medal from Buffalo, New York, a commendation from Queen Victoria, and a recognition from the Benevolent Life Saving Association of New York. In 1990 a two act play entitled *Abigail* or *The Gold Medal* was written, and produced by Port Dover's Lighthouse Theater.

Over the years there have been countless such rescues. From the residents of nearby shores, to fishermen, commercial sailors and recreational boaters, there have been thousands of cases of assistance over the years. Most of these ended in unsung heroes; persons who simply did what was called for in the hope that the long tradition of boaters helping fellow boaters would continue. Perhaps the best known modern lifesaver was Harvey Ferris whose grandfather was head keeper for the Long Point Company. Harvey was a fisherman, trapper, boat owner and innkeeper at Long Point. Over the years it always seemed to be Harvey who organized search parties and found missing sportsmen and fishermen. It was, in fact, Harvey who was first to the scene of the stricken fish tug *Ciscoe* (see chapter 10) when she came aground near Port Burwell. Harvey epitomized the spirit of lifesaving on the lake, a third generation Ferris with Lake Erie in his blood!

THE IDAHO

One of the greatest rescues within the Quadrangle was accomplished by Captain Frank Root of the Steamer *Mariposa* on Saturday, November 6, 1897. The day before, the propeller *Idaho* had left Buffalo for Milwaukee with a load of package freight. The *Idaho* was an old-timer which had been moth balled and then returned to service. She was a wooden hulled 220 footer which had been launched in 1863. Her huge port and starboard hogging arches gave her the look of a classic side wheel steamer, but she was equipped with a propeller drive. She was decked out with a traditional octagonal wheelhouse topped with a carved eagle. Looking far more like a passenger steamer than a freighter, she carried a 90 foot mast to fly the pendants and flags which had been popular among earlier passenger liners. The *Idaho* was long past her useful life as she worked the 1897 season. But freight rates were good, and business was plentiful. Expediency dictated her use until the owners could have a new steel hulled ship commissioned.

Trouble began long before the *Idaho* reached Long Point. Her old hull was working badly in the November seas. Leaks began to worsen and the pumps were at capacity trying to keep the water out of the holds. As the ship neared the Point, the winds rose dramatically. The captain considered seeking shelter behind the Point (a too familiar story) but decided that with the hull leaking as badly as it was it would be more prudent to steam for port rather than try to anchor and put an evening's strain on the hull.

Somewhere near the Old Cut the pumps began to fail. The crew formed a bucket brigade but could not keep up with the leaks. Soon the *Idaho* began to list to stern. The captain ordered anchors set, but this worsened things and soon it was apparent that the ship was about to go down. In his attempts to work the anchors on the decks, Captain Gillies was swept overboard and lost. Slowly the *Idaho* wallowed in the growing seas and sank to the bottom. As it went down, two crew members were able to crawl up the mast and attach themselves to the rigging. The ship settled in 50 feet of water with the two men perched 25 feet above the water.

Harvey Ferris, 1954.
Courtesy of MRS. H. FERRIS

The Idaho.

Louis LaForge and Bill Gill considered swimming for shore but realized that it would be a suicide mission. Instead they decided to hang on the rigging and wait for help. Their prayers were answered the next morning when Root's *Mariposa* crew spotted the two crew men frozen to the mast. Root launched a yawl to assist but the lifeboat was destroyed in the waves. In what was to become a legendary piece of seamanship. Root brought the *Mariposa* downwind of the stricken sailors, and after three attempts put the 350 foot steamer right alongside the mast of the Idaho and held her there while his crew chopped the frost bitten sailors from their icy perch.

THE BEALS

In late September 1876, a three masted schooner loaded with lumber was heading from Port Burwell to Dunkirk. In the early evening a nor'easter blew up with winds of 40 miles per hour. Rather than continue beating upwind, the captain of the *Beals* decided to seek shelter in the harbor at Erie.

The ship's crew was relieved to see the harbor lights just as darkness was falling that night. Unfamiliar with the channel entrance, however, the *Beals* went hard aground about a mile east and to the south of the channel entrance. The patrol from the lifesaving station soon spotted the distressed schooner, and attempted to launch a lifeboat to come to her rescue. After three attempts, it had become clear that the huge surf from the northeast winds would make launching a rescue boat impossible.

Meanwhile large crowds had gathered at both the south and the north piers near the channel. It was apparent to all that the crew of the *Beals* was in serious danger. The schooner had rolled over and as darkness fell, she seemed in imminent danger of breaking up.

Coxswain Clark Jones of the lifesaving station ordered the lifeboat to be loaded into a wagon and towed to the channel. Here, under the scrutiny of the cheering crowd, he and his surfmen launched the boat in the shelter of the piers. With a lantern lashed to the bow the crew rowed through the tremendous waves in the channel and disappeared into the inky darkness separating the crew of the *Beals* from safety. As the lifeboat slowly pulled toward the stricken schooner the assembled crowd could see the lantern periodically rise to the top of a wave, then disappear as the vessel fell to the trough. After more than an hour the surfmen reached the *Beals*, removed its crew and returned them to shore amidst cheering and adulation.

It was this rescue which convinced the Lifesaving Service of the folly of locating stations on the beaches. In 1868, the station was moved to a sheltered sight along the channel and its protective piers.

The Port Dover Light.

Erie Harbor Light.

Lake Erie Adventures

1. In Scotland, tourists and residents alike spend countless hours traveling to castles. We suggest that you make a similar hobby out of finding and visiting the lighthouses of the lake and of the Quadrangle in particular. Take a camera and begin your personal collection of photographs of the lighthouses of Lake Erie. It will be a challenge to find them all but you can do it!

2. When you visit the Presque Isle Lighthouse take the opportunity to walk the cement keeper's trail which leads to Misery Bay. As you do so imagine that the keeper built this path piece by piece and that this was how he supplied all of his needs. He rolled a wheelbarrow to Misery Bay, rowed a dory across the channel and returned with supplies.

3. The Barcelona Lighthouse is well worth a field trip. Stop for lunch or dinner at the nearby restaurant (on the lake) or take a picnic to the adjoining park.

4. The Long Point Light will present the greatest challenge. To get a close up picture you will need to use a boat.

5. Once you have done the Quadrangle Lighthouses you will probably be hooked. From here you can complete Lake Erie, then move on to the other Great Lakes and beyond!

COMMERCIAL AND SPORT FISHING

*T*he history of fishing in the Lake Erie Quadrangle is the story of two changing phenomena. The first is the evolution of the lake's fish biomass and how this has effected commercial and sport fishing. Gradually, the fish population has changed from species so unbelievably abundant that they were once considered a nuisance, herded into pens and killed for use as fertilizer. Over the years individual species have disappeared, reappeared, and sometimes become extinct. As the species changed and the lake's production shifted, both commercial and sport fishermen adapted and changed. The second interconnected phenomena is the evolution of fishing techniques, boats and equipment.

Sadly, it looks as though a combination of over fishing, human population growth along the lake shore, and pollution (all of which are clearly interrelated) has created a threat to Lake Erie's fish population. Both the sport fishing business and the commercial fisheries (still active on the north shore) are struggling. During the winter of 1993, for example, Misner Fisheries in Port Dover ceased operations. For years, this large fish processing plant along the Lynn River had been a Port Dover landmark. In what may have been a gesture of kindness as much

The abandoned Misner Fish Plant in Port Dover.

as one of business acumen, Olmstead (a subsidiary of Heintz Foods) bought the equipment, including Misner's fleet of fish tugs. In Port Dover, observers fear that "American Corporate" ownership and control of the fishing business spells the beginning of the end for the industry.

On the U.S. side of the lake, 1991 and 1992 were poor years for sport fishing. With the commercial industry all but defunct in Erie, sport fishing had emerged over the past decade as the primary impetus for fishing as a business. The tiny current fleet of fish tugs working out of Erie has been augmented by an incredible growth in sport fishing of all sorts. Both individual fishermen in boats and charter captains had been working American waters off Erie with downriggers over the past decade. The years from 1980 to 1990 witnessed a steady and encouraging catch for the off-shore downriggers. Catches of salmon, pickerel (yellow pike), and lake trout encouraged the development of the sport fishing business prior to the past few years, and this industry has had a significant impact on Erie's tourist economy.

Both U.S. and Canadian sport fishermen blame commercial over-fishing by the north shore fleet for the decreased productivity of game fish. During the 1993 winter meetings of sport fishermen in Erie, it was strongly suggested that there be a moratorium on trawling. Sports fishermen argue that trawling not only results in over fishing, but that it damages bottom structure as well.

Cross border criticism is not new. There are historical records of Canadians calling for a moratorium on U.S. commercial fishing as early as 1910 to protect the then popular herring population. Canadians charged that U.S. fishing boats were desecrating the entire population of herring and threatening the whitefish by over fishing from commercial steam tugs. The history of fishing in Lake Erie includes an evolving argument between commercial and sport fishermen, as well as a long conflict between Canadian and U.S. commercial interests. There have been hundreds of incidents in which authorities on one side of the lake, chased, shot at, arrested, or confiscated equipment and catches of fish tugs operating on the "wrong" side of the international line.

COMMERCIAL FISHING

Indian legend tells of the first organized fishing ventures on the lake. The Iroquois were so fearful of the lake and her sporadic fury that they avoided living close to the shore. Instead, they organized fishing parties to visit the lake shore at opportune times. Anthropologic evidence suggests that fishing parties regularly visited both Long Point and Presque Isle, setting up temporary working camps. The Indians apparently gathered the abundant species using combinations of netting and spearing, and then moved their catch back to their permanent settlements. The Iroquois dried fish for storage and subsequent food usage. They also used fish for fertilizer. On Long Point, there is evidence that the Indians made regular fishing trips just prior to the spring melt so that they could use toboggans to bring their dead from the winter for burial in the sands. They used the toboggans to return with their catch.

Erie's remaining commercial fishing fleet, 1993.

The first settlers along both shores approached fishing in a similar manner. They were primarily engaged in homesteading, but utilized late fall (after harvest) and early spring (before planting) to take advantage of the relatively easy access to food fish. Records suggest that fish were, at times, so incredibly abundant along the shores that they could be harvested with baskets. For the settlers prior to the war of 1812, fishing was a diversion either just before or after farming duties, which provided a food bonus. With such easy access to fish, it seemed that no one could ever starve in the Long Point or Erie areas. Fish were like "manna" from heaven, under-appreciated and taken for granted.

By the end of the War of 1812, fishing had grown more difficult. While fish populations were still plentiful by today's standards, it was no longer easy for anyone to simply gather them in baskets. The settlers were beginning to recall the

Some of Port Dover's fishing fleet, tied up in the river.

good old days and developed an appreciation for fish as a food staple. At the same time, the ideas of the industrial revolution were beginning to take hold. Perhaps, within this context, there would be a place in society for specialists, such as fishermen, who would trade their goods and services to others.

By the 1840s there were commercial fishermen operating on both sides of the lake. They used several variations of seines to gather their catch, and worked primarily from shore in shallow waters. The seining techniques worked best in the spring and fall, however, and commercial fishing did not really become well-established in these days because of its seasonalness. Some of the early seine fishermen added to their flexibility through the use of row boats for moving nets into deeper water. There were no processing plants or buildings associated with the fishing business until the 1850s, however, and farmers still thought of fish as a seasonal food.

During the 1850s, pound netting began to emerge in the shallows along both the north and south shores. Most of the work of the pound netters was done from shore. When boats were used, they were small enough to be drawn up on the beach. This allowed the industry to develop in numerous locations, as deep draft harbors were not needed. In the early 1850s, there was another important development in fishing. Captain John Nash from Mackinac moved to Erie and demonstrated the use of gill nets. By the 1860s, gill netting was practiced on both sides of the lake and had become more popular than pound netting.

As the competition between technologies increased, the pound netters developed larger operations. Toward the end of the pound netting era in the early 1940s, there were fewer pounder's, but each used tremendously large runs of netting. Hoover's at Nanticoke, for example, used hundreds of telephone pole sized stakes, driven 8 to 10 feet into the lake bottom, to support runs of up to one-half mile of netting.

The glue which eventually bound the industries together was the development of the processing plant. Because of the growth of gill netters and their boats, processors, such as Kolbe in Port Dover and Shaw in Erie, located in central harbor areas. This further burdened the pound netters (as well as the remaining seine netters) who were forced to move their catch to the market processors.

Centralized processing plants also helped to solidify the centers of the industry in a few specific locations. This ultimately encouraged market growth, since railroad companies along the north shore were willing to build trunk lines to fishing ports such as Port Dover. The railroads provided a bonus for the north shore ports: they brought a wave of tourists to the lake's port cities. Port Dover and its beaches, for example, became a summer tourist attraction.

In both Port Dover and Erie, the annual fishing business cycle began in February and March as fishermen organized for the annual ice harvest. When the ice had reached its thickest stage, workers would venture out with huge saws to cut it into blocks and float it to town. It was hauled to the fish market's ice houses and stored for subsequent use in packing the season's catch. During most years, ice from the annual harvest would last for the entire season. This was a festive occasion for a port city, for it reunited the fishermen after a long winter.

Seine netting on the Inner Bay.

COMMERCIAL TECHNIQUES

Historically, there have been four primary methods employed by commercial fishermen. Only one of the four, pound netting, has passed from common practice on the lakes. The four include: (1) Seining: placing a long net out in relatively shallow water and drawing it back to its origin in a semi-circular pattern. Fish are trapped at the center portion of the net. Seining continues in the Inner Bay near Port Rowan. (2) Pound Netting: the laying of a large run of standing netting in shallow water, usually at cross directions to travel patterns of fish. The long run of net leads to a maze of angles so that fish are funneled into a small pen from

Jim and Tom (1907) showing her new roof and supports.

The Smith Brothers (1927) with aft roof and side walls.

which most cannot escape. (3) Gill Netting: uses a net with square openings large enough for fish to swim into an individual opening, become trapped by their gills and unable to back out. Gill nets can be set in any depth of water at angles which are designed to intercept the moving fish. Each end of the gill net is anchored to the bottom with weights and marked at the surface with a float. Along the net itself, the bottom surface is weighted and the top has small cork floats attached. From the fishes' perspective, the gill net looks like a huge tennis net suspended at an adjustable depth between the lake bottom and the water's surface. (4) Trawling: two doors (sleds) are lowered to the bottom of the lake from the aft corners of the boat. These flat weights are dragged along the bottom and tow a huge parachute shaped net behind them. The net captures all of the fish that it encounters.

THE EVOLUTION OF THE FISH TUG

The modern fish tug, which can be seen today along both shores, is a remarkable testament to the ingenuity and engineering of the fishermen and boat builders of Lake Erie. Much of the innovation of the modern tug took place in Port Dover, Port Burwell, and Erie. The current design has remained roughly the same since the 1930s and 40s and is largely the handiwork of the Gamble yards of Port Dover, and the Paasch and Nolen yards of Erie. The Lake Erie tug design has been aggressively copied by fishermen in the other Great Lakes as well as Atlantic coast builders.

The steam tug particularly revolutionized the fishing industry in Erie. It allowed the commercial fishermen, who had formerly been restricted to the bay, to move into the open lake. This, in turn, allowed the fishermen to catch new species, in particular whitefish and herring. It also began a long tradition of contact between Canadian and American fishermen, which would ultimately lead to the hastened evolution of the tug.

As fish tug innovations and refinements were made during the early 1900s, other fishermen soon noticed and copied them. This evolution spread up and down the north shore and back and forth across the lake. When one tug full of fishermen saw a good idea, they simply went home and copied it. By the early 1950s, the current design had been fully refined, and most of the working tugs had begun to resemble each other.

The trawler Alex B at Port Dover with her trawling sled hanging on the stern.

The first fishermen to utilize boats were the 19th century seine and pound net operators. As the fish supply near shore was depleted, which forced them to extend their operations into the mid-summer, they began to use row boats to work their nets. Specially designed rowing prams were used. These prams were usually between 25 and 30 feet long, with a tremendous beam and freeboard allowing for large cargoes of fish. A metal version of this craft, which evolved in the 1940s, is still commonly seen in dock areas along the north shore.

As gill netting grew in popularity, fishermen began to use sailboats to increase their range. Typically, the vessels had a single mast or a large main mast with a relatively long boom and mainsail. With this rig, they could carry a full suite of sails while traveling to and from the nets. Upon reaching the nets, they would lower the headsails and topsails and keep a single main flying. In most wind conditions, this rig allowed them to sail up to the float end of a gill net, pull it and remove the fish, while heading the boat up into the wind. After tending a net, the fishermen pulled the long boom across the deck, made his way back onto the wind

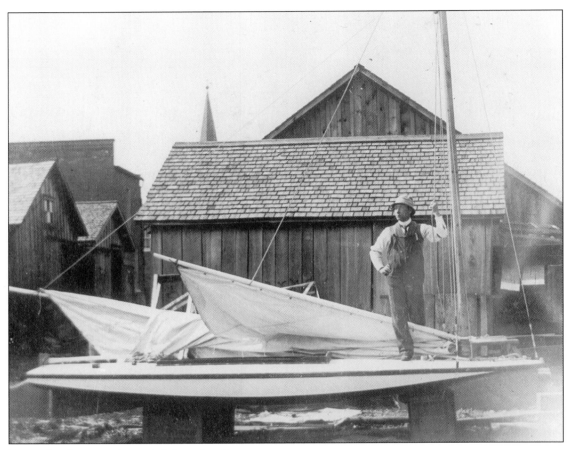

Types of sailboats used in early fishing: Port Rowan.
Photo by DONALD BUSCOMBE

and sailed to the next net with the single (easily managed) mainsail.

As steam propulsion became popular, the fishermen began to appreciate the advantages of using the steam tug. One by one, they abandoned sailboats in favor of engine driven craft. They were no longer prisoners of the elements. They could fish when there was no wind and operate much more predictably. The first steam driven fishing boats were patterned after a combination of the rabbits, which were pulling schooner-barges, and the tugs that had been developed to haul floating lumber. This is why commercial fishing boats are still commonly called "tugs."

The earliest versions, which appeared near the end of the 19th century, were open wooden boats of some 30 to 40 feet in length, with a pilot house in the center housing a steering station and the engine. The typical crew consisted of the captain, who drove; the engineer, who tended to the steam boiler and loaded it with coal; and a crew of two or three, who handled the nets. In inclement weather, crews were always a bit resentful of the captain and engineer who had the advantage of shelter in the wheelhouse. To accommodate the crew, fish tugs slowly began to evolve a rear roofed section, so that there was shelter from sun, rain and snow. By the early 1900s tugs began to incorporate canvas curtains, which could be dropped from the rear roofed areas to the side decks, providing comfort on the ride to and from the nets.

By the 1920s, most tugs were using motorized net pullers. This cut down on the size of the working deck needed to pull nets. As a result of this innovation, the canvas side deck curtains were ultimately replaced with solid sides and sliding doors so that they could be opened to work the nets. The final structural innovation, which appeared at about the same time, was a roof to cover the front of the boat from the bow to the wheelhouse. Because of its shape, this forward roof is called a turtle deck.

In the 1930s, steel construction replaced wood. The earliest tugs were riveted together, but by the mid-30s the Gamble Yard in Dover (soon to be copied by yards on both sides of the lake) was producing welded

The Mars, built in Erie about 1920.

steel tugs. Most of the welded tugs built in the 30s and 40s are still in use today. Many have been sold several times, moving from port to port and from the U.S. to Canada and back. With reasonable maintenance and continuous renovation, these early tugs are as sound today as they were before World War II.

The Kolbe company which moved from Sandusky to Erie, Pa., and then to Port Dover (and Burwell) innovated a refrigeration system for processing fish. As a part of their processing operation they were able to freeze their catch solid, making it easily handled and extending the delivery range significantly. Because of this innovation and the Kolbe's former connections in Erie, there was substantial trade between Port Dover's fish tugs and the Erie processors such as Shaw. Prior to World War II there were regular deliveries in which frozen fish were brought to Erie and tugs returned with coal.

A modern one piece trawler, the 1969 CJ Weaver steams toward Dover.

In the 50s, diesel engines appeared on the lakes and became a preferable alternative to the smokey coal burning power plants of earlier years. One by one, the tugs converted. The change to diesel created a labor savings, since the captain could handle both engine and piloting duties. Some of the old salts still claim, however, that the disappearance of coal driven engines hastened the decline of the fish population. They feel that the common practice of throwing coal dust and ash overboard, as the tugs worked the net areas, was beneficial for both water and fish. While modern engineers herald the clean burning diesel, old timers blame its pollutants, and the sudden elimination of coal dust, for the decline of fishing in the 1950s.

There were two additional refinements in tug construction. In the 50s and 60s, larger tugs were built with one piece superstructures. Rather than having the wheelhouse, rear roof, and turtle deck as three separate entities, the topsides were constructed as one unit. In the mid-1960s, when trawling began, an "A" frame roof structure was built over the side door. In many tugs, the door itself was enlarged by cutting an opening into the roof. The "A" frame and larger door opening allow for the handling of the end of the trawl net, which contains all of the fish (the cod end) as it comes aboard.

CHANGING FISH POPULATIONS

The history of Lake Erie's fish, by species, is a sad story. It recalls a resource which was obviously mismanaged. In the earliest days of commercial fishing, every imaginable species was commonly caught in pound and seine nets. Sturgeon, for example, were considered a major nuisance since their immense size often did damage to netting. The Hoover fisheries of Nanticoke, reported, near the turn of the century, a daily catch of 100 sturgeon in their pound nets. Several of these fish were in excess of 200 pounds. In those days, sturgeon were often converted to fish oil.

The two prized fish in the early days were the herring and whitefish. Prior to the mid-1920s, other species were largely ignored. Perch, for example, were thought of as a nuisance and discarded. During winter fishing meetings in the 1920s strategies for eradicating the troublesome perch from the lake basin were seriously discussed. Herring was a perfect fish to be sent to market. It had a firm flesh and was quite sweet. It lasted for a long time in transit without deteriorating, and it could be prepared in a variety of ways. Old timers on both sides of the lake often refer to the time period before 1920 as the "Herring Years." Between 1920 and 1925, the total Lake Erie herring catch slowly dropped from 20 to 12 million pounds. By 1930, it had fallen to less than a million pounds.

Undaunted, the fishermen turned their attention to whitefish and began to market pickerel more aggressively. They began a categorization system to distinguish between yellow and blue pickerel (pike), and started to harvest the previously ignored perch. Despite efforts to tout the benefits of pickerel and perch, the industry sagged badly in the years preceding the depression. Fortunately, some of the commercial fishermen were able to make ends meet during the prohibition era by adding harvests of "midnight herring" (booze) to their regular operations. The depression years saw a reduction in the number of tugs fishing both sides of the lake. The fishing was bad and the economy was worse. On both sides of the Lake Erie Quadrangle, the number of active fish tugs fell by about 40%.

The Depression years were good ones for the fish population. Fewer tugs soon resulted in a noticeable return of the fish. In a post-Depression burst of enthusiasm, large numbers of fishermen returned to their beloved profession. The ship yards at Dover and Erie were filled with orders for welded steel tugs, and the captains had little difficulty paying for their new boats. By 1939, the catch of blue pickerel (blues or blue pike) was up to 10 million pounds. It seemed as though the blue was taking over the role of the herring.

The Erwin, a Kolbe tug from Dover approaching Erie with a load of fish about 1910.
Photo by PAT SHOUP

Erie's Shaw Fish Company.
ERIE COUNTY HISTORICAL SOCIETY

When World War II ended, a large number of returning soldiers and sailors on both sides of the lake financed their return to the fishing business through the acquisition of low interest government loans. These veterans often received enough funding support to become captains of their own tugs. The number of tugs grew precipitously on both sides of the Quadrangle. The north shore fleet, for example, grew from 50 before the war, to 65 in 1947, 80 in 1950 and 125 by 1960. The glory days of commercial fishing had returned. To add fuel to the economic recovery, the herring reappeared. For some absolutely unknown reason, fishermen began to bring in large catches of the prized fish of the 20s. In 1947, the herring catch was reported to be almost 10 million pounds.

But the enthusiasm was short lived! By 1949 the herring catch began to decline again—falling to 2 million pounds. By the mid-1960s, the herring were gone, probably forever. To make matters worse, the blue pickerel began a steady decline in the 50s. By 1960, they were judged to be extinct; an even worse fate than that of the herring, since the fishing industry on both sides of the lake had created an image of the "blue" as the perfect food fish. It was of reasonable size, easy to clean and cook, and had a delicious mild flavor. When blue pike disappeared, both the fishing community and the consuming public began to become concerned about the lake. The 50s were also peak years for lake pollution. The media began to note the possibility that, with herring, whitefish, and blue pickerel effectively gone, Erie would soon become a dead lake.

The 60s were tough times for fishing. While the north shore waters of the Quadrangle remained pristine, bad press about the lake and its fish virtually devastated the commercial industry near Erie. Large numbers of fishermen ceased operations, and people increasingly avoided the consumption of fish. The north shore fleet carried on with the aid of the Canadian government. The ministry of fishing helped the fishermen to convert their catch to perch, yellow pickerel (walleye) and smelt. It seemed that perch populations were increasing in the wake of the species which had disappeared. In the mid-60s, catch limits were established in Canadian waters and the government established a minimum commercial price to protect fishermen from market idiosyncrasies.

Perhaps the chief boost to the north shore market was a dramatic increase in smelt. Smelt were introduced into the lower lakes in the early 60s in an attempt to provide a food chain for lake trout. Within a few short years, massive populations of the small but tasty fish were reported throughout Lake Erie. In response to this new species, north shore fishermen were encouraged to begin trawling. By the late 60s, most of the Port Dover tug fleet had converted to trawling techniques and were using a combination of trawling and gill netting. Although trawling methods were new and quite different, the government assisted the fleet with the changeover by offering grants, training, and demonstrations of equipment in an effort to shore up the fishing industry. On the U.S. side, commercial fishermen also tried trawling in the mid-60s, but the costs of conversion were prohibitive.

Unlike the Canadian government, which intervened and assisted the north shore fishermen, the U.S. government took a hands off policy with respect to financial support. In a few short years, the Erie fleet and its industry infrastructure had fallen apart. The remaining fishermen continued to utilize gill netting techniques without interference until 1982, when the Pennsylvania Fish Commission, under pressure from sport fishermen and conservationists, instituted catch restrictions. Not only were the fishermen restricted to a total poundage, but gill net opening sizes were increased. Younger fish were able to avoid capture and spawn for several years before growing large enough to be captured in the gill nets.

As of 1993, only eight licensed commercial fishermen work out of Erie. Some of them utilize small boats (under 30 feet) rather than traditional tugs in order to take advantage of a lower category of license fee. Of the eight, three are under temporary suspension for alleged catch reporting violations. The glory days of commercial fishing in Erie seem to be gone forever. In the place of a harbor full of fish tugs, processing plants, and net drying racks, there are now yacht clubs and commercial marinas.

Commercial fishermen unloading smelt at Dover, 1978.

SPORT FISHING

From the earliest days along both lake shores, the population, and particularly working class people, thought of fish as a food staple. It was relatively simple for most citizens to buy bait casting equipment and spend a few happy hours per week fishing (gathering food). Many neighborhood fishermen would happily share their abundant catches with friends and neighbors who were unable to get to the docks for a day of fishing.

During the 50s and 60s, increasing numbers of fishermen began to use small boats to get to the fish. It was quite popular to launch (or rent) a small row boat or outboard, and row a few miles out into the lake for bluepike, yellow pike, and perch. There were no catch limits. When the fish were "running," there were reports of fishermen from the 1950s rowing to shore with boat loads of bluepike.

An interesting adjunct to the commercial fishing business, which was extremely popular in the post-World War II era, was the party boat. In Erie, several fishing party boats, with 50 person capacities, operated until the early 1960s. At their peak, the boats would leave the harbor two or three times daily, taking loads of fishermen a few miles off shore to fish for blues, yellows, and perch. Evening trips were especially popular, because the lights from the party boats would serve as magnets for both the minnows and the larger fish which would follow them to the surface. Sometimes, it was said, that the blues would bite an empty hook!

Thousands of fishermen would travel to Erie from Pittsburgh and points south to take advantage of the party boat system. A factory worker from Pittsburgh could leave work on a Friday, drive to Erie, and be on the 8:00 p.m. party boat that very night. With friends, a few beers, and a bucket full of fish to take home, fishing in Erie was a bonanza. Party boats were also popular in Port Rowan, where they would take fishermen into the Inner Bay for similar ventures.

By the 1970s, the tradition of food fishing had effectively vanished. There were still a few die hard perch fishermen. But the times when almost anyone could get a bucket full at anytime were long gone. Gradually, the character of amateur fishing changed. Many fishermen became interested in fishing as a pure sport. Catch and release techniques and the use of lightweight tackle replaced food fishing for many. This new philosophy shifted the choice of catch to muskellunge, northern pike and bass. These were species which were difficult to find, and gave a great fight once hooked. Not valued as a food source, the sport fish were often caught and released simply because they were not good to eat. Food fishermen became increasingly interested in less desirable species such as crappies and bluegills.

The Jerry B, a partyboat from Port Rowan about 1928.

In a controversial move to stimulate the sport fishing business, coho salmon were introduced to Lake Erie in 1968. Given the increasing interest in sport fishing, and in catching a fish which gave a great fight, it was reasoned that salmon fishing would create an instant industry. By the middle 1970s, coho supporters seemed to be visionaries. In a business boom, fishermen began to buy record numbers of power boats and downrigging equipment. Deepwater trolling for "big fish," such as salmon had become the new trend. When the water warmed up, and the coho and other fish moved to deep water, the fishermen in their downrigger equipped boats followed them.

By the early 1980s, a charter fishing industry reminiscent of Florida's Atlantic coast sport fishing business had sprung to life in Erie. For a basic fee, the charter captain would take passengers to the center of the lake. Using a fishfinder, he would locate coho and other large fish, such as lake trout and walleye. The guide would then continue to use his depth sounder and downriggers to move lures through the schools of game fish. Happy fishermen returning with trophy sized gamefish replaced the food gathering party boaters of the 50s. It was estimated that the value of coho fishing to Erie County was $25 million annually.

The rapid growth of the charter business was short lived, however. Many, if not most, charterers were in the business as a sideline. Some utilized chartering as a way to own and operate a large boat. By the mid-1980s, it became clear that the coho populations in the lake were not matching projections. Spawning yields fell, there were problems with diseases, and the traditional argument that they were a foreign species which should not have been introduced, was increasingly heard.

The current state of the lake and its fish production seems to be driven by a new invader, the Zebra Mussel. This species, and its cousins, which have emigrated from Europe in ocean going freighters, is infesting the Great Lakes. Zebra mussels are voracious filterers. Each Zebra mussel can filter as much as two liters of water in a 24 hour period, turning a muddy or silty environment crystal clear in a short time. As an apparent result of the work of zebra and other mussels, water clarity in Lake Erie's central basin (as reported by the limnology people at Gannon University) is changing geometrically. Natural light was limited to 10 or 15 feet under optimum circumstances a decade ago. Now, it is possible to see bottom in 50 feet of water under many circumstances.

While this may seem to offer an aesthetic improvement to the waters of the lake, it provides a major shift in fish habitat. Light reaching the bottom in increasing intensity will stimulate weed growth more than ever before, changing the underwater structure significantly. The balance of organic growth will be permanently shifted within the lake. As this occurs, it is certain that some fish will suffer from the transition. Smelt, for example, appear to be declining since the proliferation of zebra mussels, threatening the entire north shore trawling industry. On the other hand, commercial fishermen on both sides of the lake report that whitefish are making a significant return.

What is abundantly clear, after watching the evolution of fishing, is how little we know about the lake and her environmental dynamics. In the 1950s, it was commonly thought that fish hatcheries could maintain the balance of fishing in the lake by providing fry of any particular species. Since that time, however, we have learned the difficulties and impossibilities of maintaining a natural process via intervention. As foreign species have been introduced, either by design (smelt, coho) or by error (lamprey eel, zebra mussel), we seem to learn the downside effects to the natural process long after the fact. Yet the damage, if that is the correct term, is already done and quite probably irreversible. What took thousands of years to evolve, after the glaciers passed by here, has been irrevocably disturbed by us, as we created our history over the past century!

THE CISCOE

Captain Buck Young started the diesel engine of the Kolbe Company's Fish Tug, the *Ciscoe* on the morning of March 22, 1955. It was a cold day in the harbor at Port Burwell, and there was a fresh breeze from the southeast. The U.S. National Weather Service's regular radio reports did not begin until April in those days, and Buck was feeling uneasy about the steel grey sky. Grumbling about how illogical it was to save a few dollars on weather broadcasts, Captain Young cleared the harbor and headed upwind. His gill nets were well offshore between Burwell and the tip of Long Point.

Still uneasy about the weather, Buck listened carefully to the ship's radio in order to determine the conditions that other tug captains were experiencing. His crew: Gordon Rockefeller, John Siskovits, Gordon Massecar, and John Wilson, were busy preparing to pull nets. It was 9:00 in the morning when they

The Ciscoe.

reached the first net marker. As the crew pulled it in, Buck became increasingly concerned about the weather. Every fisherman realizes the dangers of spring and fall storms. For the Burwell fleet, however, the dangers were even more significant. The tiny harbor lies right on the lake shore, and, in a stiff blow, the entrance way to the town docks quickly becomes a maelstrom. The Burwell fleet did not have the advantage of the Dover fleet, which could tuck behind the shelter of Long Point if they were caught offshore.

As the crew finished working its first gang of nets, Buck's concerns escalated. The wind and waves were building. The *Ciscoe's* barometer was plummeting, and radio chatter from boats up the lake indicated that they were all running for harbor. At 1:00 p.m., Captain Young made the decision to "cut and run." He turned the *Ciscoe* toward Burwell and told the crew to prepare for the return trip. The crew was relieved to be abandoning the rest of the day's nets.

By 2:00 p.m., Buck could make out the grey cliffs behind Burwell, and the crew began to feel a sense of relief. A few moments later, however, the sky suddenly turned jet black and the full fury of Lake Erie's worst storm in three decades was upon them. Even though they were only five miles from the harbor, the blinking light disappeared in the first blast of wind and snow. Gradually, the shoreline became obscured, leaving the *Ciscoe* pitching wildly on 15 to 20 foot seas and uncertain of her exact location.

By 2:30 p.m. the tug was fully enveloped in a blinding snow squall. Captain Young was afraid that he would either run aground in the shallows near Burwell, or worse yet, miss the tiny harbor entrance and slam into the concrete retaining wall. As he pondered his dilemma, a huge comber lifted the *Ciscoe* helplessly to a height of more than 20 feet and slammed it sideways into its trough. Alarmed that he was getting into shoal waters and worried about the boat, Young swung the wheel 180 degrees and headed for deeper water and sea room.

Buck decided to head toward Long Point. Steaming slowly upwind would be easier on the boat, and if conditions eased he could always come about and coast downwind for Port Burwell. On the odd chance that conditions remained this difficult, Buck hoped to duck around behind the tip of the point and find shelter along the north beaches, as the Port Dover fleet had often done. In retrospect, this seems like a logical and prudent decision. For, Buck could not have realized that conditions were going to continue to deteriorate.

As the *Ciscoe* slowly inched her way eastward, the winds built to a steady 80 miles per hour. When darkness fell at 4:00 p.m. that afternoon, Buck knew that they were in serious trouble. The crew was hunkered down inside the wheelhouse and holding on for dear life. Visibility was next to zero. Because of the events of the day, the high winds, and the 25 to 35 foot waves they could not tell exactly where they were. Young began to second guess his decision. He began to realize that it would be foolhardy to try to round the tip of the point under the deteriorating circumstances. By 8:00 p.m., the *Ciscoe* was beginning to show the tolls of the struggle. Waves had crested over the top of the turtle deck and shattered all of the wheelhouse windows. As the *Ciscoe* took water over her decks, it ran right through the wheelhouse soaking Young and his crew. The tug had also taken on quite a bit of water as stray waves washed through the side doors and into the rear deck. The engine was missing badly and seemed in imminent danger of failing.

The worst dilemma, however, was not knowing their position. Buck feared that he had been washed too far to the north, and that he might get into the shallows near the tip of Long Point. Suddenly, the crew looked up to see a virtual wall of water heading toward the *Ciscoe*. It was the largest wave that Buck Young had ever seen. The *Ciscoe* was lifted and thrown sideways down the face of this wave. All forward motion stopped. For a dizzying moment Buck, who was wedged into the pilots chair, was sure that the tug would capsize. She was iced over badly and top heavy. Somehow, however, the *Ciscoe* righted herself as Buck turned the wheel hard to starboard.

But, the insides of the tug were virtually destroyed. Nets and equipment had been swept overboard, companionways and interior doors were twisted, and almost every surface had been crushed. Then Buck noticed that John Wilson was nowhere to be seen. He, like much of the ships equipment, had simply been swept out of the wheelhouse by the fury of the rogue wave.

For a second time, Young reversed course 180 degrees looking for sea room. This time he was running away from the shoal waters of the tip of Long Point. He decided that his best hope was to head northwest. This would allow the *Ciscoe* to run before the wind toward Burwell. Despondent over the loss of John Wilson, he gave up his concerns for the tug and decided that if nothing else, he would drive the *Ciscoe* on shore close to Port Burwell in the light of dawn. He had made sporadic contact with other tugs (which were safely lying in port) during the night and realized that his friends would all be looking for him. Mercifully, the winds began to fall, and, for a brief time, Buck considered an attempt at piloting the *Ciscoe* through the tiny harbor entrance to safety. Shortly after dawn, though, the engine gave up, leaving the *Ciscoe* ice coated, wallowing in 20 footers, and drifting. By this time, captain and crew were exhausted and suffering badly from hypothermia.

On shore, anxious onlookers had spotted the *Cisco* in the early morning light and realized what had happened. The fishing community, from Port Dover to Port Stanley, had been following the drama of the *Ciscoe* through the evening, and hundreds of fishermen were gathered along the banks east of Burwell to try to give assistance. By mid-morning, the relentless winds and waves had driven the *Ciscoe* onto a sandbar some 100 feet off shore and east of Burwell. There was a large crowd of anxious rescuers on the banks above the stricken tug, hoping to help rescue the crew. But the waves and water between shore and the *Ciscoe* proved to be a major challenge. A number of brave souls attempted to swim to the stricken vessel with a rope, but were turned back by the waves and cold water. Finally, Harvey Ferris managed to row to the side of the *Ciscoe* in a small dory and pick up a crew member. As Ferris turned the small boat to return to shore it was swamped. Both rescuer and rescued were almost lost.

It wasn't until 3:00 in the afternoon that a group of Kolbe's commercial fishermen brought a steel (pound netting tender) row boat to the scene in a truck. They successfully removed Buck Young and the remaining crew. The heavy steel dory allowed the group to work together to effect the rescue. Young and his crew were taken to the hospital and treated for exposure.

THE A.B. HOOVER

March 23rd, 1956 (almost exactly a year later) was a typical early spring day for the fishermen at Port Burwell. The weather was bitter cold. There had been difficulties, of late, with fields of cake ice. But the fishing was good, and Captain John Semple was anxious to leave harbor with his tug, the *A.B. Hoover*. Clearing the town pier, the crew: Ed Grahm, Ray McDonald, John McKay, and Charley Walker joked about getting stuck in pack ice. A trapped fish tug was nothing new to fishermen. It usually meant a night playing cards and too many cups of bad coffee.

At first, there was no wind. The water was grey and had a gentle swell. As the Hoover continued, however, it began to encounter more and more ice. This kind of ice was not usually a problem. A steel fish tug could just run up over it and break its way through. By noon, though, serious difficulties began to develop. First, the ice became much more resistant to the efforts of the little tug to break through it. Then, at about 12:30 p.m., a gale began to develop from the northwest. A decision was made to turn the 53 foot tug around and return to harbor, but the ship lost steerage on the turning maneuver and became hopelessly trapped in the pack ice.

To compound matters, the pack ice began moving rapidly to the northeast. By 1:30 p.m., the crew knew that they were in trouble. The ice flow that they were riding was now moving at speeds of 10 to 15 miles per hour. As it twisted and contorted its way through the now turbulent waters, pushed by a 40 mile per hour wind, the shifting ice alternately twisted the fish tug from one side to another. Many times on this perilous ride, the tug was pushed so far to port or starboard that the crew were sure it would capsize.

By 2:30 p.m., Captain Semple began to realize that the captive ship was rapidly approaching the American coast. They could see the horizon line, even in the snowy conditions. At about 3:00 p.m., the pack ice stopped moving. At first the crew was relieved, thinking that the entire flow had reached the south shore

Storm off Presque Isle.

and that their wild ice ride had ended. Within a few minutes, however, they began to realize that their position was now even more perilous. The ice pack began to tighten, forcing the *Hoover* higher out of the water and over at a more extreme angle.

Calculating that they were only 4 or 5 miles off shore, they abandoned ship in the diminishing light, and began to pick their way across the uneven ice flow toward Erie. They soon realized that the decision to set out for Erie was probably flawed. They did not have adequate clothing for an ice walk. The light was disappearing fast, and the route from tug to shore was crooked and hazardous. Approximately one hour into the trek, Grahm slipped through the ice and was almost lost. Only a valiant effort by his four exhausted friends saved him from drowning as they succeeded in dragging him out of the icy waters.

Finally, after more than two hours the bedraggled crew, helping their frozen friend, walked up to the Presque Isle Coast Guard Station, where they received help. A Coast Guard fly over the next day produced no sign of the *Hoover*, suggesting that the pack ice had, indeed, tumbled the tug and that it had sunk. This made the crew's decision to abandon ship seem quite sound. But, several days later a lake freighter reported seeing the *Hoover* floating in the eastern basin. The ship was retrieved and put back into service.

Lake Erie Adventures

1. Visit Gannon's Historical Museum on West Sixth Street in Erie and see the fishing exhibit.

2. Visit the Port Dover harbor and take a walking tour of the commercial docks. The Ontario Ministry of Fishing keeps an office at the Commercial Harbor which is open to the public.

3. The Pa. Fish Commission station at Fairview (off Route 5) is open to the public and features a fish spawning and stocking program as is the station at Walnut Creek (just east of Fairview and also on Route 5).

4. Ohio State maintains a field station with an interpretive program at Put-in Bay Ohio. This station includes live exhibits of each lake species.

5. In Erie, the Support our Native Species (SONS of Lake Erie) Organization maintains a volunteer hatchery program at the bay front near the water department which has public programs.

6. As you encounter commercial fish tugs try to distinguish between the trawlers and the gill netters (some tugs do both). Look for the A frames on the trawlers and the power net pullers (winches) on the gill netters.

7. Visit lower State Street in Erie and take a look at the remaining fishing fleet.

Smuggling: The Underground Railroad, Rum Running and Shopping

*T*here is no well-marked border line down the center of Lake Erie. Once a boat is 4 or 5 miles offshore, for all practical purposes, it is alone. There are no traffic cops, road signs, or customs officials. If it is engaged in something illegal, who would know? This is an entrepreneurial opportunity which has been utilized in a number of different ways over the years!

The general environment for the beginnings of "untaxed trade" was, in effect, created by the American War of Independence in 1776. It is a little-known fact that many people living in upstate New York and Pennsylvania were not in favor of the war against England. Some spoke out against the revolution. Others worked actively against it.

When the war ended, many of these people found themselves in delicate positions. They worried that their loyalty to England would be held against them. After the war, they were offered the opportunity to move to Canada as United Empire Loyalists (UEL's) and join in the development of Upper Canada (Ontario). They were offered plots of land for their trouble. Naturally, many of the UEL's from the Erie area moved to locations along the lake shore near Long Point.

Two political events created the circumstances which launched the first smuggling from Erie. First, Canadian UEL's were given the opportunity to return to America after their first 10 years in Ontario. Some of Ontario's UEL's felt they had overreacted by leaving the U.S. and returned to more familiar territory near Erie. This movement across the border and back created linkages between people which transcended politics. By the early 1800s, there were a number of former UEL's living in the Erie area who continued to have pro-British feelings. Second, John Simcoe, Governor of Upper Canada, was the first political leader in the new world to outlaw slavery. As a result, a number of black people left America as Loyalists and established free communities in Canada long before the American Civil War. Several of these groups located in Ontario (as well as the better known communities in the Maritimes).

These two political phenomena soon inspired two organized smuggling ventures. First, former UEL connections in the Long Point area stimulated wheat smuggling from Erie to Port Rowan during the War of 1812. Second, and later in the century, an underground railroad was developed in Erie which delivered runaway slaves to Port Royal and Southern Ontario.

WHEAT SMUGGLING DURING THE WAR OF 1812

The first smuggling took place during the War of 1812 and was a highly profitable venture for the purpose of supplying British military forces with wheat. Because of the connections between the two sides of the lake, which were caused by the earlier cross migration of UEL's, there were many farmers on the U.S. side of Lake Erie who were concerned about friends and relatives in southern Ontario. Most ordinary citizens had difficulty relating to the political issues of the war and were more concerned about friendships and business relationships than battles and military strategy.

The years preceding the War of 1812 happened to coincide with the beginnings of schooner trade and the commercial transport of goods such as wheat. Neither nation bordering the lake was prepared to deal with such issues as customs, international trade, or smuggling. As military buildups increased on the Canadian side of the Quadrangle, including both British regulars and the Canadian militia, the demand for food stuffs soon increased beyond the domestic capabilities of the north shore milling operations at Ports Dover, Rowan and Ryerse. The mills had excess capacity, but could not acquire the needed grains. To move supplies from eastern Canada would have required tremendous transportation efforts. Logically then, the best place to acquire grains and other supplies was from Erie. To make this trade desirable to American merchants, the military was willing to pay a premium price for their goods.

The preferred ports of entry for these early grain smugglers were Port Rowan, which could be accessed through the area near where the cut would later appear or Port Royal a few miles to the west (Figure 11-1). Schooner captains from Erie were able to make either sail in one tack. The return to Erie could also be made in a single tack, thus making it less obvious that they had been across the lake delivering a cargo of grain. Had the schooners attempted Port Dover, the return trip to Erie (after rounding the tip of Long Point) would have resulted in their ships not being able to sail high enough against the wind to reach port.

The destruction of Dover by Campbell added fuel to the ongoing smuggling operations between Erie and Ontario. The burning of the town and the absence of able-bodied men from their homes along the north shore sparked an organized mission to send wheat across the lake. Campbell was already receiving

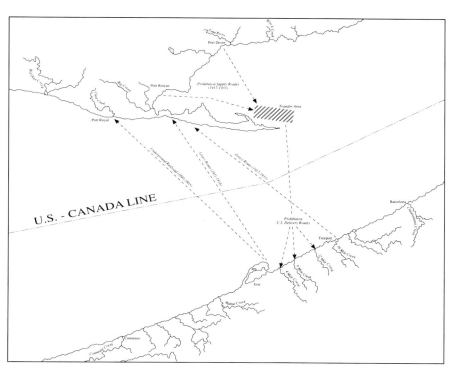

Figure 11-1
Smuggling Ports of call.

criticism from his superiors for his actions but he argued that the smuggling of wheat by American schooner merchants justified his attack of the mills. This attention was responsible for beginning the first military interdiction against smuggling on the lakes.

Naturally, this smuggling was considered an act of sedition by United States officials, but there was little concern among the participants, because of the frontier nature of the Pennsylvania coast. It was the dawn of the era of schooner trade on the lakes, and there was money to be made in the business. So, the first known smuggling system emerged. While Campbell and Perry sailed the lake looking for enemy troops, the farmers of the Erie area were feeding them.

THE UNDERGROUND RAILROAD

The history of Erie, Pa. is replete with tales of slaves being smuggled to Canada. There is more testimony from "elders" about these events than documented history. But, it is clear that Erie was an important termination point for the Underground Railroad. Legend has it that there were tunnels leading from the downtown areas near West Sixth Street to the bay front and public dock areas. There are testimonial reports of tunnels leading from the original Reed Mansion (now the Erie Club at Sixth and Peach) to the waterfront. Since the Reed family owned a steamship line, it seems entirely logical to presume that this was the case.

Ontario was, of course, a wonderful destination for blacks. Once there, they were taken in by black UEL communities that had been established in the Chatham area on land grant farms. The original black UEL's and the runaway blacks established a number of primarily black communities in southern Ontario in the days prior to the abolition of slavery in the U.S. Today's community of Dresden, Ontario is an example of this phenomena.

Because of the circuitous nature of the smuggling of the runaway slaves, it is unclear where they were put off in Canada. Testimonial evidence suggests that many were released at Port Royal (Figure 11-1) which is a few miles west of the base of Long Point and well removed from the prying eyes of authorities.

Even though it would seem to have been easier for runaways to cross the river near Detroit, the added land travel greatly increased the danger of apprehension. From Port Royal they made their way north toward Ingersoll where they were assisted by local church groups.

RUM RUNNING

After the Civil War ended and normal commerce resumed on Lake Erie, there was little interest in smuggling until Prohibition. As both the U.S. and Canada moved into those (1917 to 1933) exciting times, the lawmakers of the two countries inadvertently created a set of interacting regulations which sent entrepreneurs on both sides of Lake Erie into hyperactivity. On the U.S. side, even though it was illegal to purchase whiskey, there was a tremendous demand for the product. In Ontario, while it was illegal to purchase or drink alcohol without a prescription, it was entirely legal to manufacture and sell it. What an opportunity!

On both sides of the Lake Erie Quadrangle, entrepreneurs purchased, repaired, and built vessels for the express purpose of transporting whiskey. In the Port Dover and Port Rowan areas, boats regularly cleared customs with cargos of whiskey bound for Cuba, Venezuela, or Jamaica. (It was illegal to ship whiskey to the U.S.) These ships would leave the Canadian side for such foreign ports and return to harbor 12 hours later. And these were the relatively legitimate traders.

Others simply loaded fishing trawlers with untaxed whiskey. They set off on trips to the Outer Bay to fish and somehow transferred their cargos to waiting U.S. vessels. For the fishermen, this side business was a wonderful economic bonus. Clearly, the fishermen were well equipped to enter the smuggling business because of their knowledge of the lake. The Canadian vessels had to transfer their cargos to waiting American boats. Their favorite place along the whole of Lake Erie was Long Point, because of its secluded coves. It was approximately half way between Erie (a favorite port of entry) and the Canadian mainland, and remote from authorities on either shore.

By the middle of the Prohibition era, the waters between the Ports Dover & Rowan areas and Erie, Pa. had become a virtual highway for rum running. The authorities on both sides of the lake became increasingly wise to these practices, and to the involvement of fishermen. The challenges and risks grew. In Erie, the Coast Guard became aggressive in its enforcement efforts. They would take a cutter to Long Point and wait in hiding for Canadian vessels to appear. Then they would actually open fire as transfers were made between vessels.

Undaunted, the rum runners purchased faster, specialized speed boats (grey ghosts or no-names) for their purposes. Toward the end of the era the favored vessels were Jardines and Bancrofts in the 30 to 40 foot range. These boats could carry a big load and reach speeds of 40 to 45 miles per hour, easily leaving the big Coast Guard cutters in their wakes. Generally they were powered by one or two 500 horsepower Liberty Aircraft engines.

In Erie, boat builders began to receive winter contracts to produce special speed boats. The primary operating specification was that the boat had to be able to outrun the Erie Coast Guard Cutter. The lake lore of Erie has it that, once a rum runner made it through the channel unchallenged by the Coast Guard and tied up at the public pier, he was safe. The city officials had apparently seized the opportunity of the day by taking a cut. On today's east slip access to the public dock, there is a restaurant called "Smugglers." It is said that the rum runners would gather there to consummate deals after successfully negotiating the lake and avoiding the U.S. Coast Guard.

As the "heat" increased in and around Erie, activities moved to the beaches near Harborcreek and North East and to the Cascade docks at the west end of the bay. By the middle of the prohibition era, vast quantities of whiskey were being off-loaded at points along the shores east of Erie (six, eight and twelve mile creeks were favored areas). There is a famous story about an order of Catholic Sisters who operated a summer retreat and conference center on the lake shore near Harborcreek. A wonderfully generous man offered to be the caretaker during the 1920s at almost no salary. Somehow, during the prohibition era, that man became a millionaire. During his tenure, he was known to the sisters for his generosity in gifting them, from time to time, with bottles of whiskey (for medicinal purposes of course)!

The grey ghosts would pull close to shore near the appointed locations and use flashlights wrapped in carbon paper to send signals to shore. This system minimized the chance that the light could be spotted from far off. On the beach there would usually be four or five fast cars (Cadillac and Peerless were models of choice) with a driver and helper in each. Once the shore party had returned the signal the speedboats would

A grey ghost, armor-plated speed boat.

run as close to the beach as possible and the drivers worked furiously to transfer the load (before authorities could be alerted) either wading out to the speedboats or using row boats.

In Erie there was a well-known fisherman and dock builder named Joe Divel who owned hard hat diving gear which he used in his maintenance work. Like many others he became a deliverer during the era. His special tactic for outwitting the Coast Guard was to drop a cargo of whiskey overboard in one of several previously marked (by him) areas just before the cutter could catch up to him. He would return the next morning and dive for the "buried treasure." We interviewed a former assistant of his who worked with him the year before he entered the seminary to study for the priesthood. The ex-assistant told us how he learned sailor language one morning. The grizzled old salt and his soon to be young seminarian assistant trundled out to the sight of the loot and while keeping a watchful eye open for authorities descended to the floor of the bay. There was a strange and pungent odor to the water and within moments of the dive, worst suspicions were confirmed. The corks had failed!

Along with organized crime figures, a number of individuals on both sides of Lake Erie grew wealthy during Prohibition. In Port Dover, Port Rowan, and Erie there were many otherwise solid citizens who somehow became quite wealthy during those tumultuous years. The Canadians were primarily involved in manufacture and delivery (export), while the Americans specialized in receipt and marketing (import). Much of the sale of illegal spirits went on at speakeasies (such as The Dardanella Club on upper State Street, Murphy's on East Lake Road, and the Amber Club on Buffalo Road) which were common in both Erie and Harborcreek. In most cases friends and neighbors recognized these activities, but accepted them as entrepreneurial ventures. This was perhaps more true in Canada, where the act of selling was, itself, quite legal.

In the early 1970s, we sailed to Port Rowan and met an old timer fishing on the Port Rowan pier. He told us of how he had made quite a nice living as a youngster during rum running days. The latter days of the era were marked by the use of high-powered, armor-plated speedboats from Dover and Rowan. The U.S. Coast Guard would lie in wait along Long Point and fire at these boats as they offloaded to equally fast American boats. Because of their superior speed, the only dangerous time for the rum runners was when they were loading. The Coast Guard's best hope was to catch them behind Long Point in midst of a transfer. Most often, however, the participants would see the cutter and run. Frustrated, the Coast Guard would riddle the sides of their boats with machine gun fire as they escaped. The smugglers were unhurt as long as they kept their heads down inside their "grey ghosts."

The Coast Guard would return to Erie and call Canadian authorities on the evenings when they had actually shot up the side of a rum runner's boat. Canadian revenue agents would then make their way to the town harbors the next day, looking for boats with bullet holes. Our old timer friend told of the "gravy" days, when he and his young colleagues would walk the Dover and Rowan piers at dawn looking for bullet holes. They would then contract to repair them for 50 cents per hole. The only stipulation was that all repair work had to be finished before the police showed up!

By the late 1920s the activities of the rum runners on the U.S. side grew ugly and dangerous. First the Coast Guard began a practice of confiscating the grey ghosts on "suspicion." Any unnamed 30 to 40 foot speedboat with high powered engines would be summarily commandeered by the Erie Coast Guard and moored in Misery Bay. The rum runners were forced to hide their speedboats, often mooring them in Canadian ports. Next the guardsmen began to retrofit these no-names and use them to chase down the smugglers. Inspired by the potential of having their own grey ghosts, the Coast Guard concocted their best strategy yet. In what was to become the last straw for local smuggling, the Coast Guard commissioned its own special duty chase vessel. Under the command of Captain James Haglove, a 42 foot Jardine was launched and equipped with three 500 horse power Liberty engines. That ship was said to be capable of speeds in excess of 60 miles per hour. Haglove's mission was specifically to clean up rum running in the Erie area and he approached this challenge with abandon. He was, in effect, the "Elliot Ness" of Lake Erie. With his fast chase boat, capable of outrunning the smugglers and his absolute disregard for regulations and protocol, Haglove soon became a major obstacle in a once smooth delivery system. Captain Haglove used paid informers to gain information about delivery times, and commonly violated international rules by lying in wait for transfers near Long Point. He was even known to have taken boats into custody in Canadian waters. Most frightening was Harglove's no nonsense "ask first and then shoot" policy. He had no compunction about opening fire on the rum runners if they did not immediately surrender.

The City of Dresden.
GREAT LAKES HISTORICAL SOCIETY

Problems in the delivery systems and shortfalls in supply soon caused conflicts among the once cooperative onshore delivery gangs. By the 1930s they were hijacking each others loads, shooting each other and rapidly converting a once friendly and profitable "importing business" into an ongoing gang war which effected customers from Buffalo, to Pittsburgh and Cleveland.

The definitive prohibition story from the Quadrangle, however, is the sinking of the *City of Dresden* off the base of Long Point near Port Rowan on November 18, 1922. As the $65,000 worth of whiskey floated ashore townspeople gathered and "stored" it for safekeeping. The *Dresden* story has been told many times and is the subject of contemporary Corby's Whiskey advertisements. Townspeople still recall the many stories of how and where they hid the contraband as well as the exciting tales of the searches which were conducted by authorities for the next several days.

But there was tragedy connected to the *Dresden* as well. The 50 year old steamer was well past her prime and had been pressed into service to earn quick money running booze. To compound matters she was in the lake in November and had encountered a fierce storm that day. Even though the captain managed to reach the relative security of Long Point and the ship went down less than a half mile off shore, his son drowned in the mishap and the ship was a total loss.

LIGHTHOUSE KEEPER TALES

Throughout prohibition there were lighthouse keepers stationed at the tip of Long Point. For decades, these wonderfully friendly and helpful persons lived in quiet isolation at the tip of the Point, separated from the mainland by more than 25 miles. In addition to maintaining the integrity of the lighthouse, most of them saw themselves as guardians. They had a long standing tradition of being helpful to all boaters who happened by.

The prohibition era keepers told many smuggling tales. For them, the events of the day were melodramas played out on the stage of Lake Erie. The most common story was the "old broken engine routine." Thinking, perhaps, that the keepers were more naive than could be humanly possible, a Canadian deliverer or an American receiver would drive to within a few hundred yards of the lighthouse and drop anchor. The captain would then wade to shore and report engine trouble, asking to use the radio phone. After contacting a colleague from the other side of the lake, the captain would offer his gratitude, return to his ship and either wait to be met by another vessel, or drive off for a meeting in another location. In either event, the engines would somehow always seem to get repaired.

As interdiction increased, the keepers were on hand to watch the antics of both the Coast Guard as they tried to catch the smugglers, and the smugglers as they tried to avoid capture. It did not take long for the keepers to develop a sense of tactics from both "sides." One typical maneuver for the Canadians, who knew that they were about to "get caught," was to jettison the bags which held their whiskey in hopes that they could return to retrieve the cargo at a safer time. This was a common strategy for the fishermen who were doing smuggling as an adjunct, since there was no way that they could outrun the authorities.

Often, the keepers would keep track of these activities and help themselves to some of the jettisoned cargoes. Sometimes, the fishermen made this practice inviting and easy by marking the submerged whiskey, so that it would look to the untrained eye like a fish net marker buoy. Just as often, the jettisoned cargoes

The Inner Bay was a favorite place for staging illegal booze runs.

would break apart during storms and the lighthouse keepers could do their "shopping" for spirits by simply walking the beaches and keeping an eye open for floating bottles or crates.

The smuggling business was not always "good sport," however. In the summer of 1929, keeper Lorne Brown and his wife were walking the south beach behind the lighthouse when they spotted a floating object some 100 yards off shore. Thinking that it might be a keg of whiskey, Lorne swam out to investigate. To his shock he discovered a body clothed in a dark three piece suit, white shirt and tie (definitely not fishing wear) with three bullet holes. Apparently someone had crossed the wrong person!

MODERN DAY SMUGGLERS

The smuggling business calmed down after the repeal of Prohibition. Aside from the odd commercial fishing violation, there were few smuggling problems between Long Point and Erie until the 1970s. Again, the forces of enterprise presented business opportunities, and the wheels of illegal commerce turned.

In the early and mid-1970s, it became increasingly difficult to smuggle illegal drugs into the U.S through traditional southern routes. As the interdiction efforts of the U.S. Customs officials expanded, more drug traffickers began to select Canada as a port of entry. Naturally, the easiest way to move these goods into the U.S. was to take them across the unguarded parts of the border. Throughout the past two decades, there has been little or no interest in guarding the shores of Erie, Pa. or its surroundings from foreign incursion. This clearly makes the movement of illegal drugs from the north shore to the Erie area an attractive alternative.

It is unclear how much of this traffic went on during the past decades, but law enforcement officials at all levels have expressed concern. For a short time in the late 1970s, the Coast Guard Cutter *Ojibwe*, from Cleveland patrolled the lake off Erie in an attempt to create a visible presence.

By the middle 1980s, prices had shifted so dramatically in favor of U.S. goods (which were dramatically cheaper), that a new problem arose. Amateur smuggling, also known as unreported cross border shopping, became common. There had historically been a customs outpost at Port Dover, which had (over the 1970s and early 1980s) busied itself with the task of inspecting visiting American vessels. But when Canada passed its 7% goods and services tax (GST), it soon became apparent that the probable smugglers would now most likely be the innocent looking Canadians, who were steaming out of Port Dover or the Inner Bay en route for Erie and its discount stores. By filling the holds of their yachts with clothing, toiletries, and other small expensives, the typical Ontarian could gain a price advantage and also avoid both provincial tax and GST.

By the late 1980s, Canada Customs had undercover agents watching discount stores in Erie. These agents recorded the names of visiting Canadian yachts. They would then search the Canadian vessels as they returned from the U.S. As Canada Customs expanded these activities, more than a few Doverites were surprised by a sudden police visit following a holiday weekend in Erie.

Recent years have also seen some professional smuggling aimed at exploiting price differentials. The pros have been working in the areas of cigarettes and alcohol. Currently the "best" business opportunity is in cigarettes. A pack costs as much as $7.00 in Canada (as opposed to $2.00 in the states), thus creating a major opportunity. It has been estimated that approximately 30 percent of the cigarettes sold in Ontario are black market products that have been smuggled in to avoided taxes levied by Ontario. This may give new meaning to the term "cigarette boat."

The desolation of Long Point makes it a perfect place for illegal activities.

In the early 1980s, there was a boater and apparent modern smuggler in Port Rowan. He was said to be involved in selling American whiskey in and around town. It seems as though he was crossing the lake to Erie in a 38 foot cruiser, filling up, and then returning to Port Rowan in the Inner Bay, where there was no customs station. Both he and his boat disappeared one summer evening under mysterious circumstances. He was known to have rented space in a storage building east of Erie, Pa. He was also seen buying large quantities of alcohol at various state stores in Pennsylvania and New York. Witnesses saw him loading his boat one afternoon and heard him shove off to return to the Inner Bay late that same evening. But the boat was never seen again. Just one more mystery for the Lake Erie Quadrangle.

Lake Erie Adventures

1. Do some informal research about the Prohibition era. Look up your elderly friends and talk with them about rum running and speakeasies.

2. Try to find a Corby's Whiskey ad in a magazine with its popular description of the *City of Dresden* incident.

3. The next time you visit the Millcreek Mall pay attention to the number of Ontario license plates.

4. If you are from Ontario and you have not yet done so, plan a shopping trip but don't forget to declare your purchases when you return!

OTHER ADVENTURES:
SWIMMERS AND ICE WALKERS

*P*erhaps a better title for this chapter might have been, "Because It's There!" The relatively short distance between the tip of Long Point and Erie's Peninsula has captured the attention of several adventurers. Warm August nights and moonlit winter evenings alike have tempted them into thinking that such a short jaunt would be a simple matter. And, given exactly the correct conditions it could conceivably be. The problem, of course, is finding that one right day or night when the adventure is "scheduled" to happen.

Some have actually acted out their fantasies by attempting either a summer swim or a winter walk across Lake Erie. It should not be surprising that the bulk of these events have bisected the Quadrangle. This is clearly due to the fact that the distance here is the shortest across the central lake basin. In statute miles, a straight line trip from Long Point to Erie's Peninsula is only 27 miles. From the point to Harborcreek or North East is even closer (approximately 25 miles).

The adventure bug seems to have bitten more Americans than Canadians. Indeed, over the years it has been Americans who have made all of the attempted crossings. Perhaps Canadians are likely to think of the lake in terms of the distance between the mainlands (rather than the relatively short distance from Long Point) and regard the U.S. shore as being 50 or more miles away. Somehow, people from the U.S. side have a romantic notion that the Canadian mainland is just a few miles behind the tip of Long Point, and thus fail to understand the true nature of the undertaking.

There have probably been thousands of youngsters who dreamed about swimming or ice-walking the lake. They hop into the calm water at the beach and swim a mile on a warm summer day then find themselves harboring such fantasies: "If I can swim a mile, why not 10, or 20? Why not the lake?" A similar fantasy can occur on the ice. Someone walks across Erie's sheltered bay on a sunny February afternoon and realizes that they have just covered 3 miles. So why not 27?

There are more reasons "why not" than "why." But these reasons are not so obvious to those who don't understand the lake. Nor has reason dissuaded all of the potential adventurers. Over the years, a number of brave (or foolhardy) souls have defied logic and taken the plunge. They ignored the dangers, the risks of failure, the skeptics and the odds and simply did it!

THE SWIMMERS

The challenge of swimming Lake Erie has been touted for decades. No endurance trip has developed a more sinister reputation. Swimmers who have easily crossed the English Channel have stated that they would never attempt this stretch of water. Cold Lake Erie temperatures, coupled with less buoyant fresh water, and tricky unpredictable winds and strong currents have been too formidable a challenge for "outsiders." It was always clear that if a swimmer was ever to make it, he or she would probably be a local who could patiently wait for the optimum weather. Such a vigil could easily take two or three weeks, and requires having resources and support personnel poised and ready to go at a moment's notice.

With luck, a mid-August day might bring the essential combination of relatively warm water and flat seas needed to assist in the quest. It is equally possible, however, that a year or more might pass in which no such window of opportunity presents itself. Given the odds, who would attempt such a mission and how would they do it?

A study of past attempts to swim the lake reveals some important information for future swims. First, it is clear that the early swimmers and their coaches did not know enough about the lake or its navigation. In the 1960s, for example, a former great local high school swimmer named Mary Haffey began a series of failed attempts. On her first try, she departed Erie's Peninsula and set off for the tip of Long Point with a cadre of support boats and coaches. Mary may have been one of the most talented swimmers to try the swim, but any sailor could have told her that this course was foolhardy. How could she have expected to hit the tip of the Point from that angle? Given prevailing currents, she surely would have been thrown off course and driven to the east of the Point, where she would either face an up current swim back to the point, or an additional 20 mile trek to the Canadian mainland near Nanticoke.

Later, Mary's support crew came to the realization that they were doing things backwards. On their final attempt, they left Long Point and headed for the Peninsula. In retrospect, this was almost as flawed a plan because it was also an up-current swim aiming for a rather small target. Many Erie residents can still remember the heart breaking night of Mary's last attempt in the early 1960s. She had easily swum to within a few miles of Erie and reports were circulating that her success was imminent. She had missed the tip of the Peninsula, however, and was well east of her target. She found herself only 3 miles off Erie's east shoreline, but also 3 or 4 miles east of Presque Isle.

Her crew made a command level decision to have her swim toward the Peninsula, directly up current. After she had, in effect, swum in place for more than 2 hours, they reconsidered and headed directly for the east side of town, even though the landing would not be quite as glamorous. But about that time, the summer offshore breezes began to pipe up and Mary again found herself swimming into a 15 knot breeze. After a few hours of this, she was exhausted and had to be pulled from the water.

Mary Haffey had swum more than far enough and long enough to cross the lake on more than one occasion. On her last attempt, she was painfully close to land. For almost 5 hours, she swam first in one direction, then in another without making progress. Her failure to reach shore was heart breaking for the entire community. It was also a lesson for future swimmers.

Other swimmers, one of whom was 44 year old Alaskan college professor Harry Briggs (1965), made attempts over the years, but none of these received much attention. Nor did any of these attempts come close to success. In Briggs's case, for example, after much ballyhoo regarding his experience, conditioning and cold water adaptability, he was pulled from the water because of hypothermia. The inside story was that he was on a tight schedule and made the attempt far too early in the season to be able to take advantage of the short warm water window.

PAT BUDNEY AND TIM HUGHES

In 1975 two young YMCA lifeguards announced preparations for the swim. As locals, they had the advantage of being able to wait for the correct weather window. Their support team was also well aware of past attempts and the logistical problems of the crossing. That summer was a good one for the two youngsters. They were blessed with warm water and a relatively stable weather window in mid-August.

Using the most sophisticated navigational techniques yet, the two swimmers left Long Point on August the 19th, and headed for Erie. As they continued their swim, two important lessons were learned by the support crew. First, it was a mistake to try to have one support crew for two swimmers. In a distance event such as this, where elapsed times are extensive, and each swimmer will sooner or later experience physical difficulties, it is unrealistic to think that one swimmer can wait for another during delays. Each swimmer should be allowed to proceed at his own pace.

Sometime during the night, Budney became nauseous and had to stop to recover. Tim Hughes, who was feeling fine at the time and making great progress, was forced to stop and wait for his friend. After some time, Budney revived himself and got a second wind. Unfortunately, during the wait, Hughes began to experience hypothermia from the inactivity and started to gradually deteriorate. Less than two hours from shore, he was pulled from the water.

The second lesson was a familiar one. The navigational team had underestimated the current. The swimmers swam a long semicircle, completing the trip by heading up current from well east of the Peninsula. At 2:15 a.m. on August 20, Budney walked onto the beach and claimed victory over the lake. He had swum 26 1/2 hours to accomplish this feat and was greeted by accolades from the community and the press. The beach where he landed was ultimately named after him to honor the achievement.

The event was somewhat tainted by the fact that Tim Hughes, his friend and training partner, who had stopped swimming for almost an hour to offer encouragement, had not completed the journey. The crew realized that if their course had begun from a point several miles further west, along Long Point's south beaches, allowing the swimmers to drift directly down onto the Peninsula, or if there had been two support teams, both swimmers might have made it.

CAROL MALLON

A final lesson in logistics was learned by Gannon student Carol Mallon in 1986. A YMCA lifeguard and member of the Gannon swim team, Carol was clearly a talented distance swimmer. Harland Zeller, a Budney and Hughes coach saw Carol swimming miles and miles in the pool and began to have recurrent thoughts of the earlier swim. He talked to Carol about swimming the lake and learned of her "secret" fantasy. She had long dreamed of swimming Lake Erie and quickly made a pact with Zeller, her boss at the YMCA, to begin training.

Acting as Carol's coach and manager, Zeller understood the importance of navigation and came to Gannon for computer-based assistance. He was advised, at the onset, to aim for North East and to leave from the tip of the Long Point, but he dreamed of having Carol repeat the success of Budney, with better navigation. To facilitate this objective, current computations were recorded over several conditions, and a "best" departure point was calculated some 7 miles west of the tip of the Point.

Even with sophisticated navigation and Carol's immense talent for distance swimming, the attempt failed and taught a final important lesson. Carol's support team, which should have been independently managed, was inadequate. Zeller had lined up dozens of boats whose owners all expressed a willingness to help. But what these "volunteers" did not understand was that they would have to be prepared to drop everything at a moment's notice (regardless of other commitments) to leave with the swimmer when a window of opportunity presented itself.

When Carol's "best day" appeared on the weather maps, all but three of the volunteers were busy, out of town, or working. Of the three volunteer boats, one would not start, and the occupants of another became violently sea sick and had to return before the swim actually started. This left a small runabout, the navigation boat, and a canoe to tend to the swimmer. Within the first minutes of the trip, the canoe sunk and was lost (one more wreck off Long Point's south beaches) forcing the runabout to serve as tender. It soon became apparent that the runabout would not have enough fuel.

Even though the weather turned out to be ideal for that swim, and Carol was making great progress and in excellent spirits, the swim was terminated after some 8 hours. A decision was made to pull the swimmer before she used too much energy and to return after a few days with more support vessels. Unfortunately, the lake had some other ideas. That weekend, there was a severe northeasterly blow which stirred up the lake's surface, cooling water temperatures by almost 5 degrees. Carol returned the next week to make a renewed attempt with more than adequate support, but she had missed the window of temperature opportunity. The water was too cold, and a discouraged young swimmer was pulled out of the water after several hours.

BOB NORTH AND HARVEY SNELL

In 1989 Bob North, an MBA student from Gannon and a teacher/swim coach from Iroquois High School, decided to attempt the swim. Bob had pondered the challenge for years, but had never found the energy or the time to invest in the project. Over the few years before the swim, Bob had met and talked with Harvey Snell while the two were training for Erie's Quad games. At 35 years old, Bob had been surprised to learn of his prowess at master's level competition. He had not swum competitively since college, but the training which he had done for amateur events had shown that his skills and endurance were as good as ever.

Bob's advantage over previous swimmers was his graduate school training in business. He immediately took charge of his own programs of planning and training, and he treated the overall goal of swimming the lake much like an executive would approach project management. He did research to learn why previous attempts failed. In his investigation, he immediately learned of the weaknesses of previous attempts and sought expert advice in all appropriate areas. He then divided the problem into sub-problems and found experts to help with each specialized area. Harvey Snell brought an incredible ferocity for training to the project. Those who have known

Bob North and Harvey Snell leaving Long Point.
BOB NORTH

him have always been astounded at his ability to focus on a training objective and to discipline himself to work for physical goals. Once Bob committed to Harvey he was off on a training roller coaster ride.

From the experiences of long distance swimmers the world over, and failures on Lake Erie, Bob and Harvey extracted nine problem areas:

1. Navigation … he utilized Gannon University and its computer resources to create a navigational program which would predict currents given short term weather conditions.

2. Support … a number of large boat owners were contacted and committed to make their vessels available to the project on a moment's notice basis. There would be adequate numbers to provide separate support teams for each swimmer.

3. Weather … Erie's Channel 35 and its weather staff agreed to work with Bob to help identify the best possible window of weather opportunity.

4. Supervision … In perhaps the most innovative component, the local Kayak club agreed to provide continuous physical supervision for the swimmers, paddling within a few feet of them, maintaining course and pacing.

5. Nutrition and Hypothermia … were treated as a pair of connected problems and were taken on by Saint Vincent Health Center. Rather than eating candy and potato chips as earlier swimmers had done, a sophisticated system of fluid replacement was designed and the fluids were heated to help fight hypothermia.

6. Psychology … the swimmers used a sports psychologist to assist them with positive imagery.

7. Training … Physical therapists, and a Saint Vincent Health Center pulmonary specialist (Dr. Ed Overfield) were used to balance aerobic with orthopedic fitness during the training period.

8. Course and Destination … Bob elected to leave the tip of Long Point and aim for the shortest possible cross-lake distance, which is North East's Freeport Beach. The plan, however, was to be flexible with regard to destination, and to adjust to the east or west if winds shifted appropriately.

9. Timing … Departure time from Long Point was calculated to miss the predictable mid-August offshore winds on arrival at the U.S. side of the lake but take advantage of offshores from the Canadian side.

For more than six months, Bob and Harvey carried on their physical training as they worked systematically through the nine problem areas. As the time of the swim approached, tensions were high. Bob had aggravated an earlier injury and was experiencing shoulder pain as he trained. It was necessary for him to slow his training cycle and to do physical therapy as August approached. It was here that the camaraderie between the two and Harvey Snell's iron will took over, propelling Bob to continue. More worrisome was the weather. That summer, the water was not warming up as rapidly as usual. It was becoming obvious that the swimmers were going to have to cope with colder than optimum water temperatures, and would have a smaller than average window of weather opportunity.

Bob North with kayak escort.
BOB NORTH

Statistically speaking, there is quite a small expected window of opportunity for a lake swim. Historical data suggests that the only dependable time is from the final week of July through the second week of August. Earlier in July the water is too cold. After the second week of August, the winds are likely to pick up again, making a crossing almost impossible. The trick is to avoid the temptation to leave too early (cold water) without waiting too long. Toward the end of the month, (as was the case with Carol Mallon) the waters cool down again, and (even worse) the winds increase.

After several frustrating "almost goes," a weather opportunity presented itself on Saturday, August 12. Amidst media fanfare, a large flotilla of support boats set off for Long Point. This attempt had everything going for it, thanks to the dedicated effort and Bob's year of project management. There was sophisticated navigation, including Loran and Radar (a first for this swim). In addition, there was medical supervision, sophisticated nutrition, and other amenities. Perhaps most important was the spirit of adventure, enthusiasm, and involvement which had evolved as a result of the support crew and their work. Support crew members later reported that the overall experience had been one of the most exciting and meaningful events of their lives! Bob and Harvey stepped into the water near the tip of the Point at 6:30 p.m. and set off on a historic swim, clearly the most sophisticated effort to date.

Problems beset Bob after several hours. His shoulder injury began to act up. Realizing that he might be able to lessen the strain on his aching joint by changing pace, he quickened his strokes. This strategy seemed to help. He began to feel more comfortable with the nagging pain, and, at the same time, started to lengthen the distance between himself and Harvey Snell. Harvey was a self taught swimmer who came to distance swimming as a necessary part of triathlon training. He was a tremendous athlete, but, he did not have Bob's skill in the water.

Later, Bob began to feel cold. Even though he was receiving a warm replacement drink every half hour, he recognized the oncoming symptoms of hypothermia. He approached this dilemma as he had the sore shoulder. He sped up his pace again. He reasoned (correctly) that swimming faster would warm him up. As Bob pounded his way toward the beaches of North East, it became apparent that the predictions regarding his arrival time were wildly incorrect. He was swimming almost 25 percent faster than he had projected, and this posed the evening's most serious problem.

The crisis occurred when Bob ran directly into the predicted offshore winds that his navigational team had so carefully sought to avoid. The plan had been for Bob to approach the final 5 miles with the sun rising and the evening offshores calming. This would remove the up wind difficulty (which Mary Haffey had faced) and add the bonus of the warming morning sun. Instead, his increased pace brought him to the 5 mile mark with a 15 mile per hour off-shore wind piping and whitecaps driving him directly offshore.

But Bob was not to be denied. Realizing how close he was he quickened his pace again and drove through 5 miles of head winds and waves to the beach at Freeport. He landed at 7:17 a.m., August 13, shattering the Budney's record by more than 13 hours and demonstrating the value of his project management training. Snell, also swimming at a faster than predicted pace, landed 2 hours later and joined the exuberant North and the support teams. It should be noted that if Bob's pace had been predicted more reliably (missing the off-shore winds) he would have easily completed the swim an hour or so faster.

In any event, Bob and Harry's swim was a success. Perhaps it was a testament to modern technology and planning. As he sat on one of the support boats cheering the swimmers on, Tim Hughes marveled at the relative ease of this swim and the sophistication which was not available for his attempt. He must still have dreams of what might have happened had that support system been available to him. When asked later if he would do it again, Bob North made a simple comment, "This is the kind of thing that you do just once in a lifetime!"

HALLI REID

When we interviewed Bob North for this chapter he told us of a protege who was training for a 1993 attempt. Halli Reid is a 24 year old swimmer from North East who had dreamed for years about the lake swim. Inspired by Bob North's accomplishments she asked him for technical and coaching assistance in her quest. Halli had actually hoped to make the swim in 1992, but she was frustrated by the weather. That year was one of the (not so rare) weather anomalies. There was no window of opportunity for a swim.

Undaunted she trained for another year and was finally able to make her attempt on August 8th, 1993. Using Bob North's pioneering swim technology, Halli left Long Point at 5:15 p.m. and stepped onto the beach at Freeport the following morning at 10:28.

Bob North on the beaches at Freeport.
BOB NORTH

ICE WALKERS

Ice walking is also a weather related activity. To hike across the lake's frozen surface, one needs ice and lots of it. There are years when the center of the lake never freezes over. There are other years when the central basin freezes over but the ice thicknesses are inadequate. And then there are the "old fashioned" winters that our grandparents always seem to recall. These are the years when temperatures drop well below freezing and remain there for several weeks in a row. Given the right year, there can be 2 to 3 feet of solid ice across the entire central basin. During these years, and only these years, a well prepared ice walker can (theoretically) walk the distance from the U.S. shore to Long Point in relative safety.

In non-theoretical fact, there are some major problems. First, there is always the danger of encountering a soft spot or hole in the ice. A prudent ice walker must be equipped and prepared to extricate him or herself from the water and then to change to dry clothing to avoid hypothermia. This requires equipment and training. A second problem is that open lake ice is not flat. It is a wind and current driven system of pressure ridges and mounds which must be climbed or avoided. This makes an apparent 27 mile walk a 50 miler with ups and downs. This kind of distance is difficult, if not impossible, to accomplish in a single day carrying equipment. The walker is left with a difficult decision. The walk might be possible in a single day if equipment is excluded. For the cautious (and prudent), equipment needs change the trip to a 2 or 3 day adventure on open ice.

Another practical problem is the desolation of the Long Point area in the winter. Even in the days of lighthouse keepers, there was no one on duty in the winter. In effect, this leaves the successful ice walker stranded at the tip of the Point with no food or shelter. He can either turn around and go back the way he came, or set off on another open ice walk across the Outer Bay for Port Dover (20 additional miles).

Walter Shaw walking the ice in 1977.
ERIE COUNTY HISTORICAL SOCIETY

Greulich taking a lunch break on the first day out.
BILL GREULICH

The first recorded walker was 19 year old Walter Lick, who accomplished the feat empty handed in 1912. There were few pressure ridges that year. Lick was able to make the journey from North East in (probably) a record time of 12 hours. Naive as he was, he strode up to the lighthouse keeper's house and knocked. By great fortune, the keeper just happened to be there that weekend doing repair work. He was astounded to open the door and find young Walter inquiring about the distance to Port Rowan. Bill Porritt, the keeper, convinced Lick to spend the evening before sending him along the beaches to Port Rowan the next day. As Lick approached Port Rowan, he fell through the ice in a spot where ice was being harvested for the summer season.

In 1963 Walter Heuser of Harborcreek repeated Lick's adventure. Traveling with only a lunch and a hickory stick, Heuser needed 24 hours to complete his journey. That year was a worse one for pressure ridges, and the most frustrating part of the journey was encountering open water near the tip of the Point. Heuser estimated that with his goal in sight, he had to walk a 10 mile circle to the west to avoid the current driven open waters near the tip of the Point. He was later quoted as saying that he would have turned back if he had not been exhausted and out of food. Most fortunately for Heuser, he stumbled into a research team from the Ministry of Natural Resources which was gathering data along the south beaches. He was taken to the keeper's house, where again (fortunately) Clayton Scofield had just arrived to do some work. Later, he was given a Jeep ride to Port Rowan, narrowly avoiding a night's exposure on the Point after his long walk.

THE CRAZY ICEMEN OF 1977

The winter of 1977 was amazingly cold. Perhaps it was cabin fever, but within a week that year there were four attempts to cross the ice. Perhaps the most infamous ice walkers were Bill Greulich and Ron Pirrello, Gannon students who completed the trek on Wednesday, February 23, 1977. Their (successful) walk began two days before Walter Shaw began his walk from Lawrence Park. Unlike Shaw, however, Bill and Ron were prepared for a long term trek and had left with a toboggan, a tent, sleeping bags and supplies. On the Tuesday that Shaw left, Craig Latimer and John Zeisenheim also set off from Girard.

Many who knew Greulich, or have heard his exploits described in taverns (on both sides of the lake) considered him to have been a bit cavalier. In fact, he had planned the trip carefully and was taking a substantially smaller risk than the other adventurers. It had been 20 degrees or less with two long cold spells of sub freezing weather that year. Greulich knew that there was 2 to 3 feet of ice on the lake. On the weekend prior to his walk, he had a friend with a private plane fly him across the lake so that he could scout for open water and judge the heights of the pressure ridges. His flight assured him that the lake was frozen solid. On the negative side, he could see pressure ridges which he judged to be 20 feet in height. He realized that the trip could not be made in one day. Prudence would require overnight camping with equipment.

Undaunted, Greulich and two companions left the Public Dock at 8:00 a.m. on Sunday morning, February 13, towing a toboggan loaded with food and equipment. The trip was uneventful for the first 25 minutes. On their way out of the channel, however, his two companions fell through the ice and had to be rescued. Soaking wet, they sought the shelter of the Coast Guard Station. They returned to Erie to rethink their strategy. That day was a busy one for the Coast Guard since they were called upon to rescue Brian Kinal and Bob Bliss who began an attempt the same day.

The next Sunday, at 8:00 a.m. Greulich and Pirrello set off again. This time, they pulled a smaller sled and took a short cut across the Peninsula to avoid the soft ice in the channel. Greulich's account of the rest of the trip can take almost as long as the trip itself, depending upon the mood and timing of the story. It is clear to any listener, however, that it was a wonderful adventure; the kind of life shaking event that stays in memory forever. To the novice ice walker, it may come as a surprise that once the first pressure ridge is crossed, some 4 or 5 miles off shore, the landscape is, as Mike puts it, "like walking on the moon." There are no clear horizon lines—only a compass bearing to the next ice ridge. And, each ridge line is a new challenge to be climbed or skirted. The pace of the trip that particular year was walk a mile, climb a pressure ridge, drag the equipment over the top, etc.

After a few hours of walking, the adventurers were clearly in the midst of a beautiful, if not surreal, place—a place where no one had ever been before or would likely ever be again. They spent their first night in the center (as best they could calculate) of the lake in a tent trying to sleep. It was freezing cold, and they felt like continuing, but they were not fully confident of their compass course and did not want to risk getting lost at night. Fortunately, the evening was crystal clear and the north star appeared, helping to affirm their location.

Refreshed, they continued the next morning and easily made shore near the tip of Long Point, where they camped the second evening. On the third day, they started across the Outer Bay for Port Dover, but somehow changed their minds about another open ice crossing, which would have been almost as long as the trip to Long Point. Instead, they doubled back to the security of Long Point and followed the north beaches to the Inner Bay where they planned to cross to the mainland. Progress was slow, however, and they stopped for a third night, making use of a keeper's cabin for warmth and shelter.

On Wednesday morning Greulich and Pirrello walked across the relatively flat ice of the Inner Bay and came ashore at Normandale, where they encountered a woman hanging laundry. She immediately knew who they were, since a search operation had been launched the day before. It seems that the Coast Guard, after "rescuing" two of the crossing parties from the ice near Long Point, had learned that Greulich and his companion (the very same people who had entered their station the previous week soaking wet and seeking shelter) were out three days and overdue. Bill had seen helicopters from time to time but, they were over the central part of the lake and he did not know of the excitement caused by the other walks to the lighthouse. But, the people at Normandale had been listening to the news, and to them the landing of the American "ice men" was an exciting event in an otherwise dull winter.

Before they knew what was happening, Greulich and Pirrello were whisked away to Simcoe where they became town celebrities. Everyone wanted to meet the crazy Americans and buy them a beer. They did not realize the agitation that they had inadvertently caused until they returned to Erie a few days later.

Greulich and Pirrello landing at Normandale.
BILL GREULICH

THE OTHER 1977 ATTEMPTS

Unbeknownst to Greulich and Pirrello two other attempts were occurring while they were en route. They both began on the Tuesday after their second departure. Walter Shaw, a 72 year old Great Lakes sailor, left his home in Lawrence Park with only a lunch and a stick, leaving word for his wife that he had gone to cross the lake. Shaw's wife, upon learning of her husbands absence, called the Coast Guard who dispatched a helicopter to look for him. Early in the day the Millcreek Emergency Helicopter spotted Shaw and landed next to him. Walter reported that he was doing fine and continued his walk. Later in the day, however, a Coast Guard helicopter spotted him and landed to reason with him about returning home with them. Shaw agreed when Coast Guard helicopter personnel assured him that there was no one at the Long Point light and that he could die of exposure out there.

The Sunday that Greulich and Pirrello left, Craig Latimer was having a few beers with his friend and landlord John Ziesenheim at John's Girard home overlooking the lake. John told Craig how he had dreamed of walking across the lake since he was a child and the two made a pact to try the trip that week. On Tuesday at 6:00 a.m., the pair left John's home, walked down Godfrey Run and began their trek across the lake with minimal food, two compasses, a sleeping bag, and sticks.

Unaware of the fact that by this time the Coast Guard was disgruntled and frantically looking for Greulich, Pirrello and Shaw, John and Craig climbed the pressure ridges west of Presque Isle and descended to a relatively smooth central lake basin. They told their wives that if it looked possible after a few hours, they would continue and that they expected the trip to take some 12 hours. Elated at the relatively flat surface of the middle part of the lake, they resolved in the beautiful dawn of the new day to go the distance. Their exuberance was soon dampened when, by mid-afternoon, they could not spot the opposite shore. They began to realize that they may have misjudged the distance and that they were in for a longer walk than they planned.

About this time, they began to see the helicopters and C-130 cargo planes which were looking for Greulich and Pirrello. The Coast Guard was flying patterns well to the east, however, and did not spot Craig and John as they moved toward the western base of Long Point. As darkness fell that night, the pair was just reaching the northern pressure ridges. It was a cloudy night with almost no natural light and climbing the ridges was difficult and dangerous. But, both men were exhausted but realized that they had to press on rather than risk falling asleep and freezing to death. At midnight they finally saw lights on the north shore. They continued, realizing that their wives would be panicked since they were more than 6 hours overdue.

At 2:00 a.m. on the morning of February 23, Craig and John stepped on shore at Long Point (the cottage community) only to learn that there is no one at home in February. There were no lights, no cars, no people. Exhausted, they found the road which leads from the provincial park to the causeway and began walking west. As they continued, they realized that their best hope might be to break into a cottage and seek shelter from the bitter cold.

As they were picking a target, they noticed a single cottage with a light. There was a car in the driveway! By an incredible stroke of luck a lone cottager had been working on his property and decided to stay overnight. Unhappy as he was to answer the bell at 3:00 a.m., the cottager called the police who escorted the tired walkers to a hotel for the night.

Postscript

Just in case our readers have gotten the wrong idea, we feel compelled to say, "Don't try this!" We feel equally sure that the authorities on both sides of the lake would echo this advice. One new problem with an ice walk is the increased thermal activity at the Nanticoke Power Generating station. Now that this plant is up and running at capacity, it has had a dramatic effect on water temperature. Many feel that Ontario Hydro is the cause of the open water winters which have allowed commercial fishing to continue throughout the winter in the Outer Bay and beyond for most of the past decade.

As if to send a message to would be adventurers, a group of ice walkers who apparently wanted to try to set a record were greeted with a stiff fine as a result of their efforts the next year. A threesome from Erie was driven to Port Rowan in the winter of 1978, where they were taken by jeep to the tip of the Point and then walked the somewhat shorter distance to North East (the route of Bob North's swim). After the accolades and media attention had calmed down, they were issued citations by the U.S. Customs Department for failure to properly report back to the U.S. after visiting Canada. This was clearly a case of bureaucracy trying to save future ice walkers from themselves.

Lake Erie Adventures

1. Wait for the dead of winter and take an ice walk. Be sure that the ice is thick enough and stay in the bay area close to shore and fishermen who can help if you have any trouble. About an hour should be enough to convince a reasonable person not to try a long distance trek.

2. Go to your favorite swimming pool and do some laps. While you swim you can dream about swimming the lake. Then take a shower and go home.

Yachting and
The Erie-Dover Tradition

T he two city relationship has been fueled by boating friendships since the 1800s. Early on, it was the fishermen who visited each other on opposite sides of the lake. Later, it was excursion ferry traffic which brought the cities together. In the 1920s, bands from each city would regularly reciprocate on the first weekend of July by celebrating Canada Day in Dover and the 4th of July in Erie. But since the end of World War II, it has been the pleasure boating community which has bonded Port Dover with Erie.

Sailors and motor boaters alike have regularly made the trip across the "pond." It has become a boating tradition to take vacation trips, weekend holidays and other excursions across the center of the Quadrangle. For Erie's pleasure boating community, Port Dover has been a favorite destination since the turn of the century. Sailors find the cross-lake trip an easy one-day voyage because the winds and currents make the trip to Long Point, and then into Dover, an easy one-tack sail. For motor boaters, all that is needed to cross the lake to Long Point is a relatively short period of flat water.

In addition to the allure of the relatively short trip across the lake, the mystery and charm of reaching a "foreign" country enhances the trip. For Canadians, who spend considerable time watching Erie TV (and Millcreek Mall commercials), Erie is an equally exciting destination. In both cases, the yachting community always seems to extend itself to visiting boaters by offering rides, directions, friendly advice, and other hospitality.

Canadians who visit Erie can choose between three Yacht Clubs and or anchor in the quiet of the Presque Isle Marina. Many Erieites would be surprised to hear accounts of two week vacations spent by Canadian sailors entirely within the confines of Erie's Bay (with side trips to shopping malls, restaurants, and theaters). The opportunities on the Canadian side are equally delightful. Visiting U.S. boaters can anchor at Long Point or Pottohawk, visit Port Dover's Yacht Club and marinas, and take a trip into the Inner Bay.

During summer months, there is a constant stream of pleasure boat traffic between Erie's harbor and the tip of Long Point. Even in the absence of navigational equipment, it is generally a simple matter to judge one's course by comparing it to the courses of other vessels traveling the corridor between the tip of the Point and the Erie channel light.

THE ADVENT OF PLEASURE BOATING

In some ways, it was the decline of the schooners during the late 1800s which paved the way to today's pleasure boating community. The many woodworkers who contributed to schooner building needed a new way to make a living and to apply their boat building expertise. The era of the 1890s, with its great prosperity, led to an interest in the building of pleasure yachts. Many individuals already owned small rowing boats (some of which carried sailing rigs). These were relatively easy to build and did not need to be of great quality, since they generally operated near shore. Modeled after the rowing dories of commercial and military ships, these privately owned rowing prams began to appear in the mid-1800s for recreation, fishing, and transport.

As the victorian period began, more and more families were attracted to the beautiful waters of Lake Erie. People began to have free time for recreation and the water was a natural magnet. The upper class tended to use private boats for pleasure, rowing or sailing them just for the fun of it. The working class was more pragmatic, acquiring and using small boats for fishing to augment the family food supply. By the turn of the century in Erie, there were boat rental agents offering rowboats or small sailboats for lease during the summertime. Along the bay front in Erie there was a rush to establish boathouses, which working class families used for fishing equipment and boats. Similar boathouses appeared near Port Rowan, Long Point, and Port Dover. Often, a group or club would share expenses and maintenance duties of a single boathouse.

As the turn of the century demand for pleasure boats grew, some of the traditional schooner builders adapted their operations and began to build sailboats and rowing prams for private use. It was becoming apparent that the recreational boat industry might exceed the old schooner building businesses as a source of revenue. Many builders, for example Paasch in Erie, were active in both businesses. They created commercial vessels such as fish tugs and work boats, as well as wooden sailboats built to customer orders.

By the late 1800s, a number of wealthy individuals in Cleveland, Buffalo, Sandusky, and Detroit had commissioned sailing vessels for the purpose of racing, which were almost as large as earlier commercial schooners. Sailboat racing (yachting) began to grow in popularity. Races were held locally and along the lakes in these recreational creations of the schooner builders. There was competition among builders to develop a reputation for designing the fastest sailing vessel.

Dave Bierig's Anemonie, a 1953 Paasch creation looks as beautiful today as she did 40 years ago.

The recreational boating industry grew rapidly after World War I, when economic boom times reappeared and the gasoline engine was adapted to marine use. Small boat builders along the lakes began to turn out reasonably priced motor boats. These boats were attractive to the working class and held the promise of both pleasure boating and efficient fishing. For the first time, national companies such as Chris Craft appeared. They offered lines of recreational power boats for the general public. Power boat racing in sleek speedboats with modified airplane engines began to appear throughout the country, capturing the attention of the general public. Motor yachts of substantial size also appeared. These appealed to yachtsmen who did not wish the expense or agitation of commissioning and crewing a large sailing vessel. The expertise of the Great Lakes schooner builders energized the growth of an entire new industry which grew faster and faster until the Depression years.

The Depression's short glitch in the growth of pleasure boating did not really effect the builders. In most cases, the small builders were able to redirect their interests to the repair and maintenance of commercial vessels such as fish tugs or the "special order" craft which were in demand during the latter years of prohibition.

The 1950s ushered in a new growth spurt for the recreational boat business, but ultimately began the end of the era of wooden boat building. During that decade, as North Americans became enthralled with the notion of boat ownership, they simultaneously became disenfranchised with the work involved in maintaining the traditional wooden boat. By the mid-1960s, it had become clear that the future of the industry would lie in the production of fiberglass boats. Plastics promised low maintenance boats which might last indefinitely and could be built at a lower cost than traditional wooden craft. In addition, the fine woodworking skills previously needed for the "woodies" were not required. As the 1970s rolled along, boat builders sprang up all over the country and entered the glass boat market. Regional builders such as MFG in Union City soon developed reputations for producing quality boats at a reasonable price. Many of these manufacturers offered both sailing and motor boats and produced a variety of trailerable models. Trailer boating opened the market to consumers who could store boats in garages and driveways and use them when the spirit moved them. Fiberglass boats brought hoards of new boaters into the market in both the sailing and power boat businesses.

By the mid-1970s, fiberglass builders had abandoned the limiting traditional wooden designs. The new "plastic" boats offered more space per water line length than the old woodies (with rib structures). This innovation soon caused consumers to become interested in larger boats and gave rise to an increase in the demand for what was heretofore considered a large yacht. Slowly, the old wooden sailing and motor yachts passed away. Boat yards began to fill with plastic 25 to 40 footers. As traditionalists grumbled, a new generation of boaters happily indebted themselves to own these modern, care free yachts. Class boat sailing (especially the old woodies like stars and lightnings) declined as the rush to own bigger and better yachts evolved.

By the mid-1980s, the escalation of growth in the boating business was almost unbelievable. In both the Erie and the Long Point areas, new marinas sprang into existence and thousands of new docks appeared. It seemed clear that recreational boating and its peripherals would replace the traditional marine industries, commercial fishing, and freight. But trouble was on the horizon for the emergent recreational boat industry. First, the glass boats seemed to last forever. With reasonable care, most 30, or 40 year old glass boats still seemed to be as "good as new." In terms of the market for boats, this meant that the marine industry was quite different from automobile industry (after which it had been originally

ILYA Fleet ghosts through the Erie channel at dawn.
Photo by BARRY HAZLETT

patterned). Used boats never seem to disappear. They just keep on competing with the new ones that are being produced. By the mid-1980s, boat manufacturers began to face the fact that the used market was their number one competitor. The boat market was so absolutely unique that literally no one in the business understood it.

Economic factors also appeared in the 1980s to trouble the growth of the marine industry. First was the escalation of petroleum costs. As the primary material in a fiberglass boat, rising fuel costs quickly drove prices of boats up. To exacerbate these costs, environmental awareness grew, and producers began to fully understand the dangers (to workers) in the lay up process of fiberglass hulls. Work place protection quickly drove costs even higher. The final economic blow to the industry was a combination of the "bad" economy of the late 1980s and the declining demographics of the purchasing market segment. By the early 1990s, the industry had faltered. Boat manufacturers who had dominated the business, like C & C Yachts in Niagara on the Lake, went bankrupt, followed by dealers, brokers, suppliers and others.

THE YACHT CLUBS

The glue which has historically cemented recreational boating through good times and bad has been the yacht club. Throughout the Great Lakes, clubs of boaters began to emerge near the turn of the century. Unlike commercial marina businesses, which came and went in various locations (depending upon the business environment of the time), yacht clubs were comprised of individuals whose interests in boating were long term and intense. Although the early yacht clubs began with a primary interest in sailing, the common agendas of sailors and powerboaters have always knit members together into a powerful force. Yacht clubs have traditionally directed their corporate energies toward the establishment of boating facilities, ongoing programs to enhance knowledge and safety, and the encouragement of legislation which improves water access for the general public.

The preeminent clubs within the Quadrangle include the Erie Yacht Club (1895), on the U.S. side, and the Port Dover Yacht Club (1905 and 1946) on the north shore. Both had their origins in the Inter Lake Yachting Association (ILYA), which was formed in the early 1880s to encourage and stimulate sailboat racing. ILYA members from Buffalo, Cleveland, Sandusky, and Detroit were already involved in sailboat racing and were interested in a central location which could be utilized in Lake Erie circuit racing.

Erie Yacht Club.

ILYA members were connected to Erie by virtue of the Buffalo yacht *Corsair*, which had been brought to Erie in 1879 and regularly participated in Lake Erie Races. Her owner F.H. Ball was quite successful. He raced the 30 foot schooner and was a member of Erie's first boating club "The Undine," which failed in the 1880s. Fellow Erie Sailor E.O. Beigler also had considerable success racing his yacht, the *Wanderer* and worked with Ball to interest the ILYA in Erie.

In 1894, a contingent of yachtsmen led by George Bliss founded EYC at the foot of Myrtle. The facilities opened on July 4, 1895 and immediately became a sanctioned station of the ILYA. The early club (like other yachting clubs) was quite an elite operation. Sailing and private schooner ownership was essentially the domain of the wealthy. In the early 1900s, the gasoline launch became popular,

Port Dover Yacht Club.

diffusing interest in sailing and threatening the stability of the club. The gas launch reduced the costs of boating so that working class individuals could participate. Subsequently, the launch made it difficult for the yacht racers to attract the scores of crew members needed to commission and race large yachts.

After some financial difficulties, the Erie Yacht Club emerged with a bit of a different look. The club had incorporated many more power boats and had taken on a less elite air. In 1917, EYC moved from Myrtle Street to its present location at the west end of the bay. After another brush with financial difficulty during the Depression, the club blossomed into one of the finest yacht clubs on the Great Lakes, with first class docks and a luxurious clubhouse. Today's EYC remains an important ILYA station, sponsors sailing education, and classes, and runs a number of sailing regattas each year featuring everything from the tiniest class boats to national level MORCY (Midget Ocean Racing Yacht) competitions.

The forces which encouraged the development of EYC also stimulated the creation of the Port Dover Yacht Club (PDYC). The first PDYC was formed in 1905 for the express purpose of yacht racing. Records are a bit unclear, but it seems that many of the early PDYC members were fishermen who raced their sail powered fishing boats. Others were well-to-do Port Dover residents who had purchased sail powered fishing boats after the trend to steam tugs had begun.

PDYC fell into disuse at about the same time that the Erie Yacht Club was experiencing difficulties on the south side of the lake. In 1938, George Gamble spearheaded a movement to rekindle interest in the club, and for the next few years winter meetings were held to organize and find a suitable location. In

1945, eleven members each put $50 toward the purchase of a plot of creek-side land from Kolbe Fishing Company. A charter was granted by Ontario on March 23, 1946. The first dock was constructed that same year.

PDYC had its share of economic problems in the early years. But the members were "roll up your sleeves and do it types" and they gradually built the club with sweat equity. In 1947, a small church was purchased and moved into place for a clubhouse by Harry Gamble. A channel to the club was excavated shortly thereafter.

Interestingly, members of the Erie Yacht Club took a great interest in progress at PDYC. They were anxious to have a reciprocating club in Port Dover. In the early 1950s, PDYC created a special membership class for U.S. boaters who had made a significant contribution to the growth of their club. Today's PDYC, while smaller than the Erie Yacht Club, is one of the most picturesque facilities on the lakes. It is located north of the lake along the banks of a sheltered tree lined creek. PDYC is currently an ILYA member and participates in the traditional sailboat racing circuits.

There are four additional Yacht Clubs in the Quadrangle including two in the Erie area, one at Conneaut, and one near Port Rowan. All of the clubs on the U.S. side have docking facilities. In Erie, these include the Presque Isle Yacht Club (PYC) and The Commodore Perry Yacht Club (CPYC). PYC had a modest beginning when a group of fishermen with small boats created a boating club at the head of the present day Marina Lake on Presque Isle. When the park went through extensive renovations in the late 1950s the PYC group was evicted to make way for the creation of the current marina complex. The members were given a block of state owned lands in the canal basin (today's west slip) in order to appease the members of the club. From this modest beginning PYC has developed into a fine club at the foot of Peach Street. The facility includes buildings and additional docks.

Commodore Perry Yacht Club.

Conneaut Boat Club.

CPYC also had its genesis on Presque Isle. In the early 1970s, a small group of boaters who were primarily Presque Isle Marina tenants met and formed a charter for a new yacht club. Over a 10 year period, they attracted more members, located bay front property at the foot of Walnut Street, and created an attractive facility including a clubhouse, docks, and a break wall. Given the mountain of bureaucracy which had evolved by the mid-1970s, the CPYC members displayed some incredible patience while waiting to complete their new facilities. But today's club is a beautiful monument to a group of people who (like the early Port Dover members) were willing to get their hands dirty to accomplish their objectives. The essence of CPYC is a system in which members annually work a prescribed number of hours doing building maintenance and grounds keeping.

There is a boat club just inside the break wall at Conneaut on the west end of the Quadrangle which participates in the yacht club system. The Conneaut Boat Club features modern docks, an attractive clubhouse, and an active sailboat racing program.

On the north shore, there is just one other yacht club, the Long Point Bay Yacht Club in the Inner Bay. This club has no physical facilities. It is a conglomeration of sailors and powerboaters from various locations in the Inner Bay who organized in the 1970s for the purpose of sponsoring sailboat races and other boating activities. Like CPYC in Erie, they ultimately hope to establish and build a physical facility somewhere in the Inner Bay. Most of the members keep their boats at St. Williams, and therefore the St. Williams harbor has become the unofficial home of LPBYC. There have been two stumbling blocks in the development of this club. First was the dramatic drop in water levels in the late 1980s. Many of the most active sailors in the LPBYC were forced to move their boats out of the Inner Bay, and much of the popular racing schedule of the club had to be abandoned. The slow migration of sailboats out of the Inner Bay was hastened by the opening of Port Dover's new municipal marina in the late 1980s. By 1990, the racing fleet, the glue which had held LPBYC together had essentially disappeared. Second was the growing difficulty with environmental permits to build a marine facility like a club. The good old days when a gang of members could take sledge hammers and shovels and dig a club into the side of a beach disappeared soon after the early days of Port Dover's Yacht Club. By the 1990s, permits were required to apply for permits.

Presque Isle Yacht Club.

SAILBOAT RACING

Sailboat racing has been a popular sport in Lake Erie since the turn of the century. Few persons in the general public realize the extent or the competitive level of racing which continues in both the Erie and Port Dover areas. The Erie Yacht Club has continued to sponsor national class boat as well as auxiliary racing. In a typical season, two or more national or regional level competitions are held in Presque Isle Bay. There are also regular weekly and special races. Events such as the August Multiple Sclerosis (M.S.) Regatta, The Mayor's and Governor's Cup races, and the Dover Day's Race are annual events which can be viewed by the general public. For the M.S. Regatta, there are spectator boats available to the public at the Erie Yacht Club. In addition to the EYC racing circuit, both Presque Isle and Commodore Perry Yacht Clubs sponsor regular sailboat races. Racing is also quite popular in Port Dover and is sponsored there by Port Dover Yacht Club.

Sailboat racing falls within two general categories: class boat racing and auxiliary racing. In class boat competition, each competitor has exactly the same kind of boat. The competition, like horse racing, is on a boat to boat basis. The first boat across the finish line is the winner. In auxiliary racing (usually for larger

Close quarter tactics rounding Long Point.
Photo by BARRY HAZLETT

sailboats), each sailboat has a designated handicap. This means that the first boat across the finish line may not be the winner, because it may be required to give time to the second or third boat across the line. Theoretically each competing boat is assigned a fair overall "rating," which is the means by which it can be compared in a particular race to any other boat. Ratings are based on boat size, shape, and sail configuration.

If one boat is rated at 170 and another at 150, then the boat with the lower rating must "spot" the boat with the high rating the difference of 20 (seconds per mile). Although there are different ratings systems, the intention of each is to create a situation where each boat has exactly the same probability of winning, so that outcome is dependent upon sailing skill. In practice, ratings systems work differently for various boats, depending upon conditions. Some boats have a rating advantage in high winds, others in low winds, etc.

While sailboat racing seems confusing at first, it is really quite easy to understand. The typical race course is a triangle which includes a starting line monitored by a committee boat. The starting line itself is designated by a flag on the committee boat and one other flag, usually set from the boat at right angles to the wind (sometimes a permanent buoy or shore marker is used). The start consists of a series of three gunshots at 5 minute intervals including a 10 minute warning, a 5 minute warning, and then the starting gun. During the warning periods, the competing sailboats jockey for position on the start line according to sailing right-of-way rules. Each captain attempts to be the first to cross the line (boat moving at full speed) as the final gun goes off.

Once the race has started, the boats typically race upwind (tacking back and forth) to the first mark. After rounding this mark, the boats will usually put up colorful spinnakers (downwind sails) and head downwind to a second mark. In most races, after the second mark is rounded boats sail to a third mark, drop their spinnakers, and return upwind to the original starting line. There are exceptions to these basics. Sometimes a special race may call for a downwind or off the wind start. Often a course will feature the typical three leg triangle course plus one or two additional legs.

Deck action aboard Bill Burke's Mary Lou approaching Long Point.
Photo by BARRY HAZLETT

The trick in understanding sailboat races is to find the starting line and then to try to pick out the first race mark (which is almost always directly upwind). The sailboats will remain on the downwind side of the starting line during the pre-race jockeying for position. In a large race, there may be two or more starting groups with boats divided by size and or competitiveness. When this is the case, a large percentage of the participants will not seem to be jockeying for position at the start. Immediately after the third gun, which is the starting signal for the first group, the second set of boats will begin to jockey for position at the starting line. The start gun of race number one is the 10 minute warning signal for them.

The start of a sailboat race is extremely exciting. In general, the boats which gain an early advantage are difficult to catch because they sail off into clear air. The intensity and excitement of the start followed by the tactics on the actual course are now understood by many non-sailors as a result of TV coverage of the

America's Cup races. But there is no better way to view this sport than to see it live. For Erie or Dover folks, a grandstand seat is easily available. Races are generally on Wednesday evenings at 7:00 and are best seen from a boat. Boaters who are sure to stay downwind and well out of maneuvering distance from the sailors will be welcomed to any race, especially if they are careful with their wakes. Land bound spectators can get the best view in Erie at the foot of Lincoln Avenue. In Dover, the best "seats" are on the cliffs to the east of town along Old Lake Shore Road.

DISTANCE RACES

In the long histories of both the Erie and the Port Dover Yacht Clubs, there have traditionally been a number of summer sailboat races which feature a lake crossing. The names of the races have changed over the years but the spirit remains. A distance race creates excitement and camaraderie which is not rivaled by many other competitive events. Some of these events are cooperative races between other clubs and attract large numbers of participant boats. The annual Interclub (ILYA) race, for example, often features 50 or more competing sailboats.

Often such long distance races are made up of a series of racing legs. Each leg takes a day or more to complete. Boats may race from Erie to Dover, then from Dover to Dunkirk, on to Buffalo, etc. Racing from Erie to Dover or visa versa is a long tradition dating back to the early 1900s. The tradition includes sailboats from a number of classes. For such long distance races, the absolute best "seats" are along the Erie Channel shortly after the start time. From this vantage point, it is possible to see all of the boats close up and to watch tactics as the competitors deal with the congestion of the narrow channel.

Lake Erie Adventures

1. Take your binoculars and a lawn chair and watch a weekday evening race. A phone call to the local yacht club will tell you of the racing schedule. Be sure to see the start!

2. Find out when the ILYA (usually in June) regatta is scheduled and get to the channel in Erie to watch. Here you will be able to see the entire fleet close up, but you will have to get up very early (usually about 5:30 a.m.). Take a camera.

3. In late August the Erie Yacht Club sponsors its annual M.S. Regatta which is open to the public and includes spectator boats.

4. The Erie Yacht club offers both adult and children's sailing lessons to the general public. Sign up!

5. Buy a sailboat. You can find one in absolutely any price or size range. There are car top boats available on the used market for $200 which can offer most of the joy of the hundred thousand dollar models.

6. Sign up for the Power Squadron's annual boating course.

Modern Marine Disasters

Over the past 30 years, losses of property and life have decreased significantly within the Quadrangle, as they have on the Great Lakes in general. Yet, many of the traditional dangers continue to exist, including problems of weather, and navigation near the shallows of the two peninsulas. Advances in modern navigational aids, improvements in commercial and recreational vessels, and better rescue technologies have, however, more than compensated for these continuing dangers.

Ship-to-shore radio, for example, is now so inexpensive that most modern pleasure boaters are equipped and listening regularly. Other tools for modern navigation include radio direction finders, which allow boaters to determine relatively accurate positions; Loran, which gives nearly exact locations; and the newest advance GPS, which uses satellite technology to produce precise positions. Like most electronics, prices have fallen rapidly. A reliable Loran unit, for example, can now be purchased for less than $200. The ability to know exact positions while under way has greatly reduced navigational error. In combination with inexpensive depth sounders (or fish finders) boaters can now easily avoid problems of being lost or running aground.

The Ashram.
Photo by NADINE MITCHELL

The queen of navigational tools, of course, is radar. Radar units give precise positions relative to land masses and warn of other boats. Radar has undoubtedly helped to avert many disasters over the past 50 years. Even in the days when it was cost prohibitive for all but the large freighters, the technology helped substantially. Commercial freighters used it to avoid collisions with other vessels. These days, radar has become almost affordable. Fishing tugs and other commercial vessels are all radar equipped. Many large pleasure vessels also have radar units aboard. If radar has one fatal flaw, however, it is that it makes some captains a bit too daring, especially in foggy conditions. And if a vessel which is in the way of the radar carrier is small, or if the operator is not paying close attention, there is room for error.

In June of 1984, for example, the Frew family was participating in a sailboat race from Port Dover to Erie. We left the starting line at 7:00 a.m. on Sunday in our 30 foot sailboat the *Ashram* and were among the fleet leaders rounding the tip of Long Point in a thickening fog. The winds were light and we were making only 3 or 4 knots. After an hour, the visibility had become so poor that we could barely see the bow of the boat from the stern. I sat below trying to determine our position relative to the shipping lanes. I worried that we could be in danger from traffic crossing at right angles to our course. Suddenly, there was a change in the regular sounds which the boat and sea conditions had been making. It was enough of a change to capture the attention of my (then) 16 year old son who was at the helm.

Out of nowhere, a wall of dull red metal appeared astern. We made a sharp turn to starboard and watched with our mouths open as a coal freighter passed us to port within 30 feet. We could see in the portholes and smell breakfast cooking as the freighter passed by. I hailed the ship's captain to ask if he had seen us and to tell him of the other racing sailboats in the vicinity. The captain had not seen us and suggested that it was rather stupid to be out in such conditions. The freighter was heading from Nanticoke to Ashtabula and caught us by surprise by coming from our rear. We had been flying a radar detector and worrying about freighters crossing our course. In the fog that morning, we never heard the 700 foot vessel until it was upon us. What a lesson!

The coal freighter captain's words of wisdom were good ones. They remind us of the reason for most modern problems, being out in weather that is inherently dangerous. Of course, the reasons for using poor judgement always make sense at the time. A sailboat race, the rush to get somewhere, the end of a boating vacation, great fishing … these are among the rationalizations that lure recreational boaters to the sea when better judgement would advise staying in port.

For those who make a living on the lake, however, there is no choice. As long as there is a shipping season, the freighters go to sea. Commercial fishermen similarly must go out to take advantage of the early (March) and late (December) fishing. And commercial tug and barge traffic continues throughout the season. So, long before and after the fair weather pleasure boaters have basked in the relatively calm seas of summer, there are ships plying the lake. And, it is the spring fog or fall storm which is most likely to cause a modern commercial disaster.

The following stories represent a collection of marine disasters from the past 30 years. While it is clear that a single life lost makes a property loss pale by comparison, our stories include both.

THE GUS

In 1971, Robert Heinrich of Erie was faced with a classic boat buying dilemma. He could either purchase a new fiberglass boat (the type that wooden boat traditionalists scoffed at) or a veteran woody. Being an adventuresome and romantic type, he purchased and refitted a 46 foot wooden sloop. It would have been impossible to purchase a fiberglass sailboat of the same size and opulence for what it cost to launch the *Gus*.

The Gus

To complete the romantic vision of the first voyage of the *Gus*, the owner was married at the Erie Yacht Club aboard the *Gus* and departed for a honeymoon voyage on his beloved project boat. But troubles began on the lake crossing. The old wooden hull began leaking badly and Heinrich worked furiously to pump the water out fast enough to keep her afloat.

Greatly relieved to see the relative safety of Long Point, the *Gus* rounded the tip and proceeded close to the north shore within sight of the comforting beaches. Heinrich was hoping to make it to port, perhaps in the Inner Bay, where he could effect a repair. Unfortunately, the *Gus* tripped on the sand bar guarding the Inner Bay off Pottahawk and ran hopelessly aground. Some 99 years after the schooner *Gus* (1872) ran aground going through the cut at the opposite end of the Inner Bay, the modern *Gus* was similarly trapped.

Stuck on the bar, the wooden hull began to come apart in the pounding surf. In a matter of hours, she had driven herself into the sand and rolled to a 45 degree angle. Within days, the *Gus* was literally breaking apart with contents floating in all directions. Boaters from the area began to pilfer the remains and within a few weeks, the hull broke up completely. The deck section washed into the Inner Bay and the hull and ribs remained, becoming a part of the sand bar.

Originally optimistic that the *Gus* could be salvaged, Heinrich left the boat with what little he could gather and walked to shore along the sand bar to seek help. When it became clear that salvage would be impossible, he returned to Erie, where he raised the boom and mainsail as a burgee over his furniture store (Heinrich Feigle's at Eighth and Greengarden) and as a monument to the fated trip. The salvaged rigging flew there in effigy for more than a decade.

THE ALETHA B

On Sunday March 24, 1974, the *Aletha B* left Dover to trawl for smelt in the Outer Bay. The 56 foot trawler was driven by Captain Allan Perry and crewed by his brother Wayne. The weather soon deteriorated to 25 to 30 knot westerly winds and the seas, even in the Outer Bay, built to almost 10 feet. The *Trimac*, captained by Terry Hagen, was also trawling in the Outer Bay and was in visual contact with the *Aletha B*. Fishing was slow but steady that day, and it was midday before the boats began to fill with smelt. The rising winds and cold temperatures were creating a freezing spray which began to collect on the rigging.

At about 2:50 p.m., there was a radio message from the *Aletha B* to the fishing trawler *Trimac* asking for assistance. Captain Hagen headed the *Trimac* toward the area where the *Aletha B* had been fishing but found the vessel upside down. As the crew of the *Trimac* watched helplessly, the *Aletha B* slipped below the surface and disappeared. They searched the waters for the crew but found no trace.

As the *Trimac* searched the area, they too, began to experience difficulty. With a full load of fish, growing seas and the weight of ice in the superstructure, the trawler began rolling, coming dangerously close to foundering herself. Reluctantly, the *Trimac* turned toward Dover and fought her way back to port through 12 foot waves. Unfortunately, both Perry brothers drowned. The *Aletha B* was located a few days later and raised. She was returned to Port Dover, refitted, and rejoined the commercial fishing fleet where she continues to work today.

Dover Rose and Ciscoette towing the partially submerged Stanley Clipper back to port.

THE STANLEY CLIPPER

On April 30, 1984, two tugs from the Misner Fisheries fleet were trawling for smelt in the open lake along the south shore of Long Point. At about the same time that they had filled up with smelt, a southwest wind began to rise. The *Stanley Clipper*, a 62 foot tug, and the *Ciscoette* rounded the tip of the point at about 1:00 p.m. that afternoon in a hurry to get back to Port Dover before the waves built up. They were running loaded in extremely cold water and concerned about the rapidly deteriorating weather.

Within a half hour, the winds had built to a steady 50 to 60 miles per hour with gusts to 70. Waves were running at 15 feet. Both vessels began to tack into the waves and slow their speed to minimize pounding. At about 2:00 p.m., the crew of the *Ciscoette* lost visual contact with the *Stanley Clipper*, even though they were only separated by a half mile. They were able to see her on radar, however, and were in constant radio contact with Captain James Saunders and his crew, John Mummery and Daryl Clement.

Suddenly, there was a transmission from the *Stanley Clipper*'s radio. This final message was, "We're going over … Oh my God, what a way to go!" The *Ciscoette* radioed for help and began a search. They were soon joined by other tugs as well as air rescue crews. The search continued until dark and resumed the next morning. Several articles from the tug were found, indicating that the *Stanley Clipper* had gone to the bottom. Given the 40 degree water, the only hope for the crew was that they somehow got off the boat and made it to shore on Long Point's north beaches.

By morning of the third day, however, hope had evaporated. Later that day, the sunken *Stanley Clipper* was located by a fish tug approximately 4 miles east of Pottahawk point in 38 feet of water. OPP divers searched the wreckage but found no signs of the crew.

On Sunday May 20th, three fishing tugs from the Misner fleet raised the *Stanley Clipper* with air bags. This operation was only a partial success, since they could not get the hull high enough to pump it. The vessel was towed to shallow water and re-sunk. A few days later, a salvage company came to the assistance of the tugs with a crane and the *Stanley Clipper* was raised and pumped dry. That evening, the *Dover Rose* towed her back to her berth in the river where she was refitted and subsequently returned to service.

Captain Saunder's body was found on June 13th near Dunville. The bodies of the crew were also recovered. Daryl Clements was found near Bluff Bar on June 26, and John Mummary was discovered west of Port Dover in August.

The Stanley Clipper, tied up 1993.

THE TOYA

The story of the *Toya* will cause sailboaters to cringe in terror; not because of the loss of a life, but for the sudden and bitter end of a dream. This is the story of a vision that almost every boater has had at one time or another. In July of 1985, the Frew family visited Port Rowan in the *Ashram*. We berthed at Bluebill marina, an organic project which had been developing over the past 3 years.

The marina manager and his wife were wonderful hosts and spent many hours telling us of their plans for an extended cruise. They had been involved in the creation of the new marina, but their real love, and reason for being in the marina business, was bobbing invitingly at Bluebill's largest pier. She was large sloop named the *Toya*. The manager and his wife had built her from a bare hull. The *Toya* was a three year project, and that summer as we toured her, it was obvious that she was nearing completion.

The Toya in 1986.

The proud owners shared their dream with us. They planned to sail out of the bay that fall and take the *Toya* down the barge canal and then down the intercoastal to Florida and the Bahamas. Perhaps they would return without the boat the next summer to run the marina, but in any event they hoped to get into the charter business in southern waters with *Toya* and to semi-retire. Their care and their dreams showed in the interior of the *Toya*. She was truly opulent, with careful attention to detail. She looked out of place in the Inner Bay, where she was clearly the largest sailboat.

On August 31, 1985, the *Toya* left the Inner Bay in a northeasterly breeze and headed east along the inside of Long Point. The owners were on a shake-down cruise and anxious to see how she would fare in the large seas of the open lake. They rounded the Point and spent time sailing in the open lake before coming about to return to Bluebill. With a rising northeasterly of 15 to 20 knots, the ride home promised to be an exciting one.

Rounding Long Point always requires caution. The sand bar which extends from the tip of the point to the east following the sculpted contour of the peninsula is unpredictable. It can move north or south in a matter of weeks, filling in former deep areas and creating hazardous shoals in places where a boat could have sailed only days earlier. Even more importantly, the faces of the sand bar are at times quite steep. A person who is attentively watching a depth sounder may find depths changing from 40 feet to 5 in a matter of a few yards.

Rounding the Point in an easterly wind of high velocity is especially dangerous, since a bump on the bottom can quickly lead to a grounding from which a boat cannot recover. In a westerly, a bump on the bottom is followed by the boat losing momentum, but the wind and waves will move the vessel toward deeper waters. In an easterly, when momentum is lost, a sailboat stands upright (stops heeling) and begins to be driven on shore. In no time at all, a sailboat will twist its own keel into the sand and, in effect, bury itself. As soon as the boat stops floating, the forces of wind and sea begin their destructive process and in very little time a boat can become a wreck.

Somehow, on their return trip around the tip of Long Point, the *Toya* made this fatal error. On her way around the point, the *Toya* was steered to close to the tip. She ran aground, and slowly washed herself into an irretrievable position. The crew abandoned the *Toya* in waist deep water and walked ashore at the tip of the Point. They attempted to contact a salvage crew, but the weather deteriorated and it was several days before an organized technical attempt could be made. By that time it was simply too late. The *Toya* was a structural wreck.

In December of 1985, there was a tremendous sustained storm on Lake Erie. Water levels rose high enough for boats in winter storage along the river in Port Dover to float off of their cradles. During that storm, the *Toya* settled below the water's surface and was lost. In late summer of 1991, we visited the tip of the point on a low water September day and found the *Toya's* bow pulpit above the surface, about 100 yards off shore. Most of the hull is now buried in sand.

THE CAPTAIN K

Some 312 years after the first commercial sailing voyage on Lake Erie by the *Griffon*, another *Griffon* was steaming at full throttle toward Long Point. This *Griffon* was a 234 foot Canadian Coast Guard ice breaker and buoy tender. It was March 18th, 1991 and the *Griffon* was setting navigational buoys in anticipation of the upcoming boating season.

The Griffon

Unlike the first *Griffon*, this vessel was well aware of the existence of Long Point. In fact, her mission that day was to set the buoys which mark shoals and navigational bench marks within the Outer Bay. Captain Gordon Stogdale was apparently in a hurry to complete his work, since he had ordered the *Griffon* to steam at top speed, some 12 knots. It was midday as the *Griffon* passed to the north of the tip of Long Point. The radar operator noted a contact which seemed to be a fishing trawler running parallel to the course of the *Griffon*. There was a heavy fog that day and a gently rolling sea. Captain Stogdale had ordered the fog horn on board to be silenced for the sake of the deck crew who were preparing buoys prior to laying them.

Once satisfied that he had cleared the tip of the point, Stogdale turned the helm over to 28 year old third officer William Bennett. Bennett had only 40 hours of experience at the helm and had never operated the *Griffon* in fog or at top speed. He considered slowing down and running the fog horn, but he did not want to countermand the captain's orders. It was known on board that Stogdale did not like it when replacement helmsmen changed things such as the throttle. The crew of the *Griffon* knew that the commercial fishing fleet would be out that day, but they had heard that the smelt were running in the open lake well to the north and west of the tip of Long Point. As they steamed through the Outer Bay toward Port Dover, they did not expect to encounter trawlers.

Earlier that morning, the 56 foot *Captain K*, along with a dozen other fishing tugs, had left Port Dover's commercial harbor to fish for smelt. The *Captain K* was captained by Gary Speight. The crew included Dean Felker and 19 year old

John Walsh. All three were from Port Dover. It was early in the season, but the ice had cleared and fishing was good. The *Captain K*'s radar was not working, but it was simply not economically feasible to miss a day's fishing while waiting for a repair. More than a few fishermen have gone to sea over the years with defective electronics.

Apparently, the *Captain K* was having a good day because captains from the other trawlers reported seeing her turn to return to port shortly after noon. One of the other trawlers reported that he and the *Captain K* had almost run into each other while fishing. They came up on each other late in the morning and had to steer hard to avoid a collision. The trawler captains knew each other well. Even in the fog, they were relatively assured that the slow fishing speeds and their knowledge of each other's patterns would ultimately help avoid problems.

The Captain K

At 1:30 p.m. the *Griffon* was continuing at full speed toward its next buoy laying location off Port Dover. Captain Stogdale was having lunch. Bennett, still at the helm, was growing uncomfortable with the foggy conditions. Suddenly, he spotted the *Captain K* in the fog. Bennett steered hard to avoid a collision, but heard a sickening crunch as the *Griffon*'s ice breaker bow literally collapsed the wheelhouse and port side of the smaller fishing trawler. The *Griffon*, which was approximately 200 times heavier than the *Captain K*, came about in an attempt to render assistance, but no sign of the *Captain K* could be found. The *Griffon* radioed for assistance and anchored at the spot of the tragedy, where it remained for several days attempting to assist with salvage operations.

A massive search was launched for the *Captain K*, but no sign of the crew could be found. Divers were able to locate the sunken ship in 115 feet of water, but the hull was so badly damaged that they could not get inside to confirm that crew members were trapped inside. The mystery of the missing crew was solved 13 days later, when a salvage vessel was brought on sight to raise the hull. It was learned

The Captain K being raised.

that the collapsing wheel house had instantly killed the two crew members, and that the Captain had drowned. All of the bodies had been trapped inside the trawler.

The *Captain K* affair continued for almost two years in and around Port Dover. The tragedy enraged the community. There were always dangers involved in fishing, and fishermen had died before. But to be run down by a Coast Guard ice breaker steaming at full speed in fog with no warning horn seemed a horrible indignity. Funeral services for the fishermen drew an unbelievable crowd for such a small village. Everyone, from Port Dover's most prosperous businessmen to the motorcycle gang friends of crew member Dean Felker, found time to share in the grief of Port Dover that day.

On January 22, 1993 the affair came to a symbolic end when court proceedings in Simcoe found Captain Stogdale guilty of three counts of dangerous operation of a vessel. Bennett was acquitted. During the proceedings, it was learned that the radar unit aboard the *Griffon* was of such antique vintage that to miss a reading from a fish tug in the fog was not surprising. An electronics expert testified that a more sensitive modern unit aboard the government vessel might have helped to avert the tragedy. The legal culmination of the affair came on April 21 when Stogdale was sentenced to a year in prison.

IT WILL NEVER END

The sea is essentially dangerous. It is rewarding, beautiful, exciting and romantic, but it is and will always be dangerous. It is particularly threatening to the persons who must go out in all kinds of weather to make a living. There have been other tragedies within the Quadrangle in recent years. In 1940, Vernon Bravner drowned while trying to reach shore off Port Dover from his burning fish tug. In 1955, John Wilson drowned when his fish tug, the *Ciscoe*, was grounded on Long Point. Two fishermen died at Port Burwell in 1975, when their fish tug burned. In that same year another Burwell fisherman died when the tug *South Side* rolled over.

Fortunately, most pleasure boaters have fared better in recent years. While there is still a predictable number of drownings each year among fishermen and other recreational boaters, advances in electronics and improved rescue capabilities have greatly minimized these occurrences.

Lake Erie Adventures

1. At Port Dover the town has memorialized the commercial fishermen who have died by dedicating benches to them on the municipal pier. Visit the pier and read the names.

2. The *Stanley Clipper* is tied up near the Port Dover Harbor Museum. It is hoped that it will soon become a floating museum piece and a part of the facility.

THE CONTINUING SAGA OF THE ATLANTIC

We puzzled over how to conclude for several weeks. We were groping for an idea that would somehow connect maritime history with our reader's "modern" lives. From our perspective, the regional history of Lake Erie is a continuous flow of events which leads from the "past" to "now" and toward the future. We continue to see the many ways in which the events of past years, decades and centuries influence our current lives. But how could we describe this in a final chapter? Should we preach, give warnings about the potential loss of our regional marine heritage, or tell another story? We decided to be storytellers and the idea for an integrating tale came to us quite suddenly on a winter day at Long Point.

It was a bitter cold day in late January 1993. We were walking the beach in front of Dave Stone's cottage, watching in awe as a slate grey snow squall moved down the lake. Dave commented on how excited he was about spring and his annual shipwreck lecture for the grade 13 kids at Port Dover. Dave mentioned that kids were always the the best audience. They were excited about shipwrecks and schooners. As we walked, he recalled the absolutely most excited youngster that he had ever encountered—a teenager named Mike Fletcher, who he had met in the

1970s. Mike was more than just interested in the wreck of the *Atlantic*, a ship whose story connects the 1850s with today. Mike was so obsessed that he made the *Atlantic* his life's work! As Dave recalled his long relationship with Mike, we instantly realized that we had hit upon the concluding story for our book. We would tell a final tale; one which began more than 150 years ago!

BOUND FOR WISCONSIN

In the summer of 1852, a group of Scandinavian families made their way from Europe to New York City. Like many settlers of the day, they were headed for Milwaukee, where they hoped to join the already thriving northern European communities there and to make a new life in America. The immigrants had endured a long passage across the ocean and were tired after traveling in steerage accommodations. They had struggled to live out of the single trunk that each family was allowed to bring on the voyage. Their steamer trunks contained clothing, food for the long voyage, and basic necessities for life in the new world.

The immigrants had made the transatlantic trip, the transfer to the Erie Canal, and the long trip to Buffalo from New York. As they boarded the *Atlantic*, their enthusiasm grew. They were in a festive mood on the evening of Thursday August 9th, 1852; about to depart on the last leg of their long journey. It was a beautiful summer night on Lake Erie and while the general treatment of "coach class" passengers on the lakes was not comparable to that of first class guests, it was still much better than the steerage conditions endured on the ocean crossing. Enthusiasm was also quite high because of the shorter and supposedly less dangerous steamer trip up the lake. The *Atlantic* was a 267 foot, 1,155 ton side wheel steamer. She was state of the art for the 1850s; opulent and fast. Her interior was fitted out in finely finished hardwoods. The galley featured beautiful china with the name of the ship embossed on the plates. During her first year in the water (1849), she set the record from Buffalo to Detroit of 16 hours and 30 minutes.

The Atlantic.
MIKE FLETCHER

THE ATLANTIC ENTERS THE QUADRANGLE

Captain J.B. Petty entered the Quadrangle at about 1:30 a.m. A light fog was filling in around Long Point as the *Atlantic* made her way through calm seas, past the tip of the Point and to the south of the lighthouse. At the same time, the 275 foot propeller *Ogdensburg* was steaming through the Quadrangle in the opposite direction. The *Ogdensburg* was headed from Cleveland to the Welland Canal; a course that crossed the path of the *Atlantic.*

At about 2:00 a.m. the crew of the *Ogdensburg* suddenly spotted the *Atlantic* immediately ahead in the haze. They reversed their engines and tried to change course, but hit the port side of the *Atlantic* just forward of the side wheel. The first reaction of both crews was to assume that the damage was cosmetic, since the collision had not been at full force. After a momentary inspection, each vessel continued on course. The crew of the *Ogdensburg* reported that the *Atlantic* never even missed a stroke of its paddle wheel. Captain Petty was quite proud of the strength and speed of his vessel!

Within a few minutes, however, the *Atlantic*'s engineers reported that water was coming into the engine room and that the ship was in serious danger. The crew roused most of the sleeping passengers and tried to get them to move to the starboard side to stop the *Atlantic* from listing. The passengers (mostly unable to understand English) panicked and ran for the bow. Many jumped overboard as others attempted to launch the lifeboats.

The captain realized that the fires in the engines were in grave danger of going out because of the rapidly rising water in the ship. He turned the *Atlantic* toward Long Point and began to run for shore. The activity of the panicked passengers, however hastened the list of the boat, and, about six miles from the beach, the bow list became so great that the *Atlantic* took on enough water to put out the fires in her engines. Dead in the water, she began to sink off Long Point in the deepest part of Lake Erie.

Fortunately for the 250 survivors, the crew of the *Ogdensburg*, who watched the *Atlantic* as she changed course, heard the screams of terror and circled back to help. It was also fortunate, at least for some, that the *Atlantic* sunk bow first. In the relatively calm seas, trapped air in the stern section caused the vessel to pause for a time with its bow stuck 165 feet below on the bottom and its stern floating. Large numbers of survivors made their way from the sinking bow to the floating stern and were hanging on to the aft sections as the *Ogdensburg* approached. The exact number drowned that night is not clear. Some estimates placed the toll at 250 others at 300.

The *Ogdensburg* proceeded with all survivors to Erie where the frightened and demoralized passengers and crew were treated. A hearing was held later in Erie. The *Ogdensburg* was found to be at fault for the accident. Months later, a judgement in Ohio (home port of the *Ogdensburg*) found the *Atlantic* responsible.

BURIED TREASURE

After the tragedy and loss of life had been dealt with, attention turned to the cargo. Most of the concern was about the $35,000 in gold coins reported to be in the ship's safe. It was also estimated that as much as $250,000 in additional cash and valuables was aboard, along with a strong box holding $700.

In the late summer of 1852 an organized salvage attempt was sponsored by American Express. They hired Johnny B. Green, a famous Buffalo salvage diver (then called a submariner), to recover the ship's safe and strong box using his "diving armor." Green had a schooner, and a rubber diving suit with a copper helmet, but he had never made a dive to the depths of the *Atlantic*, some 165 feet below the surface. Green made three tries on the first trip. On two dives his pumps failed because of the depth. On the third he got stuck in the ship's smoke stack. During his dives he experienced severe pains, but ignored them. He returned to Buffalo, resolved to make equipment modifications and to try again the following week.

Green was back at the *Atlantic* after several days but his crew quickly grew discouraged with the project. As fall 1852 approached Green withdrew from the wreck reasoning that he needed more resources and time.

In 1853 and 1854 Johnny Green revisited the *Atlantic* several times and dove it retrieving artifacts for which he was given rewards. He later admitted that he had been stalling in the hopes that American Express would give up its interest in the ship. Meanwhile he was diving other wrecks in order to raise capital for another attempt. By 1855 Green had raised the cash needed to design new and improved diving armor and to purchase a new schooner, the *Yorktown*. On August 14 he sailed to the *Atlantic* with a crew of 18 men. It took him a while to relocate the wreck, as it had shifted, turning approximately 90 degrees from southwest to

Elliott P. Harrington (second from the left) and his brother-in-law, James Philips (third from the left) recovered the Atlantic's American Express safe in 1856.
MIKE FLETCHER

southeast. Green attached grappling hooks and marker buoys to the bow and stern. He then began a series of dives with his new equipment, finally reaching the cabin after 6 days of diving. On August 23, he found the safe and attached a marker line with a surface buoy to the railing outside the cabin window. The next day (August 24) Green returned to the *Atlantic* with a saw, cut open the cabin wall in front of the safe and moved it to the deck of the *Atlantic*.

With his prize in sight, Johnny Green returned to the surface a final time to get a line and hook. The strain of the dives, however, proved to be too much. Green was quite suddenly debilitated by pain. He became so ill that he was unable to move a muscle, stand, or straighten his posture (he was "bent").

He was taken by his crew to Port Dover for treatment. Doctors there were unclear about the nature of his symptoms and doubted that he would live. He survived, however, and was subsequently taken after 2 weeks, on his own schooner, to Buffalo for care. After a week at Buffalo he was taken to his home in Boston where he spent 5 months bedridden. Although he would never fully recover, Green was absolutely determined to complete his project. On June 27, 1856 he left Buffalo for the "final" dive. Unable to find his marker buoys he used hired divers to relocate the *Atlantic*. When it came time to dive, however, the divers refused to go down. Crippled with pain, he crawled into his diving gear for the last time in his quest for fame and fortune. He descended on July 4th to find the safe missing. His efforts had gone unrewarded, and J.B. Green lived the remaining years of his life a bitter, defeated, and sick man.

THE MISSING GOLD

There were originally two theories regarding the missing safe and its gold. The first was that the safe, itself, shifted and that J.B. Green, in his debilitated condition, simply could not find it. It could (it was said) have fallen through a collapsed deck section. This possibility kept interest in the *Atlantic* quite high for many years during the middle 1800s.

One believer in this notion was Lodner Phillips, the inventor of the first Great Lakes submarine. In 1853, Phillips traveled to the site of the *Atlantic* by schooner and launched his one man pedal-operated submarine in an apparent attempt to reach the wreck. Lodner was a bit circumspect about exactly what he was doing, and some historians are unconvinced of his specific attempts to reach the *Atlantic*. Unfortunately the submarine sprung a leak and Phillips beat a hasty retreat for the surface. Undaunted, Phillips affected a quick repair and (fortunately) decided to attempt an unmanned test dive. He lowered the sub on a cable to see if it would leak. The cable parted and the sub now sits somewhere near the *Atlantic*.

The second, and clearly more probable theory regarding the missing safe, developed as a result of the activities of Elliot Harrington in and around Port Dover during 1856. Harrington, who was a submarine wrecker of almost equal fame to Green had heard of Green's attempts and decided to organize his own independent party. Harrington who was from the Barcelona (Quadrangle) area anchored off the point near the *Atlantic* with a party of three other men in the schooner *Fletcher* on June 18th. Over a 4 day period Elliot Harrington reported making 18 short dives (of 3 to 11 minute durations as opposed to Green's 20 to 30 minute periods). On the final descent Sunday the 22nd (just days before Green was to return for his final dive), Elliot Harrington reported that he sawed open the stateroom and removed the safe.

There is much confusion about the details of the salvage from this point forward. It is interesting, for example, that Harrington claimed there were no marker lines attached and that he had not seen a safe on deck. This confusion led to supposition that there had been more than one safe. Green later claimed that Harrington had also taken a strongbox as well as a trunk with valuables. Harrington denied this. It seemed from the activities of Harrington that he had originally hoped not to report his recovery to American Express. Green, however, learned of the Harrington expedition when he returned to Buffalo empty handed and informed the company's lawyers. Ultimately American Express went to court and demanded that Harrington turn over the valuables in exchange for a reward, Even then, however, there were discrepancies. Harrington claimed that he had inadvertently destroyed thousands of dollars in his mother's attempts to dry the money. Several securities seemed missing from the safe, etc.

In the end Elliot Harrington became a relatively wealthy man. Johnny B. Green did not fare as well. He tried to carry on as a salvager but he was never able to dive again. Even though he was a relatively young man (31 years old) his salvage career ended when his schooner sunk the following year. Green retired, wrote a short book about his diving career and lived out his life as a "renowned expert" on Great Lakes salvage. During the Civil War years Green became a fixture on lake freighters, riding the lakes with the sailors. Most of the owners would let him travel at no cost. He would hold court in the bunk rooms telling his stories of diving on the wrecks of the lakes. Legend has it that he died and was buried at sea in 1865, a twisted and crippled old man of 39.

OTHER SALVAGE ATTEMPTS

A group of American adventurers organized in 1872 and in 1873 made an ill-conceived attempt to raise the entire ship. They believed that the gold was probably still aboard. And even if it wasn't they could salvage the belongings of the passengers. They were unprepared to deal with the strategic problems of equipment in such a remote location and ultimately gave up the attempt. They had cables attached to the ship on two separate occasions. Both times, weather conditions deteriorated, creating high waves which threatened to split the cables.

Near the turn of the century another group of divers came to the wreck of the *Atlantic* in newly developed one-atmosphere suits. Looking like modern space suits, these diving chambers protected the wearers from the bends. However, they were clumsy and made hand manipulation almost impossible. History suggests that these divers were counting on finding lots of "valuables" within the first class cabins. It seems from current evidence that the one atmosphere divers used grappling hooks from above to pull the *Atlantic*'s topsides apart and then made repeated attempts to root through the cabins looking for gold, jewelry etc. They soon announced that the attempt was a failure. They concluded in 1910 that there was nothing aboard the ship but a "bunch of junk."

In 1953 Harry Gamble, Port Dover boat builder, and resident mechanical genius, organized another salvage attempt. His group planned to salvage the wreck by diving on it. Aware of the dangers of deep water diving, the Gamble crew quickly realized the technical difficulty of this venture and retired from their operations at the end of the summer resolving to build a diving bell and return the following year. Harry certainly had the skills and ingenuity to complete the project. Apparently, however, business opportunities distracted him, and his group never persisted with their plans.

During the 1960s and 1970s the precise location of the *Atlantic* continued to be unknown. The early salvers had been secretive about their activities. Harry Gamble had reported that the ship which he was diving during the 1950s was east of Long Point and in 200 feet of water. A number of north shore divers continued to be interested in finding the wreck, but the depths near the point, along with the relatively easy access to other wrecks in shallow waters, kept them distracted.

Meanwhile, Dave Stone's friend Mike Fletcher was evolving his own life-long obsession with the wreck. He completed primary historical research and skillfully interviewed locals. Mike spoke with Gamble and learned of his dive location. He was skeptical of Gamble's information since it placed the *Atlantic* east of the Point. Ultimately, he dove it to learn that while there was a steamship there, it was not the *Atlantic*. Mike reasoned that the *Atlantic* had to be west of the tip of the Point and some 4 to 6 miles off shore. He began a systematic search of the deep trench off Long Point. By this time, he was a commercial diver with state of the art scuba equipment.

Ships wheel of the Atlantic underwater.

In 1984, Mike received a tip from commercial fishermen that they had been snagging nets on the bottom a few miles west of the tip of the Point and some 5 miles south. One late summer evening, Mike and two friends traveled to the Loran location that he had been given and prepared to dive. As he entered the water, he realized that this location was directly in line with the spot on the cliff bank in Port Dover where he had spent summer afternoons as a child gazing south and thinking about the *Atlantic*. Descending, he had a premonition that after all these years he had finally found his wreck.

His first dive was a partial success. There was a sidewheel steamer there but was it the *Atlantic*? Several more dives were required to absolutely identify the ship, but the engine serial number, the decorative wooden torch from the wheelhouse and some china conclusively marked this ship as the *Atlantic*. Lost and in obscurity for more than 80 years she was now in the capable hands of the young boy who had been dreaming about her since the 1950s. Mike began visiting the *Atlantic* on a regular basis, charting her, taking photographs and collecting loose artifacts which were in danger of sinking in the surrounding silt. His relationship with the *Atlantic* began to mature as he sent queries to the federal government asking how she could best be preserved. He did not, as suggested by the one-atmosphere divers, think of the *Atlantic*'s contents as a bunch of junk. Instead he could see the steamer trunks of some 350 immigrants who didn't all make it to the new world in the remains of a beautiful victorian style steamer. Each trunk contained the story of a family, and where it had come as well as hopes and aspirations for the future.

The *Atlantic* rests in 165 feet of water. A descent to that depth represents quite an athletic feat. Even using relatively sophisticated scuba gear, a diver at that depth is in great danger, and can only spend a brief time (7 or 8 minutes) on the wreck site. On his earliest dives, visibility was near zero, and the ship was literally covered with trawl nets which had become tangled on the wreck over the years. These conditions made dives to the *Atlantic* treacherous.

By the late 1980s, Mike had established his own repair and salvage business and had acquired the sophisticated gear required to minimize the dangers of such a dive. Over the years he added a dive boat (the *Kenteau)*, a decompression chamber, and mixed gas helmet diving equipment with television cameras and lights. This equipment makes it possible for him to spend extended periods on the wreck site. Still, mistakes at such depths can be life threatening.

As he continued his work, Mike registered his find with the Canadian Minister of Wrecks and proceeded with his systematic survey of the ship and her contents. The *Atlantic* has settled into the silty bottom so that much of her under water structure is (floating) below the surface of the silty lake bottom. Her upper (first class) cabins and decks have caved in (probably the work of the one-atmosphere divers) and the stacks have fallen, but otherwise she is in nearly perfect condition. Over the years, Mike has brought the loose artifacts to the surface for donation to museums. He has not, however, tampered with any of the surfaces, such as walls or bulkheads or removed steamer trunks. Except for the damage caused by the sinking, the early salvage attempts, and the collapse of the stacks, the ship was in structurally whole condition (prior to 1990).

Mike was careful to record his findings with pictures over the years. He has also catalogued and reported the artifacts which were removed. In 1992, thanks to a combination of clear water and the mussels which have begun to attach themselves to the wreck, he was able to make a video tape of the *Atlantic* using underwater cameras and lights.

THE MAR DIVE AFFAIR

During the summer of 1990 a secretive group of Americans who were camping at St. Williams, in the Inner Bay, attracted the interest of the Port Dover fishing community. Every day for several weeks, the Americans would launch a 22 foot outboard in the Inner Bay, drive through the Turkey Point channel out

Mike Fletcher on the Kenteau.

along the inside of Long Point and anchor in the deep waters near the *Atlantic*. Rumors of these men and what they might be doing grew rapidly as the commercial fishermen watched their activities over the summer. They did not seem to be sport fishermen. And whenever a fish tug would approach, the Americans would seem to make efforts to disguise what they were doing.

In Port Dover, Mike began to fear the worst—that someone was about to lay claim to the ship which had been his lifelong obsession. Word of Mike's find had spread through town and beyond by this time and it was only a matter of time until others would come to investigate. Yet Mike wasn't sure what, if anything, he should do. When Mike first began to remove the loose artifacts, he notified federal provincial authorities of what he was doing. They did not respond, however, leaving Mike unclear about how to proceed.

During the summer of 1991, Mike's worst suspicions were confirmed. The American group, went public, identifying itself as Mar Dive Inc. They issued press releases in California, Pennsylvania and Ohio, announcing that they had located the long lost wreck of the *Atlantic* and that they had purchased the salvage rights to the vessel from the company which had previously owned them. Through a quirk of business fates, the original salvage rights had belonged to a company which had evolved into an existing California-based Corporation. With legal assistance the Mar Dive Group had purchased the salvage rights for a minimal fee from the existing corporation.

There were two other interesting developments in the Mar Dive legal claim. First, as a part of incorporation they had secured private backing for their venture. They seemed to have a significant amount of capital for launching the project. Secondly, they completed a legal action in which a California judge declared the *Atlantic* to be under the jurisdiction of the State of California.

In mid-summer of 1991, in a punctuating media event, divers from Mar Dive descended to the *Atlantic* with cameras rolling and brought up a number of artifacts. In a staged media event, the Mar Dive people made a statement indicating that they had located the wreck and that there were literally millions of dollars worth of valuables aboard. They made a number of vague suggestions about establishing a "Mel Fisher" (Key West treasure hunter) type operation in some lucky city on the American side of the lake, and disappeared leaving a buoy on the wreck site.

THE RETURN OF THE WAR OF 1812

For Canadians, this was the most hostile action since Campbell's burning of Dover in 1814. Most Ontarians, seeing the Buffalo or Erie TV coverage declaring a well known wreck lying in Canadian waters to be the property of the State of California, were more than a bit miffed. To add insult to injury, here was a group of Americans, violating provincial law on television by removing historical artifacts from Ontario waters.

Without realizing what they were doing, the publicity effort of Mar Dive was soon to cause their undoing. The Ontario government, stirred by Mike Fletcher, reacted to public outrage and declared the Mar Dive operators to be in violation of Provincial law. A warrant was issued for the arrest of the Mar Dive people, and the Canadian media began a long and consistent attack against the American group.

The Mar Dive group, possibly recognizing that their project was in danger, began a counter publicity campaign, emphasizing their own altruistic intent. They promised to return some of the artifacts to descendants of the original owners. They also tried to make "connections" on the U.S. side of the lake contacting officials of more than one American city to make inquiries about that cities's interest in hosting a research center which might mean 10 to 20 local jobs. In Erie, they contacted officials at Mercyhurst College hoping to develop a relationship with the Anthropology Department.

In 1991 the Mar Dive affair came to a head in the center of the Lake Erie Quadrangle. At the site of the *Atlantic* on July 19 there was a convergence of forces. Mar Dive arrived with a constable from Erie, Pa. to attach a notice (from

Mar Dive people at the site of the Atlantic, "Arresting the Wreck."

the State of California) to the Buoy marking the wreck site. Accompanying Mar Dive, were several vessels containing the media and interested onlookers. A number of Canadian boats also showed up including Mike Fletcher in the *Kenteau*. Finally, the Ontario Provincial Police (OPP) showed up in their own boat with an arrest warrant. Because of the media coverage, it was well known within the Canadian communities near the lake that the event was going to occur.

As the Mar Dive people bolted their California court proclamation to the Buoy, declaring the Atlantic to be under the jurisdiction of the State of California two things happened. Some of the Canadian onlookers drove to the wreck sight, examined the canister with its proclamation, read it and then later removed it as a symbolic protest. Apparently, California judges have less authority in Canadian waters than they were led to believe. This action was overshadowed, however, by the excitement of the attempted arrest which followed. The OPP approached the Mar Dive boat with a warrant to arrest its occupants. Upon hearing the arrest decree the Mar Dive boat fled for American Waters, some 5 miles to the south, with the OPP in hot pursuit. Once in U.S. waters the Mar Dive boat stopped. The OPP boat shut down a few hundred yards away in Canadian waters and the two groups sat staring at each other. A stalemate! The ghosts of the old rum runners must have chuckled that day.

MIKE FLETCHER: HERO AND GOAT

The *Atlantic*'s long saga is not yet ended. On the Canadian side of the lake, a series of hearings will begin in the fall of 1993. The purpose of these hearings will be to decide who owns the wreck, what to do about the Mar Dive encroachment and the best ways to handle other cases which might arise. They are not to be touched. With respect to the *Atlantic* in particular, there is a warrant for the arrest of the Mar Dive people. If they enter Canada, they will be prosecuted. There is now also a special radar vigilance by the OPP and the Canadian Coast Guard at the wreck site. If a boat lingers near the wreck an alarm is set off by a radar beacon from the Long Point Lighthouse. A sign has been attached to the wreck buoy designating it a protected site and warning of the illegal nature of the removal of artifacts.

While the events surrounding the *Atlantic*, and Mike Fletcher's preservation activities have made him somewhat of a local hero, he (like Mar Dive) is being sued by Ontario for removing artifacts. Although he has continuously reported his activities and registered all artifacts for eventual donation to museums, he has been charged under the same act in which Mar Dive was charged. So while he was credited with a longstanding interest in the ship and with raising public consciousness regarding Ontario's marine heritage, the bureaucracy has placed him in the same category as the American salvors whose intentions were to sell the artifacts. To make matters worse Mike is caught up in a series of expensive lawsuits between himself and Mar Dive.

Mike Fletcher has become a guardian of Lake Erie and her maritime history. At great personal cost he has taken upon himself the responsibility to protect and preserve a small but incredibly important piece of her history. We asked Mike, once, what his friends and family thought about what he was doing. His response came easily. "They think I'm a fool," he said. "Why should I become obsessed, involve my family, spend all of my free time and risk financial ruin?" The answer to this question may be more obvious to us than to Mike's friends or even to Mike himself. Mike Fletcher is caught up in the spirit of the Lake that he loves so much. He sees himself as the protector of the *Atlantic* as well as the other beautiful deep water shipwrecks which lie within the deep trench off Long Point.

For Mike, history has become real. It is a stream of events connecting all of us to our predecessors in time. For Mike, the history which is most real is the history of the water which brought the Iroquois, the Europeans, the Schooners, the Steamers and all of the rest of us, in different but personally important ways, to the edge of Lake Erie. Mike Fletcher has grown from a youngster, who like so many from both shores, once sat at the edge of the lake and dreamed about what

Port Dover diver Mike Fletcher.

might be at its bottom. Little did he realize as a 10 year old playing on the beaches, or as an 18 year old listening to a Dave Stone lecture that he would become an important part of the history of the lake. Unfortunately for Mike, Lake Erie's waters are not yet …. "Waters of Repose!"

CONCLUSIONS …. FOR NOW

Obviously, the recording of history is paradoxical. Since by its very nature, history is ongoing in a very short time what is in print becomes incomplete. New tales and new events occur. What remains constant for those of us who read and write books such as this, however, is an attraction to the water itself. Is it the mystery that it holds for us, or the repose that it offers as it captures our imaginations and focuses our attention? To be honest we really don't know.

In the process of sharing our own obsessions we have revived the spirits inhabiting the Lake Erie Quadrangle and rekindled our own connections to the waters of Lake Erie. Perhaps our efforts will have initiated or nurtured your own spirit of adventure and intrigue concerning the relationship between people and the water. Who knows what the researching and reading of these tales profits us … what connection each of us uniquely makes to those who navigated, explored and wondered about these waters before us. The only certainty is that, indeed, there is a connection to them and to the water itself. And there will continue to be as over and over …

We are led
to the waters of repose …
where the great spirit
refreshes our souls.

Lake Erie Adventures

1. The best way to understand the details of Mike Fletcher's work with the *Atlantic* is to acquire and watch the video tape which he has produced. The tape includes the history of the ship, interviews with Mike and underwater footage of the wreck site (S.S. *Atlantic* Preservation Project, P.O. Box 1198, Port Dover, ON, Canada N0A1N0).

2. Our final suggestion is to read. There are volumes on the history of the Great Lakes and most of these are quite easily available. The Great Lakes Historical Society in Vermillion, Ohio offers an attractive membership program, provides a regular catalogue of offerings and maintains a lecture series.

REFERENCES

ANNUAL REPORT OF THE LAKE CARRIERS ASSOCIATION. 1992, Cleveland: The Lake Carriers Association, George Ryan, President

Andrews, Capt. W.D. 1900, THE LIFEBOAT, Toronto: Wm. Briggs President

Barrett, Harry B. 1977, LORE AND LEGENDS OF LONG POINT, Don Mills Ontario: Burns and MacEachern

Barrett, Harry B. 1977, THE PIONEER HAMLET OF PORT DOVER, Port Dover: The Dover Mills Heritage Association

Baxter, R.R. 1961, THE ST. LAWRENCE SEAWAY, New York: Preager

Bowen, Dana Thomas. 1954, LORE OF THE LAKES, Cleveland: Freshwater Press

Bowen, Dana Thomas. 1956, MEMORIES OF THE LAKES, Cleveland: Freshwater Press

Bowen, Dana Thomas. 1952, SHIPWRECKS OF THE LAKES, Cleveland: Freshwater Press

Buscombe, Donald A. 1974, PORT DOVER SCENES THROUGH CHANGING TIMES, Port Stanley: Erie Shore Publications

Claridge, John R. 1991 LOST ERIE, Erie: Erie County Historical Society

DeGeorge, Theresa. 1974, "Commercial Development of the Port of Erie," THE JOURNAL OF ERIE STUDIES, II, 2, Fall

ERIE TIMES NEWS, Select Archival Information

THE ERIE STORY, Select Archival Information

THE FRONT PAGE, 100 YEARS OF PORT DOVER NEWS, 1988, Kitchner: Allprint Company

Greenwood, J.O. 1993, GREENWOOD'S GUIDE TO GREAT LAKES SHIP-PING, Cleveland: Freshwater Press

Grinde, D. A. 1972, "Niroglycerine and Erie's Harbor," THE J. OF ERIE STUDIES, I, 2, Fall

Hatcher, Harlun and Waltz, Erich. 1963, A PICTORIAL HISTORY OF THE GREAT LAKES, New York: Crown Publications

Heilman, R.L. et al. 1986, GREAT LAKES TRANSPORTATION IN THE EIGHTIES, Milwaukee: University of Wisconson Press

Hilton, George. 1962, THE GREAT LAKES CAR FERRIES, Berkley: Howell North

HISTORY OF ERIE COUNTY, PA, 1884, Chicago: Warner Beers and Co.

HISTORY OF THE GREAT LAKES, Volume I. 1899, Chicago: J.H. Beers & Co.

HISTORY OF THE GREAT LAKES, Volume II. 1900, Chicago: J.H. Beers & Co.

Kolb, Charles, 1987, "Atlas of Great Lakes Indian History," THE JOURNAL OF ERIE STUDIES, XVI, 2, Fall

Kuhrt, Jo Ann 1976, "A Study of the Erie Yacht Club," THE JOURNAL OF ERIE STUDIES, V, 1, Fall

LAKE ERIE PIPELINE AND GAS WELL LOCATIONS, 1993, London, ON: Telesis Oil and Gas

LLOYDS OF LONDON MARITIME DISASTER ANNUALS, 1880 through 1929

LONDON FREE PRESS: Select Archival Material

MacMurray, Helen, and MacMurray, Peter. 1980, PORT DOVER YACHT CLUB: A HISTORY, Port Dover: The Port Dover Yacht Club

Marchwinski, P.J. 1983, "Following History Through The Erie Extension Canal," THE JOURNAL OF ERIE STUDIES, XII, 2, Fall

Mills, James Cooke. 1910, OUR INLAND SEAS, Chicago: McClurg & Co.

Milner, Bruce et al. 1972, LAKELORE A HISTORY OF FISHING ALONG THE NORTH SHORE OF LAKE ERIE, Simcoe: Norfolk School of Agriculture

Muller, Mary M. 1992, A TOWN AT PRESQUE ISLE: A SHORT HISTORY OF ERIE, PA TO 1980, Erie: Erie County Historical Society

OPERATIONS OF THE U.S. LIFESAVING SERVICE. 1881, Washington D.C: The Treasury Department

PORT DOVER MAPLE LEAF: Select Archival Information

PORT ROWAN GOOD NEWS: Select Archival Information

Prothero, Frank. 1973, THE GOOD YEARS, Port Stanley: Mika Publishing

Prothero, Frank and Prothero, Nancy. 1987, TALES OF THE NORTH SHORE, Port Stanley: Nan Sea Press

Ratigan, Wm. 1977, GREAT LAKES SHIPWRECKS AND SURVIVALS, Grand Rapids: Eerdmans Publishing

RESOURCE MANAGEMENT PLAN FOR PRESQUE ISLE STATE PARK, 1993, Pennsylvania Dept. of Environmental Resources

Severance, Frank. 1977, "The Career of Daniel Dobbins Parts I and II," THE JOURNAL OF ERIE STUDIES, VI, 2, Fall and VII, 1, Spring

SIMCOE REFORMER: Select Archival Information

Spencer, H. R. 1972, "Joe Root: Hermit of Presque Isle," THE JOURNAL OF ERIE STUDIES, I, 2, Fall

Stone, Dave. 1988, LONG POINT LAST PORT OF CALL, Erin: Boston Mills Press

Walker, Barbara and Walker, Warren. 1963, THE ERIE CANAL; GATEWAY TO EMPIRE, Boston: Heath Co.

INDEX

Design, composition and printing management
  Meridian Creative Group
  Erie, Pennsylvania

Art Director
  Chuck Benson

Production Coordinator
  Michele Bliss

Production Artist
  Randy Sanfratello

Printing Coordinator
  Andrew Scott

Cover Photo
  Art Becker

Cartography
  Amy Marshall
  Gene Pilch

Production Facilitators
  Linda Donico
  Deb Rieger